THE NFL, YEAR ONE

Related Titles from Potomac Books

Tailgate to Heaven: A British NFL Fan Tackles America
—Adam Goldstein

*Football's Most Wanted™: The Top 10 Book of the Great Game's
Outrageous Characters, Fortunate Fumbles, and Other Oddities*
—Floyd Conner

*Football's Most Wanted™ II: The Top 10 Book of
More Bruising Backs, Savage Sacks, and Gridiron Oddities*
—Walter Harvey

THE **NFL,**
YEAR ONE

The 1970 Season *and the* Dawn *of* Modern Football

BRAD SCHULTZ

Potomac Books
An imprint of the University of Nebraska Press

Library of Congress Cataloging-in-Publication Data
Schultz, Brad, 1961–
   The NFL, year one : the 1970 season and the dawn of modern football / Brad Schultz.
     pages ; cm
   Includes bibliographical references and index.
   ISBN 978-1-61234-502-4 (hardcover : alk. paper)
   ISBN 978-1-61234-503-1 (electronic)
   1. National Football League—History—20th century. 2. Football—United States—History—20th century. I. Title.
   GV955.5.N35S38 2013
   796.332'64097309047—dc23
   [B]

                                         2012050980

First Edition

For Lance Rentzel,
in hopes that he has finally
conquered his demons

CONTENTS

INTRODUCTION

Ordinarily, when we look at the history of the National Football League (NFL), we tend to do so from either a very small or a very large perspective. The very small could include a single game or play, and certainly the memories of most NFL fans fall into this category. We are all familiar with the "Ice Bowl," "The Catch," "The Immaculate Reception," and dozens of other singular moments. Looking at the NFL from a larger perspective usually means by decade, such as the tumultuous early period of the league in the 1920s, or the romanticized "Golden Age" of the 1950s.

The 1970 NFL season usually does not merit much attention. It is sandwiched between the Packers dynasty of the 1960s and the Steelers dynasty of the 1970s and is often overshadowed by the Joe Namath Super Bowl in 1968 and the Dolphins perfect season in 1972. That the 1970 season ended with an unspectacular thud—the "Blunder Bowl" between the Colts and Cowboys in Super Bowl V—is also why football writers tend to consign it to the scrapheap of sports history.

But the 1970 season is fascinating for so many reasons—particularly because it was the first time that teams from the NFL and former American Football League (AFL) played together on a regular basis. The newly merged and realigned league created instant geographic rivalries. The Jets and Giants played for the championship of New York, the Bengals and Browns began an Ohio rivalry that was dominated on both sides by Paul Brown, and the

Cowboys and Oilers consummated a long-standing Texas feud. These games gave the NFL a sheen of freshness.

"There was a feeling of stepping into the unknown as teams were playing for the first time," said sportswriter Jerry Green, who covered the NFL for forty-one years for the *Detroit News*. "There was a haughtiness about the NFL. It was the establishment; the superior league."

Green was there for some of the most important moments of the 1970 season, including the first *Monday Night Football* game and Tom Dempsey's record-breaking 63-yard field goal.

"Alex Karras [of the Lions] was laughing as they lined up," recalled Green of Dempsey's miracle kick. "I was standing next to the elevator waiting to go down to the locker room because I figured the Lions had the game won.

Saints' owner John Mecom was standing with me and said, 'Hold on, I want to watch this.' Afterwards in the Lions' locker room, someone knocked a hole in the blackboard. I found out later it was [coach] Joe Schmidt."*

The 1970 season is also important in that it was where the seeds of the modern NFL were planted. A short players' strike before the first kickoff foreshadowed bigger labor issues, which continue to plague the league today. Artificial turf and "soccer-style" kickers both came to prominence in 1970, developments that would have important ramifications on the league in future years. And Super Bowl V, even for all its flaws and foul-ups, would help launch the Super Bowl into a national obsession, the roots of which could be seen in the immediate success of *Monday Night Football*, which became a cultural phenomenon.

"I was surprised it was so successful, but this was when football was starting to overtake baseball as the most popular sport in America," said Green. "*Monday Night Football* was part of that. [Director] Chet Forte and Roone Arledge made it go. Their contribution to professional football is immense."

The AFL-NFL war is a fascinating story, and even though the two leagues had officially merged in 1966, there was still plenty of bad blood between teams and individuals in 1970. The former AFL teams still believed

---

*All quotes taken from a personal interview with Jerry Green, August 12, 2011. Green is one of only four men who have covered every Super Bowl. The others are Jerry Izenberg of the *Newark Star-Ledger*; Dave Klein, formerly of the *Star-Ledger*; and Edwin Pope of the *Miami Herald*.

they had to prove themselves, even after winning the previous two Super Bowls—a situation that made for some interesting games.

I chronicle many of these games in detail, framed against the backdrop of this rivalry, such as the Minnesota Vikings' desire to get revenge on the Kansas City Chiefs for their Super Bowl IV humiliation, and the cultural importance of *Monday Night Football*, which began with the Cleveland Browns and New York Jets in the first week of the 1970 season. It was also a year of huge personalities. George Blanda went from reject quarterback to hero of America's aging middle class, while Paul Brown finally had a chance to get back at the man who had ended his Cleveland Browns dynasty. There are also those who suffered. The St. Louis Cardinals and Dallas Cowboys fell victim to their own tortured histories, and football fans in Green Bay and Washington mourned the passing of legendary coach Vince Lombardi.

Lombardi's Packers had dominated the 1960s, but as the 1970s began, the playing fields had been leveled. With a few exceptions, almost every team in the league believed it had a chance to win the Super Bowl. The year 1970 was one of the most competitive and unpredictable seasons in NFL history, with four of the six division races not settled until the final weekend. It was a season that fulfilled Commissioner Pete Rozelle's dream of parity, an idea that is still alive and well in the NFL today, both on and off the field.

On a personal note, I have somewhat selfish reasons for writing about the 1970 NFL year. My family was living in Dallas at the time, and I was about as fanatical a Cowboys fan as one can be at nine years old. We subscribed to both the *Dallas Morning News* and the now-defunct *Times-Herald*, in part so I wouldn't miss any information about the team. We went to a few games, although not all of them, and those home games we didn't attend I listened to on the radio. (NFL blackout rules prevented showing the game within seventy-five miles of Dallas.) In an age before NFL Properties got serious about its merchandising, my room was filled with Cowboys paraphernalia, including a waste basket, posters, notebooks, and anything else I could get my hands on.

To a young boy, the game was a mythological battle and its players were like gods. Bob Lilly, I was told, went to our church in north Dallas, but I never did see him (and certainly not during the season). When word spread that the recently traded Lance Alworth had bought a home in our neighborhood, it created quite a sensation. I was disappointed I never got to see "Bambi," although we did play street football with his son occasionally.

I got emotionally involved with the team, which was a mistake for several reasons. My favorite player, Lance Rentzel, was arrested midway through the season for exposing himself to a girl about my age. My #19 pajamas went into the closet, never to be worn again. Then of course, there were the devastating losses—54–13 to the Minnesota Vikings, 38–0 at home to the St. Louis Cardinals, and after the team had rebounded and looked ready to win it all, 16–13 to the Baltimore Colts in the Super Bowl. I did not take the loss well, even for nine—I sobbed afterward and got so mad I tore down the Cowboys posters from my wall.

At this point, some might ask why this book isn't about the 1971 season, when the Cowboys vindicated themselves and finally won a Super Bowl. To me, the 1970 season is infinitely more fascinating. In 1970 the Cowboys still played their home games in the Cotton Bowl, where tickets were inexpensive and easy to get. By the following season, the team had moved to the more sterile Texas Stadium, where getting season tickets required buying bonds to finance stadium construction. It was a forerunner of the personal seat licenses that so many teams now use to generate millions of dollars.

Personal seat licenses, labor unrest, salary caps, and drug testing are all part of the modern NFL. In many ways, that NFL began in 1970, one of the most important years in the history of professional football.

★ 1 ★

THE WAR

When you go to fight a big gorilla, you don't hit him lightly.
You hit him with everything you've got!
—Former NFL coach Jimmy Johnson[1]

OPENING SKIRMISHES

Jimmy Johnson was one of the NFL's most quotable coaches during his five-year tenure with the Dallas Cowboys. After Dallas beat the San Francisco 49ers for the 1992 NFC Championship, Johnson greeted his team with what would become his signature line: "How 'bout them Cowboys!"[2] When the teams met a year later for a rematch, he correctly predicted, "We will beat the 49ers, and you can put that in three-inch headlines."[3] (Not surprisingly, Johnson majored in industrial psychology while in college.)

Johnson loved to use the "gorilla" quote above as a motivational tool, especially when his team was an underdog. It probably got quite a workout in Johnson's first season in Dallas when the Cowboys went 1-15. But it only took him three years to turn the Cowboys into the NFL's gorilla—leading them to three Super Bowl championships between 1992 and 1995. "Give Johnson credit; all the credit," wrote Jim Reeves of the *Fort Worth Star-Telegram*.[4]

The NFL that Johnson and the Cowboys dominated in the early '90s is in many ways the beast of sports organizations. Then, as now, its unparalleled power, popularity, and presence allowed it to tower above all other leagues and organizations, and the NFL of 2013 is a multi-billion dollar global conglomerate. In its valuations of NFL teams, *Forbes* estimates that the thirty-two franchises in the league annually bring in a combined $8.3 billion in revenue. The Cowboys are currently ranked the most valuable at $2.1 billion, but even the "poorest" team, the Jacksonville Jaguars, is worth $770 million.[5] It's hard to believe that when the NFL began in 1920 as the American Professional Football Association, the team entrance fee was $100.

"There wasn't one hundred dollars in the room," recalled NFL founding father George Halas of the twelve men who met at a Canton, Ohio, car dealership, "but still each of us put up one hundred dollars for the privilege of losing money."[6]

Perhaps more important than the money is how the NFL has ingrained itself into the public consciousness. In the fall, Sunday has become a day reserved to watch football, tailgate, or gather with friends and enjoy the NFL experience. "Super Bowl Sunday" is now an unofficial national holiday; a day where even non-football fans gather around their television sets (or monitors) to watch the biggest game of the year. Since the first Super Bowl in 1967, which was televised on two networks, the game telecast annually draws about a third of the total U.S. population, and the audience keeps growing. In 2012 Super Bowl XLVI between the Patriots and Giants was the most watched show in the history of American television with 111.3 million viewers.[7]

The passion that professional football engenders led other leagues to challenge the NFL. The World Football League (WFL) began play in 1974, competing directly with the NFL by playing much of its schedule in the summer and fall. The WFL also went after star NFL talent, and signed many established players, like Calvin Hill, Larry Csonka, and Kenny Stabler, to huge salaries once their NFL contracts expired.[8] With strong attendance in the early part of the 1974 season, the WFL seemed on solid ground.

But that ground soon turned into quicksand. It turns out that most of the ticket sales were actually giveaways, and by the end of 1974 the WFL was losing millions. "They papered the house in Philadelphia and lied about it," said WFL founder and commissioner Gary Davidson, "and everything started downhill from that point."[9]

Dozens of players went unpaid, and on the next day after the Birmingham Americans beat the Florida Blazers to win the WFL championship, authorities seized the Americans' uniforms, equipment, and office furniture. In October 1975 the league's ten remaining teams officially pulled the plug.

"When you are fighting the establishment you do what you can," said Tommy Reamon, a running back who was the WFL's rushing leader and most valuable player in 1974. "There is room for another league, but the NFL, the establishment, would never let anyone compete with them."[10]

That was a lesson never fully learned by the United States Football League (USFL), an upstart competitor that began play with twelve teams in 1983. At first, the USFL did not try to compete directly with the NFL, instead playing its entire schedule during the spring and summer. Unlike the WFL, the league had both a national television contract (with ABC and ESPN) and solid attendance figures (an average of twenty-four thousand per game). The first USFL championship game, won by the Michigan Panthers over the Philadelphia Stars, was held on a neutral field in Denver and attracted more than fifty thousand fans.

Perhaps misled by its modest success, the USFL made a fatal mistake— directly taking on the NFL. The league moved its schedule from spring to fall, and decided to get in a bidding war with the NFL for college football talent. USFL teams signed Heisman trophy winners Herschel Walker, Mike Rozier, and Doug Flutie to multi-million dollar contracts. Walker's contract with the New Jersey Generals was for a record $1.5 million at a time when the league salary cap was $1.8 million per team.

Initial fan interest waned and USFL teams began losing money. Despite winning two USFL championships in three years, the Philadelphia Stars lost $17 million, while Edward J. DeBartolo Sr. lost $11 million as owner of the Pittsburgh Maulers.[11]

In 1985, in part spurred by Donald Trump, who had taken over ownership of the Generals, the USFL went all-in on its fight with the NFL. The league filed a $1.7 billion anti-trust suit, claiming that the NFL had pressured networks not to televise USFL games in the fall. On July 29, 1986, after forty-eight days of hearings, a federal jury found the NFL guilty of monopolizing professional football, but awarded the USFL only one dollar in damages. Since anti-trust suits automatically treble damages, the USFL got three dollars for all its trouble.

The NFL sent the USFL a check for $3.76 (76 cents worth of interest), but the younger league never cashed it. "They didn't even spell out our league name," said USFL executive Steve Ehrhart. "They even double-signed it."[12]

The decision signaled the death-knell for the league, which at the time was $163 million in debt. On August 1, USFL owners voted to suspend the 1986 season, hoping to win an appeal. When the verdict was upheld in court, the USFL was officially dead. If the USFL had received its $1.7 billion, "there would have been some kind of amalgamation [with the NFL]," said Ehrhart.[13]

"I really think [the USFL] would have made it if it stayed in the spring, not moving to the fall like Trump wanted, to challenge the NFL," said Michigan Panthers quarterback Bobby Hebert. "You know, the Panthers were more popular than the Lions."[14]

It's difficult to call the XFL a direct challenge to the NFL, because neither the NFL, football fans, nor even the XFL itself took the league seriously. It was the brainchild of professional wrestling entrepreneur Vince McMahon, who wanted a league that embodied his World Wrestling Federation (WWF) principles: action, high drama, and over-the-top entertainment. The league began play in 2001 as a joint venture of NBC and the WWF, playing in the winter to avoid direct competition with the NFL. Attendance and ratings were fairly strong for the league's first four games on February 3, 2001, but after the curiosity factor wore off, interest plummeted and NBC eventually pulled out. The XFL lasted only one season, officially ceasing operation in May 2001.

The XFL, USFL, and WFL all had the misfortune of bad timing. "I think the WFL was the best deal I ever did," said Davidson, "but it was at the wrong time."[15]

The timing for a rival league was better in the 1940s, when the NFL was still a somewhat shaky ten-team operation struggling to match the popularity of professional baseball and college football. Several NFL teams merged operations during World War II just to stay afloat—during the 1943 season the Philadelphia Eagles and Pittsburgh Steelers played together, and in the 1944 season the Steelers merged with the Chicago Cardinals. (Sportswriters derisively called these combinations the "Steagles" and "Car-Pitts.")

Thus, when the All-America Football Conference (AAFC) began play in 1946, its founders reasoned that the booming post-war economy would create more interest in the pro game. The AAFC had eight teams, including franchises on the west coast, which was still somewhat virgin territory for professional leagues. Even before the league kicked off, its owners hoped to eventually create a "World Series" of pro football by having the AAFC champion play the NFL champion. "Let them get a ball, draw a schedule, and play a game. Then I will talk to them," answered NFL commissioner Elmer Layden.[16]

The AAFC played its first game in the fall of 1946 and seemed to prove its owners right regarding the interest in more pro football. At the first regular season game on September 6, more than 60,000 fans watched the Cleveland Browns beat the Miami Seahawks, 44–0. Later that season, Cleveland set a new attendance record when it beat the Los Angeles Dons before 71,134 fans. At its height in 1949, the AAFC was ahead of the NFL in attendance by more than 10,000 fans per game. In addition to opening the west coast, the AAFC proved to be forward-thinking in terms of race. The league had several black players, including future Hall of Famers Marion Motley and Bill Willis, who both played in Cleveland.[17]

But there were also disturbing signs for the AAFC. Several teams were in dire financial straits, leading some to fold or change cities. It also hurt interest that the Browns so badly outclassed the rest of the league. In the AAFC's four seasons, Cleveland lost only four games and won the championship each year. And despite its own rules prohibiting the signing of NFL players, a bidding war for college players broke out that would end up costing both leagues millions of dollars. By 1949 it became obvious that some kind of settlement would have to be reached, and on December 9, the NFL absorbed the Cleveland, San Francisco, and Baltimore franchises.[18]

There was still plenty of lingering acrimony when the new thirteen-team NFL opened play in 1950. "The worst team in our league could beat the best team in theirs," Washington Redskins owner George Preston Marshall said of the NFL prior to the merger.[19]

Hoping to drive that point home, Commissioner Bert Bell scheduled the Browns to open the season against two-time defending NFL champion Philadelphia. Cleveland humiliated the Eagles, 35–10, in a game that went a long way toward cementing the merger.

"For four years, Coach [Paul] Brown never said a word, he just kept putting that stuff on the bulletin board," said Browns quarterback Otto Graham. "We were so fired up, we would have played them anywhere anytime, for a keg of beer or a chocolate milkshake. It didn't matter."[20] The Browns went on to win the NFL championship that season and won two more titles in the next five years.

THE FOOLISH CLUB

The 1950s were a time of tremendous growth for the expanded NFL, thanks in large part to the advent of television. Many point to the excitement of the 1958 championship game, televised nationally by NBC, as the defining moment in the evolution of the modern NFL. The Baltimore Colts' 23–17 win over the New York Giants in overtime captured the attention of the entire sporting public.

"I still think the biggest game we ever had in the league was the Colts' win over the Giants," said former NFL commissioner Pete Rozelle. "I think that was the first game that got television coverage across America. It reached fans who had never seen pro football before."[21]

At that time, Lamar Hunt was just a twenty-six-year-old former third-string end from Southern Methodist University. But his daddy was H. L. Hunt, a Texas oil billionaire who was perhaps the richest man in the country. Spurred by his love for football and fueled with his family's fortune, Lamar Hunt set out to acquire a franchise in the growing NFL. When efforts to buy an existing team failed, Hunt met with Bert Bell in an attempt to bring an expansion team to Dallas. The NFL had tried Dallas before with disastrous results—in 1952 the New York Yanks relocated as the Dallas Texans, but the team was ignored by fans and ridiculed by the press. The Texans eventually became wards of the league before moving to Baltimore and becoming the Colts, so Bell and league owners were understandably reluctant to try their hand again in Texas.

Unable to break into the NFL, Hunt had enough money, and enough rich friends, to start his own league. On August 14, 1959, six owners met in Chicago to announce the formation of the American Football League, which would begin play in 1960 with teams in New York, Houston, Denver, Los Angeles, Minneapolis, and Dallas. Oakland would later replace Minneapolis, and Buffalo and Boston would join shortly thereafter. Besides Hunt, the league featured hotel mogul Barron Hilton (Los Angeles), sportscaster and entertainer Harry Wismer (New York), and another Texas oil millionaire, Bud Adams (Houston). Despite their seeming wealth, Oakland managing partner Wayne Valley called the group the "Foolish Club" for taking on the established NFL.[22]

The NFL immediately set out to undercut the fledgling league. In late 1959, NFL owners announced their own expansion plans, including the cities of Minneapolis and Dallas where the AFL wanted to operate. The announcement prompted Max Winter, who originally agreed to own the AFL's Minneapolis franchise, to switch allegiance to the NFL. It also meant that Hunt would face direct NFL competition for his new team in Dallas. But the AFL did have some advantages, including a national television contract with ABC, which allowed AFL franchises to evenly distribute broadcast revenues. It was a novel concept in a time when individual NFL teams were still cutting their own television deals. It didn't bring in much money—about $25,000 per team in 1960—but it did help, since several AFL teams were struggling financially. "The American Football League adapted it from the start," Hunt said of the revenue sharing, "and the NFL copied it two years later after efforts had been made by their commissioner Pete Rozelle."[23]

In 1965 NBC paid $36 million for the AFL contract, a long-term deal that most experts agreed "purchased the survival" of the younger league.[24]

The AFL also benefited from the NFL's television blackout policy, which prevented home teams from televising games locally. That often left an empty slot in the late Sunday afternoon television schedule, which the AFL gladly filled with its own games. "It was like letting a vacuum cleaner salesman in your home on a Sunday," said AFL broadcaster Curt Gowdy. "Once you let those guys in the door, some of them are pretty good."[25]

But the main weapon used by AFL owners was deep pockets and a willingness to spend big money on college football talent. In 1960 the Houston Oilers signed Heisman Trophy winner Billy Cannon of LSU to a contract for $100,000, even though he had already signed a contract with the Los Angeles Rams. The dispute ended in court and the AFL's eventual legal victory precipitated all-out war between the two leagues.[26]

The bidding wars escalated to the point that, in 1965, the AFL's New York Jets signed quarterback Joe Namath to a three-year, $427,000 contract, which at the time was the biggest deal ever for an athlete in a team sport. That same year, the NFL's Atlanta Falcons and AFL's Houston Oilers were wrangling over linebacker Tommy Nobis, a senior at the University of Texas.

During the orbital flight of Gemini 7, thousands of miles above the earth, astronaut Frank Borman radioed back to mission control, "Tell Nobis to sign with Houston."[27] Despite that, and the promise of a herd of cattle as part of his contract, Nobis went with the Falcons.

The fight for Nobis reflected the cutthroat intensity of the NFL-AFL bidding wars, and stories of high intrigue abounded. Both leagues often employed "baby-sitters" whose main job was to keep a drafted player sequestered and unable to meet with representatives of the other league. "I had a limousine to take me everywhere," said Nobis. "I was really getting the royal treatment. I thought they were just being nice, but I finally figured it out after awhile."[28] At one point, the NFL's Operation Hand-Holding program employed eighty people.

The AFL may have lost Nobis, but it had its own tricks. The Chiefs' Lloyd Wells posed as a magazine writer to lure Otis Taylor away from the Cowboys, even sneaking Taylor out of the hotel through a window. Raiders executive Al Davis helped keep lineman Harry Schuh away from the Rams by sending him on a Hawaiian vacation. "We had to pull an escapade," said Davis. "We had to get him out of the hotel."[29]

In addition to new college talent, the AFL also relied heavily on NFL castoffs. Future Hall of Famers Don Maynard and Len Dawson were both released by NFL teams before finding success in the AFL. Another Hall of Famer, quarterback George Blanda, played as a backup in the NFL for a decade and briefly retired before deciding to try his hand with the new league. As it turned out, Blanda led the Houston Oilers to the first two AFL championships, played fifteen additional seasons, and thus had the longest pro football career in history. "Even some of my own brothers used to put the AFL down," he recalled. "They'd say to me, 'Yeah, George, you're having some great years down there at Houston. Too bad it's not in the real league.'"[30]

Blanda and other AFL quarterbacks had a field day in the new league, which emphasized passing and scoring. Much of it had to do with offering fans something different from the NFL, which in the early 1960s was dominated by Vince Lombardi's emphasis on defense and running in Green Bay. As a result, the AFL got the reputation as a pass-happy league with pinball offenses. In 1961 the AFL champion Houston Oilers averaged nearly thirty-seven points a game for a fourteen-game season, which was more than a touchdown a game better than the NFL champion Packers. The AFL had two receivers, Charley Hennigan of Houston and Lionel Taylor of Denver, break the one hundred-catch mark for a single season. And in 1967, Joe Namath of the Jets became the first quarterback ever to pass for more than 4,000 yards in a single season.

But for all its offensive power, the AFL continued to get nothing but derision from the NFL and its fans. "They looked down their noses at us," said Nick Buoniconti, a linebacker for both the Boston Patriots and AFL expansion team Miami Dolphins. "They insulted us, calling us 'minor leaguers' and the AFL a 'Mickey Mouse' league."[31] Those in the NFL were happy to feed the flames of resentment. "I hated the AFL," said former Cleveland Browns owner Art Modell. "I hated them for a long time and didn't want to do business with them."[32]

"The NFL was trying to kill us," said Jets' lineman John Schmitt. "They were trying to put the AFL out of business."[33]

For some AFL teams, that was a very real possibility. The Raiders lost half a million dollars in their first year and survived only after receiving a $400,000 loan from Bills owner Ralph Wilson. The situation was even worse in New York, where by 1962 Titans owner Harry Wismer could no longer afford to meet his payroll. The league took over the team, which was eventually purchased by Sonny Werblin and renamed the Jets. Even oil-rich Lamar Hunt was having problems. When someone told his father, oil tycoon H. L. Hunt, that the Texans were losing around a million dollars a year, H. L. reportedly replied, "Well, if he keeps that up, he'll be broke in 150 years."[34]

But not even H. L.'s oil money could keep the Texans in Dallas. The Texans and Cowboys shared the city for three seasons, but eventually Lamar Hunt realized one team would have to go. In 1963 the Texans relocated to Kansas City as the Chiefs and became one of the most successful operations in the AFL. At the time, Hunt joked that he lost a coin flip with Cowboys' founder and owner Clint Murchison Jr., but others took a more practical view. "We had guys from the state of Texas on the roster that didn't want to move," said Texans/Chiefs quarterback Len Dawson. "But [Hunt] was more concerned about the league succeeding."[35]

Despite financial problems and franchise relocations, the AFL managed to stay in business. The Houston Oilers won the first two championships and nearly won three in a row, but in 1962, after two overtimes, the Texans beat Houston 20–17 in what, at the time, was the longest professional game ever played. San Diego won the title in 1963, thanks mainly to its explosive offense headlined by receiver Lance Alworth. That same season, the Chicago Bears rode a suffocating defense to win the NFL championship, leading fans and players to speculate what would happen in a possible Chargers-Bears matchup.

"Of course we would've won," said former Chargers running back Paul Lowe. "With our defense, our offense, our bench strength, we had no weaknesses. We knew we had a better team [than the Bears]."[36] According to Alworth, "I would've given anything to play in that one. In '63, I was saying, 'Line 'em up.'"[37]

After the Chargers' dominating 51–10 win over Boston for the 1963 title, AFL commissioner Joe Foss publicly challenged the NFL to a championship game between the two leagues. He wrote NFL commissioner Rozelle, "On behalf of the AFL, I reissue an official challenge to the NFL for the first game to be played at the conclusion of the 1964 season. The establishment of a 'World Series' of professional football is necessary to the continued progress of our game."[38]

At the time, Rozelle and others in the NFL probably shared the sentiments of *Sports Illustrated* writer Tex Maule, who predicted that the NFL champion would win such a game by 50 points. "In time," Maule wrote, "the AFL can probably field a team strong enough to give the NFL champion a struggle. But that time . . . is not for several years."[39] Even so, the same December 16, 1963, issue of *Sports Illustrated* ran a story titled, "The Two Pro Football Leagues Must Meet."

Several factors were pushing the leagues toward a merger. The AFL added the Miami Dolphins as an expansion franchise in 1966, which was a clear sign that the new league was not going away. In 1965 the New York Giants signed kicker Pete Gogolak away from the Buffalo Bills, violating an unwritten agreement between the leagues. The NFL and AFL had previously agreed not to steal players from the other league, but now the AFL retaliated with full force. New AFL commissioner Al Davis began raiding NFL rosters and convinced eight NFL quarterbacks, including stars like Sonny Jurgensen and Roman Gabriel, to sign AFL contracts once their NFL contracts had expired. He said the raids were "a preliminary strike to let them know what would happen if they continued."[40]

A MARRIAGE OF CONVENIENCE

Even as animosity boiled between the two leagues, cooler heads realized the necessity of a settlement. "We could have done our business for another 30 years," said Art Modell, "but we sought [a merger] to prolong the success of pro football before things got out of hand and we couldn't control them."[41] It also became obvious that any merger discussions would have to be kept secret, especially from strong anti-merger forces such as Al Davis. "Al's strategy was to take on [the NFL]," said future coach John Madden. "He wanted to become equal, then become better than them."[42] Davis carried a lot of weight in the league, especially after becoming the AFL commissioner in April 1966.

That same month, Cowboys' executive Tex Schramm began merger overtures with Lamar Hunt. The two met secretly at a Dallas airport, going so far as to hold their discussions in Schramm's parked car so as not to arouse suspicion.

"I always thought that if a proper plan could be worked out, peace was feasible," said Schramm. "We felt that if the NFL could come up with an acceptable plan that was good for the sport, it could then be presented to the AFL. If they liked it, fine. If not, we could settle down to an all-out war."[43] AFL owners were initially reluctant to listen because they thought the NFL was setting a trap.

"I'll never forget one of our owners saying, 'If they're lying to us, we'll have to drop the bomb on them,'" said Davis, who continued to resist a merger. "We would drop the bomb on them and sign all of their players."[44]

Schramm eventually presented the NFL's initial proposal to Hunt on May 30. "There it is," he told Hunt. "If you accept, this deal has been approved by every NFL club. If you have to alter it too much, it will blow up."[45] Negotiations went back and forth for a few days, but on June 8, 1966, two days and two months after the first secret meeting at Love Field in Dallas, a merger was formally announced. In the end, the NFL got almost everything it wanted, including:

- The two leagues would combine to form an expanded twenty-four-team league, with Rozelle as the sole commissioner. The merged league eventually grew to twenty-six teams, with the addition of New Orleans in 1967 and Cincinnati in 1968.
- AFL teams would pay indemnities to NFL teams that shared markets with AFL teams. Specifically, the New York Giants would receive payments from the New York Jets, and the San Francisco 49ers would get money from the Oakland Raiders. Total AFL indemnity payments would amount to $18 million over twenty years.
- Both leagues would immediately hold a common draft of college players, effectively ending the bidding war between leagues and drastically reducing rookie salaries.
- While maintaining separate schedules through 1969, the leagues agreed to play an annual NFL-AFL championship game beginning in January 1967. The leagues also agreed to play a series of preseason games starting later that year. The AFL and NFL would formally combine in 1970 to form one NFL with two conferences.

There was still much work to be done in 1966. The two leagues were now one, but it was an uneasy union. It more closely resembled a marriage between the Hatfields and McCoys. The bride and groom may have put on a happy face, but everyone else at the wedding wondered how long it would be before someone started shooting.

THE PEACE

ONE HAPPY FAMILY?

Even after the merger, hard feelings remained on both sides. Al Davis was particularly upset, and less than two months after the official announcement he resigned as AFL commissioner and returned to run the Oakland Raiders.[1] Much of the ill will was caused by a lingering sense of superiority on the part of established NFL teams. When AFL and NFL players sat down to discuss merging their respective players' associations into one union, AFL linebacker Nick Buoniconti was shocked.

"We had sort of an informal meeting with [the NFL players]," he said, "and they looked down their noses at us. I remember Ken Bowman, the Green Bay center, acting like we didn't even belong talking to them. Finally I asked him, 'Who do you think you are?'"[2]

Fans felt the rift just as sharply; you were either an NFL fan or an AFL fan, but not both. When New Orleans got a franchise in 1967, fans of the new team were aghast at rumors that the Saints would initially play in the AFL. "Holy smoke, it seems as if New Orleans is going to get stuck with 'that' pro league," sportswriter Bob Roesler wrote in the *New Orleans Times-Picayune*.[3] The Saints were eventually put in the NFL, forcing the Cincinnati Bengals into the AFL. "We were promised we would be in the NFL, not the AFL," said Bengals founder Paul Brown, who was an old NFL man from way back. "I wanted to come into the NFL where my old friends were."[4]

Since AFL and NFL teams would not play each other during the 1966 regular season, everyone looked to the first combined championship game in January 1967 with great anticipation. It would be the first true test of how the AFL would compete against the NFL. The winners of the two leagues would meet in a game officially called "The AFL-NFL World Championship Game"—a name that suffered from both length and pretentiousness. It was Lamar Hunt who eventually came up with the name that would resonate in the sports world for generations to come—the Super Bowl.[5] When Hunt mentioned the name at a meeting of NFL and AFL owners, he gave all the credit to his young daughter Sharron. At the time, the girl had a favorite toy. "It's my 'super ball,'" she told her father.[6]

The race to get to Super Bowl I (league owners decided to use Roman numerals to give an added air of importance to the game) was a lively one. At the time, both leagues were broken into two conferences, East and West, and the winner of each conference would meet for the league title. The Buffalo Bills had won two consecutive AFL championships based on running and defense, and in the pass-happy AFL they were the closest thing to an NFL-style team. They had demonstrated their power with a 23–0 shutout of high-scoring San Diego in the 1965 AFL title game. "That was the team that could have really played with NFL champions," said Bills' lineman Billy Shaw. "We matched up really good with them. I'd have loved to have that opportunity."[7]

Buffalo's defense was just as strong in 1966—they gave up the fewest points in the AFL—but its offense struggled, and Buffalo barely held off Boston (by a half-game) to win the Eastern Conference. Part of the problem was the absence of running back Carlton "Cookie" Gilchrist, who had rushed for more than 3,000 yards in three seasons with the Bills beginning in 1962.[8] He was similar to Cleveland's Jim Brown in many ways—both were proud men who retired at relatively young ages and were extremely powerful and durable runners.

"I told Jim Brown to his face that if I had stayed with the Browns, nobody would have heard of him," said Gilchrist, who had signed with the Browns right out of high school.[9] When the NFL voided the contract, Gilchrist played in Canada for six seasons before joining the Bills.

Meanwhile, Hunt's Kansas City Chiefs had no such problems in the Western Conference and comfortably finished three games ahead of the Raiders. Loaded with offensive firepower, including future Hall of Famers in quarterback Len Dawson and receiver Otis Taylor, and Heisman-Trophy-winner running back Mike Garrett, the Chiefs led both the AFL and NFL in scoring. They were just as dominant on defense, with lineman Buck Buchanan and linebackers E. J. Holub and Bobby Bell. The most flamboyant player was defensive back Fred Williamson, whose trademark tackle (since outlawed) was a clothesline-like blow to the head he called "The Hammer." When delivered efficiently, Williamson noted that victimized players "go back into the huddle with their heads ringing like they're hearing chimes, and their eyes full of stars and dots, and their legs twanging like rubber bands."[10]

Taylor, Garrett, Buchanan, Bell, and Williamson were all black starters in a league that opened its doors to minorities at a time when only a few such players were starring in the NFL. The move was part necessity—the league simply needed as many good football players as it could get—but it was also part egalitarian. When black players boycotted the 1965 AFL All-Star Game because of discrimination in the host city of New Orleans, the league moved the game to Houston. "We were led to believe that we could relax and enjoy ourselves in New Orleans just like other citizens," said Buffalo Bills end Ernie Warlick, one of twenty-one players who decided to walk out after a meeting to discuss the situation. "[But] we felt we couldn't perform 100 percent under the circumstances."[11]

Even though Hunt admitted that the team "never pretended we made a conscious effort to open things up racially,"[12] the Chiefs and coach Hank Stram seemed particularly enlightened on racial issues. The team had a full-time scout, Lloyd Wells, combing the small black colleges for talent. Wells helped convince the Chiefs to draft linebacker Willie Lanier from Morgan State in the same 1967 draft that the team selected linebacker Jim Lynch of Notre Dame.

"I wondered if there was going to be an open competition," said Lanier. "One day Hank called us in and said he wanted the best guys on the field, and I was going to be the middle linebacker and Jim was going to play outside."[13]

Within a few years, Lanier was one of eight black starters on the Kansas City defense, and his eleven-year career eventually led him to the Hall of Fame. "Imagine if there had been no AFL and no Kansas City Chiefs," he continued. "Maybe I have to wait five years for my chance to play middle linebacker. And five years in football is an eternity."[14]

Although the Bills had home-field advantage, the Chiefs were considered slight, three-point favorites in the AFL championship game. Trailing only 14–7 in the second quarter, Buffalo had the ball inside the Chiefs 10-yard line, but Bills quarterback Jack Kemp threw an interception into the end zone that Johnny Robinson returned for 72 yards. The turnover set up a field goal, and the Chiefs never looked back. Dawson threw a touchdown pass to Fred Arbanas, and Garrett scored a pair of touchdowns, the second coming after Williamson used his "Hammer" to force a fumble.

The Chiefs easily won their first-ever championship representing Kansas City, 31–7. Because of an AFL rule that prohibited using champagne in winning locker rooms, the Chiefs returned home and broke out the bubbly in their own locker room. "This is the second most thrilling day of my life," said Dawson after the game. "The first most thrilling is coming up on January 15."[15]

January 15, 1967, was the date of Super Bowl I, which would take place in the Los Angeles Coliseum. While Kansas City may have been something of a surprise participant, the Green Bay Packers certainly were not. Under Vince Lombardi, the Packers had dominated the NFL in the first half of the 1960s, winning three championships in five years. Lombardi stressed a conservative, fundamental approach to the game, and led by stars like quarterback Bart Starr, running backs Jim Taylor and Paul Hornung, and defensive players Willie Davis and Ray Nitschke, the Packers had become a dynasty of mythical stature.

LOMBARDI AND LANDRY

In the intervening years, countless books and articles have been written about the Packers of the 1960s, and almost all of them credit Lombardi as the driving force behind the team's success. He has become the subject of books, movies, and even a Broadway play, and his maxims for success have given him a mystical quality on a par with presidents, poets, or philosophers:

- "There is no room for second place. There is only one place in my game and that is first place."
- "Confidence is contagious. So is lack of confidence."
- "The harder you work, the harder it is to surrender."

- "Once you learn to quit, it becomes a habit."
- "It's not whether you get knocked down; it's whether you get up."[16]

In *Instant Replay*, his diary of the 1967 season, guard Jerry Kramer called Lombardi a "cruel, kind, tough, gentle, miserable man whom I often hate and often love and always respect."[17] It was Lombardi who, in 1959, took over a Packers team that had won just one game the previous season, and led them to a 7-5 record—the first of nine straight winning seasons. Kramer remembers a particularly rough practice in that '59 season when Lombardi rode him especially hard, calling him an "old cow" and the worst guard he had ever seen. After practice, when Kramer seemed unable to take anymore, Lombardi went over to him, tussled his hair and said, "Son, one of these days you are going to be the greatest guard in the league." According to Kramer, "He [was] a beautiful psychologist. I was ready to go back and practice for another four hours."[18]

The Lombardi Packers won NFL titles in 1961, 1962, and 1965, mainly behind the punishing backfield duo of Taylor and Hornung. A Heisman Trophy winner as a quarterback at Notre Dame, Hornung was a versatile player who could run, throw, catch, and kick. In 1960 he led the NFL with 176 points, a scoring record that lasted forty-six years.[19] But by 1966, injuries and age had begun to catch up with Hornung, and that season he carried the ball only seventy-six times and scored but five touchdowns. Green Bay overcame Hornung's absence with fine performances from Starr and Taylor, along with Elijah Pitts and newcomers Donny Anderson and Jim Grabowksi.[20] The Packer defense permitted a league-low 163 points (less than 12 per game), and as a result Green Bay easily outpaced the Baltimore Colts by three games to win the Western Conference with a 12-2 record.

In their three previous championship years, the Packers had beaten two established NFL powers—the New York Giants and Cleveland Browns. In 1966 they would face an up-and-coming team that would eventually become a dynasty in its own right and become known as America's Team.

The Dallas Cowboys had never had a winning season heading in to 1966, fueling speculation that the team would fire head coach Tom Landry. The team seemed to hit rock bottom in 1965 after a loss to Pittsburgh dropped its record to 2-5. After the game, Landry broke down while addressing the team. "That touched every one of us," remembered defensive tackle Bob Lilly. "Very deeply. From that point on we were much more attentive and much more diligent."[21]

Landry's outburst shocked Cowboy players because it was so out of his character. He had built his reputation as a brilliant, but unemotional, assistant coach with the New York Giants. In New York, he was credited with creating and refining the 4-3 defense, which revolutionized defensive play in the league for decades. When the Giants won the NFL title in 1956, Landry was the assistant in charge of the defense and Lombardi was the assistant in charge of the offense. With Landry and Lombardi running things, Giants head coach Jim Lee Howell noted wryly, "I just blow up the footballs and keep order."[22]

At the relatively young age of thirty-six, Landry brought his innovative mind and cool demeanor to Dallas, where Tex Schramm hired him to coach the expansion Cowboys. Woefully short on talent, Dallas took its beatings in those early years, including a winless inaugural season in 1960. But the Cowboys drafted well, acquiring future Hall of Famers in Lilly, defensive back Mel Renfro, and receiver Bob Hayes, who in the 1964 Olympic Games won a gold medal in the 100-meter dash to become the "World's Fastest Human." The Cowboys continued to add more pieces and improved to the point that many sportswriters picked them to win the NFL East in 1965.

The loss to Pittsburgh in 1965 signified a major turning point in the franchise's history. Cowboys' owner Clint Murchison had shown faith in Landry with an unprecedented ten-year contract at the end of the 1963 season. Now his team showed similar faith—winning five of the next seven games and qualifying for the playoffs at 7-7. Even though the Cowboys lost their Playoff Bowl game to the Colts, 35–3, they were not disheartened.[23] "It wasn't something we were proud of, particularly, but we knew we were going to be a lot better team," said Lilly. "We *knew* that."[24]

In the early years, Landry more often used his complicated schemes to disguise the Cowboys' weaknesses. "With our personnel, we couldn't afford to let the defense know where we were going," Landry said of his multiple offense, which was based more on deception and finesse than power.[25] But by 1966, he finally had the players he needed to make the offense work, and the Cowboys beat some teams by staggering scores—52–7 over the Giants, 56–7 over the Eagles, and 52–21 over the Steelers. Dallas scored the most points in the league and held off the Browns by a game and a half to win the Eastern Conference with a 10-3-1 record.

The most important difference in the Cowboy's 1966 season was quarterback Don Meredith, whom Landry had finally made the starter after the 1965 loss to Pittsburgh. A Texas homeboy and college star at nearby Southern Methodist University, the fun-loving Meredith had chafed under Landry's complicated offense and rigid rules. Meredith was the type to play practical jokes during practice and break into song in the offensive huddle. On more than one occasion, Landry had to tell his quarterback, "Remember, nothing funny happens on a football field."[26] Despite his laid-back demeanor, Meredith was extremely sensitive, and the growing criticism from fans and the media bothered him greatly. Gary Cartwright of the *Dallas Morning News* rode Meredith especially hard, writing after a 1965 loss to Cleveland, "Outlined against a gray November sky the Four Horsemen rode again Sunday. You know them: Pestilence, death, famine, Meredith."[27] When Landry finally named him the starter after the Pittsburgh loss, Meredith admitted that "we both started crying again."[28] He responded with an MVP-type season in 1966, throwing twice as many touchdowns as interceptions, and leading the most explosive offense in the NFL.

The 1966 NFL Championship game was a classic contrast—the young, upstart Cowboys against the veteran Packers; one team based on simplicity and power, the other on speed and finesse. "Lombardi's style of play was very different than ours," said Landry. "Lombardi had to develop the players to an emotional pitch [since Green Bay ran the same few plays over and over]. Our system is different. We must take advantage of situations that present themselves . . . we have to concentrate; we have to think."[29]

Another major difference between the teams was experience in big games, and the Packers started the championship game as if they were going to run the Cowboys out of the Cotton Bowl. Bart Starr threw a quick touchdown to Elijah Pitts, and when Mel Renfro fumbled the ensuing kickoff, Jim Grabowski ran it in for a 14–0 lead. But the Cowboys fought back, tying the game at 14. The Packers moved back in front 34–20 late in the fourth quarter, but the Cowboys refused to go quietly into the Dallas night. Meredith threw a long touchdown pass to Frank Clarke to make it 34–27, and the Cowboys soon got the ball back. With time running out, Dallas was first-and-goal at the Green

Bay 2, but a crucial offside penalty cost them 5 yards, and the game ended as Meredith's fourth-down desperation pass was intercepted in the end zone by Tom Brown.

In the winning Packer locker room, Lombardi said the game "was tremendous. Maybe it wasn't the most exciting ever played but they're all exciting when you win."[30]

The most exciting game was yet to come.

SUPER BOWL I

As the Packers and Chiefs headed to southern California to prepare for Super Bowl I, the common perception was that the Chiefs faced an enormous amount of pressure. After all, this was the game the AFL had waited six years to play—a chance to show those smug fossils of the NFL that the new league was every bit its equal. Pressure also came from having to play the intimidating Packers, and in the days leading up to the game the young Chiefs appeared star-struck.

"I looked around me and all I saw were zombies," said Fred Williamson. "These guys were scared of playing the Green Bay Packers. They were scared of playing in the first Super Bowl."[31] Williamson tried to shift some of the pressure to himself by making a series of derogatory comments about the Packers in the media. "[My teammates] see me peacocking around," he said, "maybe they'll pick it up, maybe they'll start saying, 'Green Bay Packers. Sheeit.' Whether they like me or not, personally, who cares?"[32]

In truth, the Packers had just as much pressure as the Chiefs, if not more. While Kansas City obviously wanted to win the game, the Packers felt they *had* to. A loss to these annoying upstarts would stain the honor of the NFL and humiliate the league for years to come.

"We had almost nothing to gain because we were expected to win," said Packers defensive end Willie Davis. "But if we had gotten knocked off, it would be something we would have to live with the rest of our lives. That game probably had more pressure . . . than any game, ever."[33] Green Bay lineman Bob Skoronski added, "I had never felt such a sense of urgency on [Lombardi's] part before. He said to us, 'I'll keep you there all day, all night, all week, if necessary, until you win. There is no way the Green Bay Packers are going to lose this football game.'"[34]

The pressure was coming from all sides and was felt in all quarters. The Super Bowl Committee announced that 1,049 media credentials had been issued for the game, and in another first, two different networks would telecast the game live. CBS had carried NFL games, while NBC had the AFL contract, so as a diplomatic solution both networks were allowed to carry the Super Bowl. NBC would have its own announcers, but it would have to rely on video provided by CBS.

"This was a competition between the two networks as much as it was a competition between Kansas City and Green Bay," said CBS broadcaster Jack Whitaker.[35] According to another CBS broadcaster, Pat Summerall, "There was a lot of animosity; a lot of fists swung in the lot outside the stadium. So much so, that one day we came and they had built a 10-foot chain-link fence between the CBS trucks and the NBC trucks."[36]

Whitaker may have had the best line of any of the press covering the game—during the CBS pregame show he said, "The seven year itch is about to be scratched."[37] He and Ray Scott worked the game for CBS, while Curt Gowdy and Paul Christman did the duties for NBC.

For all its buildup, and perfect 70 degree temperatures on game day, Super Bowl I was not a sellout. A solid crowd of 63,036 showed up, but the cavernous 93,000-seat Los Angeles Coliseum looked barren in many places. To make the stadium look fuller for the television cameras, the announcers encouraged fans sitting in the end zones to move to better locations closer to midfield. The disappointing attendance was somewhat offset by the fact that the telecast of the game attracted between fifty and sixty million viewers, which broke the record for a single football game.[38]

The fans in the Los Angeles area might have been concerned that the game would turn into a Green Bay blowout, which is ultimately what happened. The Packers played a very conservative first half and the Chiefs kept things close, trailing only 14–10. But Green Bay opened up both its offense and defense in the second half, and cruised to an easy 35–10 win. Starr threw two touchdown passes and won game MVP honors, but the award could easily have gone to Max McGee. Not expecting to play, the backup receiver had enjoyed a night on the town Super Bowl eve, returning to the team hotel around 6:30 a.m. But when Boyd Dowler injured his shoulder early in the first quarter, in came McGee, who had caught only four passes all year. He would go on to torch the Chiefs' secondary for 138 yards and two touchdowns, including the first touchdown in Super Bowl history.

"What do you say about a guy like that?" asked Lombardi after the game. "This was one of his finest games."[39]

With the game basically decided in the fourth quarter, Kansas City suffered another humiliation when Williamson, attempting to make a tackle, banged his head on a Packer helmet and was knocked cold. "The next thing I knew I was on a stretcher on the sidelines looking up at all that blue," said Williamson. "Man, was I embarrassed."[40]

In the winning locker room, Lombardi took one final dig at the Chiefs and the AFL. "Kansas City has a good team," he said, "but it doesn't compare with some of the teams in the NFL. That's what you want me to say, isn't it? There. I've said it."[41]

It would not take long for the AFL to catch up, but as the sun set on the 1966 season, there was no doubt that the NFL and the Packers were the premier class of professional football. "We endured a kind of pressure and scrutiny that no other team since has had to face," said Green Bay center Bill Curry. "It was a great achievement and real football people will always appreciate it. For those reasons, [the 1966 team] will be remembered as one of the great teams of all time."[42]

THE "LITTLE SUPER BOWLS"

The AFL did not have to wait long to try to avenge its Super Bowl loss. Even though the leagues would not play a common schedule until 1970, the merger stipulated that a series of exhibition games would take place starting in the summer of 1967. The games would not count in the standings, but they did give the AFL several opportunities to test itself against the NFL.[43] The series of games came to be known as the Little Super Bowls.

During the exhibition seasons of 1967–1969, the AFL would play seventy-two games against NFL teams. Normally, teams rest starters during exhibition games in an effort to look at promising rookies and free agent players, but these games, especially in the first summer of 1967, had the look and feel of a real Super Bowl. "'Exhibition' is hardly the word," wrote Larry Felser of *The Sporting News*. "From the talk around both leagues, at least some of those games if not all of them, will take on the characteristics of a vendetta."[44] "Our pride is at stake," said Dick Schafrath of the Cleveland Browns. "No NFL team wants to be the first to lose to the AFL."[45]

The first little Super Bowl took place August 5, 1967, in Denver between the Broncos and Detroit Lions. The Broncos were one of the worst teams in the AFL, having won just four games the previous season, and they had already lost their opening exhibition game to Miami, 19–2. Detroit was led by stars like defensive tackle Alex Karras, who publicly promised to walk home from Denver if the Broncos should win the game.

Playing before 21,288 fans in Denver, the Broncos stunned the Lions, the NFL, and football fans everywhere by beating Detroit, 13–7. It was the first win ever for an AFL team over an NFL team. The Broncos, who averaged only 83 yards rushing per game, seemed to run at will against the Lions, racking up 227 yards on the ground. The Lions offense struggled and didn't score its first and only touchdown until the fourth quarter. After the game, Roger Brown, the Lions' defensive tackle, expressed the sentiments of NFL fans everywhere, "The Denver Broncos . . . it didn't happen!"[46] There was no word on how Alex Karras made it back to Detroit.

Two weeks later, Denver pulled off a similarly shocking defeat of the Minnesota Vikings, 13–9. "The AFL is going to surprise a lot of people," said Buffalo quarterback Jack Kemp. "In fact, since Denver beat the Lions and Vikings, I guess it already has."[47]

It was somewhat easy for NFL loyalists to dismiss the Broncos' wins over Detroit and Minnesota as flukes, but there was no explanation for what happened on the night of August 23, 1967, in an exhibition game between the Chiefs and the Chicago Bears before more than 33,000 fans in Kansas City.

The Bears lineup featured future Hall of Famers Gale Sayers and Dick Butkus, and the team was still coached by NFL founder and legend George "Papa Bear" Halas. The Chiefs, meanwhile, were still smarting from their loss to Green Bay seven months earlier.

"Remember, this is not just another exhibition," Kansas City coach Hank Stram told reporters before the game. "They know it's the Bears they're playing."[48]

With four touchdown passes from Len Dawson, the Chiefs scored the most points ever against Chicago in a 66–24 rout. Just to make sure the NFL got the message, Kansas City, who was up 60–24, called timeout during the final minute of the game in order to score one more touchdown.

"Well, I wonder what the world will say now," said Chiefs' receiver Chris Burford. "[Mr. Lombardi] said we aren't as good as other top teams in the National Football League—like the Chicago Bears. Now maybe everyone will get off our backs."[49]

The two Denver victories and the win by Kansas City were the only AFL successes that first exhibition summer, as the NFL won the other thirteen of the sixteen games played. But the AFL won thirteen of twenty-three exhibition games the next year, and finished with a record of twenty-nine wins, forty-two losses, and one tie for the three years of the interleague games.

"There's very little difference between the leagues," said Otto Graham in 1967, the second of his three seasons coaching the Redskins. "When I came into the NFL [last year], I said the top teams in the AFL could give any team in the NFL a battle. A couple of guys almost shot me for saying that."[50]

THE ICE BOWL AND BEYOND

Despite its impressive performance against the Bears in the pre-season, the Chiefs were not able to repeat as AFL champions in 1967. The cream of the AFL that year was the Oakland Raiders, who scored the most points in either league and lost only one game all season. Newly acquired quarterback Daryle Lamonica, who came to Oakland in a trade with the Bills, threw thirty touchdown passes and won league MVP honors. The Raiders advanced to Super Bowl II after a crushing 40–7 win over the Houston Oilers in the AFL Championship on December 31. "There's plenty of pressure in the Super Bowl," said guard Gene Upshaw, "but if we keep calm it's going to be just like playing any team in any other game."[51]

That same New Year's Eve, the Packers and Cowboys played for the NFL Championship on the coldest day in league history.[52] The temperature at Lambeau Field started out at fifteen degrees below zero and with the wind chill factor, the temperature on the field at game time was around fifty-five below. (By comparison, the Raiders–Oilers game was a balmy forty-five degrees.) The special heating system under the turf failed, and as the game progressed the field froze over and became like a skating rink. The 1967 NFL Championship, forever to be known as the "Ice Bowl," would prove to the supreme test of football, manhood, and survival.

That the Packers even made the title game was something of a surprise. Beset with injuries and without Taylor and Hornung in its backfield, Green Bay finished with a pedestrian 9-4-1 record. But the Packers rallied to beat the favored Rams in a first-round playoff game, thus advancing to an NFL championship game rematch with Dallas. With less than five minutes to play, the Packers, who had failed to move the ball at all in the second half, trailed 17–14.

But in those final minutes, the legend of the Lombardi Packers came to life. Green Bay moved 68 yards and Bart Starr scored the winning touchdown on a somewhat controversial quarterback sneak with only sixteen seconds to play and no timeouts remaining. Had Starr been stopped, the Packers would have lost, but when he crossed the goal line Green Bay conquered the Cowboys, and the elements, 21–17.

"Those last five minutes are what the Packers are all about," said Lombardi afterward. "They do it because they respect each other. They are selfless."[53] Tackle Bob Skoronski added, "This game was our mark of distinction."[54]

After the Ice Bowl, Super Bowl II was an anti-climax. The Packers struggled for a bit but pulled away to beat the Raiders, 33–14, winning a record third-straight championship. The game did have a nostalgic quality to it; rumors surfaced during Super Bowl week that Lombardi would retire, and two weeks after the game he made the announcement official.[55] Sensing what was in the air, during the Super Bowl, several veteran Packers got together at halftime and decided to play the last thirty minutes for the "Old Man." After the game, they carried him off the field on their shoulders. "This is the best way to leave a football field," Lombardi told them.[56]

BROADWAY JOE

If one player epitomized the American Football League, it had to be Joe Namath. He was everything the AFL both wanted to be and promoted itself as—young, trendy, and exciting. As a star quarterback at the University of Alabama, Namath enjoyed flouting authority, even if it meant incurring the wrath of legendary coach Paul "Bear" Bryant, who suspended him for part of one season for violating team rules. Coming out of college in 1965, he signed the biggest contract professional football had ever seen with the New York Jets. He became "Broadway Joe," a man defined by "long hair, a Fu Manchu mustache worth $10,000 . . . , [and] swinging nights in the live spots of the big city . . . all that spells insouciant youth in the Jet Age."[57] Namath reveled in everything afforded a young star in New York—the nightlife, beautiful women, and constant media attention. Before he had ever played his first game with the Jets, he was featured on the cover of *Sports Illustrated* under the heading, "Pro Football Goes Show Biz."

"I believe in the star system," Jets' owner Sonny Werblin said in the article. "It's what you put on the stage or playing field that draws people."[58] Namath did everything in his power to become a star, on and off the field. A story in a New York magazine told of how Namath spent the night before one game accompanied by a lovely young woman in his apartment, serving her drinks from his white leather bar. The morning of the game, he said goodbye to the woman, put on his mink coat, and then went out and beat the Raiders. The story was true, Namath said, except that "the bar isn't white and I wasn't wearing my mink."[59]

Namath's personal life often overshadowed his enormous, but inconsistent, abilities as a quarterback. When he became the first quarterback to pass for more than 4,000 yards in 1967, he also had more interceptions than touchdown passes. In 1968, however, Namath seemed to mature. He drastically cut down on his interceptions, and instead relied on the Jets' strong defense and running game. New York won the Eastern Conference with an 11-3 record. It then used three Namath touchdown passes to beat Oakland, 27–23 in the AFL Championship, although the game was not decided until the Jets recovered an Oakland fumble late in the game.[60]

In the NFL, the Packers could not overcome the loss of Lombardi and stumbled to a 6-7-1 record. It looked like a new dynasty was in the making with the Baltimore Colts, who flattened fifteen of sixteen opponents and avenged their only loss with a 34-0 mauling of Cleveland in the NFL Championship game. Even though quarterback Johnny Unitas was hurt much of the year, backup Earl Morrall filled in so well he was named the league's MVP. The Colts tied the record for the fewest points allowed in a season and were picked as more than two-touchdown favorites over the Jets in the Super Bowl.

The only ones who did not seem to believe in the Colts' superiority were the Jets, particularly Joe Namath. Humility was never Namath's strong suit, and there was no need for him to pretend otherwise at Super Bowl III.

"Namath was the first white athlete to rise above the long-standing hallucination that public humility was the appropriate repayment for the opportunity to succeed in sports," said sportswriter Marty Ralbovsky. "Namath reveled in his self-indulgence . . . why, [he said], can't an athlete admit publicly to drinking alcohol, smoking tobacco and making love to beautiful women—if, indeed, he does?"[61]

Namath didn't necessarily set out to be controversial; he was just being himself. At least, that's what he said about comments he made at the Miami Touchdown Club during Super Bowl week. Namath accepted an award for his play during the year, and when some fans began heckling him during his speech, Namath told them, "We are going to win on Sunday, I guarantee you."[62]

As expected, Namath got the headlines as the comment appeared in newspapers all across the country. "A football player who is really good doesn't need to talk like that," answered Colts' defensive end Bubba Smith. "He plays well on Sunday and someone else will talk about it."[63]

If Namath's boasts made the Colts angry, they never showed it during the game. What took place on January 12, 1969, at the Orange Bowl was perhaps the most shocking upset in the history of professional football. Led by Namath's MVP performance, the Jets beat the favored Colts 16–7 and came within four minutes of shutting out a team that, two weeks earlier, many writers had called the greatest of all time.

"To everybody in America, welcome to the AFL," said Jim Turner, who kicked three field goals for the Jets.[64]

"I've been waiting three years for this," said defensive back Johnny Sample, a former Colt who had one of the Jets' four interceptions. "The writers said the NFL would kick the hell out of our quarterback. But players play the game, not writers."[65]

HAIL TO THE CHIEFS

Certainly, the NFL felt humiliation after Super Bowl III, but most people in the league told themselves the Jets win over the Colts was a fluke. Namath was one of those hot-and-cold quarterbacks, and in that game he and the Jets were obviously hot. The NFL was marking its fiftieth season in 1969, and its players, coaches, and fans expected to celebrate by reestablishing dominance in the Super Bowl. The AFL also celebrated an anniversary in 1969— its tenth and last season. Shortly after Super Bowl IV, the AFL would cease to exist and officially become absorbed into the NFL.

It was somewhat fitting that Kansas City became the last AFL champion. The Chiefs/Texans franchise had been the most consistent organization over the league's ten seasons, winning more games and championships than any other team. But despite having a strong 11-3 season, the Chiefs finished behind the Raiders in the Western Conference. Qualifying for the playoffs as a wild card team, Kansas City would have to win two road games to get to the Super Bowl. Relying on their punishing defense, the Chiefs beat Namath and the Jets in New York, 13–6, and then got revenge for two regular season losses to the Raiders by winning the AFL Championship in Oakland, 17–7.

The Colts could not repeat their NFL dominance, but a similarly strong team emerged in Minnesota. As part of the NFL expansion in 1960, the Vikings took their early lumps, but by 1969 had transformed themselves into a younger version of the Packer dynasty—a team built on fundamentals, defense, and a conservative running attack. The Vikings scored the most points during that NFL season, permitted the fewest, and tied a league record by winning 12 straight games.[66] They easily won two home playoff games on their frozen field, including an impressive 27–7 defeat of Cleveland for the NFL Championship.

Odds makers still did not think much of the Chiefs or the AFL, and installed Minnesota as a heavy 13-1/2 point favorite. After two straight years in Miami, the Super Bowl would shift to New Orleans for the first time, but the weather did not cooperate. Rain, sub-freezing temperatures, and even the threat of a tornado kept the game from selling out. Of more concern to the Chiefs was an NBC television story that broke during Super Bowl week. The network reported on an impending Justice Department investigation into gambling in pro football, and Kansas City's quarterback Len Dawson was among the eight pro players implicated. Dawson denied any involvement, but the story dominated the headlines and became, at least for the Chiefs, a potential distraction.

Chiefs' safety Johnny Robinson said the report would not have any effect at all, adding "the whole thing is ridiculous. [But] I know it hit [Dawson] real hard. It ate him up inside, and it looked to me as if he aged five years from Tuesday to Thursday."[67]

If the gambling allegations bothered them, the Chiefs certainly didn't show it during the game. Dawson directed a balanced attack and threw a clinching touchdown pass to Otis Taylor in the third quarter to win game MVP honors. The Kansas City defense completely stifled Minnesota's offense in a 23–7 win that evened the Super Bowl series at two wins apiece for each league. It helped legitimize the merger and the AFL teams that had been called inferior just a few short years before. "Hell, maybe we shouldn't have merged," said former AFL Commissioner Joe Foss.[68]

In the Chiefs' noisy locker room, Lamar Hunt called it "a satisfying conclusion to the 10 years of the American Football League." When it was his turn to be interviewed, running back Mike Garrett didn't wait to be asked a question. "I just want to say I remember what Vince Lombardi said three years ago about us; that we're not as good as a lot of teams in the NFL." Looking directly into the television camera, Garrett paused, and then added, "Love ya, Vince."[69]

The gambling investigation that implicated Len Dawson came to nothing. After the Chiefs' win over the Vikings, Dawson received a locker room phone call from President Richard Nixon, who complimented him on playing so well under pressure. Before the game, Nixon had called coach Hank Stram to "tell you to dismiss the rumors from your minds and go out there and play like champions."[70]

According to Bill Matney, the NBC reporter who broke the story, "Nixon killed the whole investigation. I'm not saying that Lenny Dawson did a single thing wrong. I'm not saying anyone's guilty or not guilty. All I'm saying is that Nixon's phone calls to Stram and Dawson put the whole investigation on ice."[71]

A NEW ERA

Peace officially returned to professional football in January 1970 because for the first time in ten years, there would only be one league, rather than two. The AFL teams would officially join the American Conference of the NFL, while the NFL teams (or, at least most of them) would play in the National Conference.

Organizing and clarifying the new football order would not be an easy task, although some issues were easier to resolve than others. NBC's contract with the AFL would transfer over to the new AFC, as would CBS's contract with NFC teams, and the Super Bowl was divided on a yearly basis, with NBC scheduled to televise Super Bowl V in January 1971. NFL Films would continue to shoot team highlight films and produce special documentaries, but would no longer operate AFL Films, a separate unit created in 1966 to shoot AFL games.[72] NFL Films would continue to help produce a weekly pro football highlight show called *This Week in Pro Football*, hosted by former NFL players Pat Summerall and Tom Brookshier. The previous season, Summerall had hosted the show with NBC's Charlie Jones, in a transparent nod to balance NFL and AFL broadcasters. In an era before ESPN and the Internet, *This Week in Pro Football* was the only way for many people to see game highlights, and the show was syndicated in several television markets.

The NFL and AFL had held a common draft since 1967, and the 1970 draft took place January 27–28 in New York.[73] Based on their 1-13 record in 1969, the Steelers had the top overall pick in the draft, which they used to select Louisiana Tech quarterback Terry Bradshaw.[74] Chuck Noll had taken over as Pittsburgh's coach in 1969, and he used the 1970 draft as a springboard to build a Steelers dynasty that would go on to win four Super Bowls in the '70s. Bradshaw and Pittsburgh's third-round pick defensive back Mel Blount would both make the Hall of Fame, while its second-round pick, Ron Shanklin, would become a Pro Bowl receiver.

As usual, there were as many misses as hits in the draft.[75] Third overall pick Mike Phipps (Cleveland) and fourth overall pick Phil Olsen (Boston) never lived up to their draft position. Fifth overall pick Al Cowlings (Buffalo) later made a name for himself, but it would be on a southern California highway with Bills teammate O. J. Simpson, not on the football field. The merger also meant the end of the Playoff Bowl, a game that matched the losing teams from the first round of the NFL playoffs. The last Playoff Bowl took place on January 3, 1970, in Miami, where the Rams whipped the Cowboys, 31–0. Only 31,361 showed up at the game, suggesting that it had outlived its usefulness. Another game that faded into history was the AFL All-Star Game, held January 17, 1970, at the Astrodome in Houston. That night, quarterback Mike Livingston scored the last touchdown in AFL history on a 12-yard run that helped the West beat the East, 26–3. John Hadl, San Diego's quarterback, was the game's MVP.

One of the thorniest issues the NFL had to face was realignment. The league needed three NFL teams to move to the AFC in order to balance the conferences at thirteen teams apiece. Because hardly any established NFL teams were willing to make the move, Commissioner Rozelle sweetened the pot by offering relocated teams three million dollars. The Colts were the first team to take the offer, and by May 1969 the Steelers and Browns agreed to join them in the AFC.

Seemingly more difficult was trying to figure out how to set up divisions within the conferences. Eight months of negotiations failed to produce any results, as did a special meeting that ran thirty-six hours, going so long that Browns owner Art Modell noted, "two of my suits went out of style."[76] The issue was not settled until Commissioner Rozelle's secretary, Thelma Elkjer, pulled the new alignment out of a hat. The Cowboys, Giants, Redskins, Eagles, and Cardinals would play in the NFC East; the Vikings, Bears, Packers, and Lions in the NFC Central; and the Rams, 49ers, Falcons, and Saints in the NFC West. The AFC East included the Colts, Jets, Dolphins, Bills, and Patriots; the AFC Central the Steelers, Bengals, Browns, and Oilers; and the AFC West had the Raiders, Chiefs, Chargers, and Broncos. "There is some unhappiness," said Rozelle, "but I talked to some of the owners and they thought it was a fair shot and a satisfactory solution."[77]

It was a bit easier to develop a new playoff format. Each conference would qualify four playoff teams—the three division winners and a "wild card" team from the non-division winner with the best record. The NFL also created a master schedule for the next eight seasons. Each year, a team would play two games against opponents in its own division (home and away), various in-conference games, and a set of games against a specific division in the other conference.

The league wanted to keep the AFL-NFL rivalry going in the annual Hall of Fame preseason game, played each year in Canton, Ohio. Starting in 1971, the game would match an AFC team against an NFC team as part of the weekend festivities honoring Hall of Fame inductees.[78]

COMINGS AND GOINGS

Three players who would eventually make the Hall of Fame retired before the 1970 season began: guard Billy Shaw of Buffalo, linebacker Sam Huff of Washington, and defensive lineman Henry Jordan of Green Bay. Shaw's teammate Jack Kemp also retired and went on to represent the Buffalo area in Congress for eighteen years. His long political career included unsuccessful runs for both the presidency and vice presidency. Journeyman quarterback Tom Flores retired after the Chiefs' Super Bowl win and went on to win two more titles in the 1980s as head coach of the Raiders.[79]

The summer before the 1970 season brought two tragic losses to the football world. On June 16, Bears' running back Brian Piccolo lost his battle to cancer. Piccolo's story, particularly his friendship with Bears' teammate Gale Sayers, was later documented in the 1971 movie *Brian's Song*. Then on July 21, when his unit came under heavy fire, Bills' offensive lineman Bob Kalsu became the only active NFL player to be killed in action in Vietnam. With the war raging, many players had used deferments or political connections to avoid service, but Kalsu satisfied his ROTC commitment and arrived in Vietnam in November 1969. "I'm no better than anybody else," he said at the time. "I gave 'em my word. I'm gonna do it."[80] Two days after Kalsu's death, his wife gave birth to their first child. James Robert Kalsu Jr. never got to meet his father, but he later said, "I'm equally proud he made the decision. That's the kind of man I want to be, to have the integrity that he had."[81]

With heavy hearts, and a very real sense of the unknown, the NFL was ready to start its 1970 season.

WEEK ONE:
Kansas City Chiefs at Minnesota Vikings

LYING BEHIND A LOG

NFL schedule-makers have always had a touch of the dramatic. In 2002 the expansion Houston Texans played their first-ever game at home against their new in-state rivals, the Dallas Cowboys. The prime-time television game marked the return of football to Houston for the first time since the Oilers moved to Tennessee in 1997. Commissioner Paul Tagliabue called it "The Texas Super Bowl," and a crowd of 69,604 watched the Texans win, 19–10. "I wouldn't say we ambushed them," Houston nose guard Seth Payne said, "but I don't think they expected what they got."[1]

An even more dramatic opening game took place in 1950. The NFL had just absorbed three teams from the All-America Football Conference, and league commissioner Bert Bell wanted to teach the AAFC upstarts a lesson. How much influence Bell had over the schedule is debatable, but it hardly seems coincidental that in the opening week the Browns had to play in Philadelphia. Cleveland had won all four AAFC championships, while the Eagles had won two consecutive NFL titles.

Bell probably figured the Eagles could show the Browns a little humility, but in his wildest dreams the NFL commissioner could not have foreseen the Browns' dominating, 35–10 win in a game that was not even as close as the final score. "It was no upset," Eagles tackle Bucko Kilroy said afterward. "Man for man, they were just a better team."[2] Browns coach Paul Brown usually avoided praising his players, but after this game couldn't help it, "I think today we were the best football team I've ever seen."[3]

Twenty years later, the NFL schedule set up a similar matchup in Minnesota. On opening day, September 20, 1970, the Vikings would get a chance to end eight months of anger and frustration by hosting the Kansas City Chiefs. In Super Bowl IV, the Chiefs had not only beaten the NFL champion Vikings, they had humiliated and physically punished them. Despite being listed as almost two-touchdown favorites, Minnesota had looked confused and listless as it lost the last-ever game between NFL and AFL champions, 23–7. "We've been lying behind a log for eight months waiting for this game," said Vikings' coach Bud Grant, in typical understated fashion.[4]

His players were not quite as reserved. Particularly grating for them was the Super Bowl IV highlight film created by NFL Films, in which Chiefs coach Hank Stram wore a microphone. Much of Stram's commentary was interesting, if not outright funny, such as his advice that the Chiefs offense "keep matriculating the ball down the field," and his repetitive demand that they run "65 Toss Power Trap" for their first touchdown. But some of it was also very critical of the Vikings, including his observation that Minnesota looked "flat as hell" early in the game. When the Vikings had trouble covering the Chiefs' receivers on a particular play, Stram said that safety Karl Kassulke looked like he was in a Chinese fire drill. "Sure, I was embarrassed," said Kassulke, who had seen the highlight show over the summer. "Every defensive back gets beat now and then. But I'd damn sure like to stick that ball in Stram's ear on Sunday."[5]

Both teams returned to the new season with essentially the same rosters that played in Super Bowl IV. The Chiefs got very little help in the 1970 NFL draft; they selected offensive lineman Sid Smith of University of Southern California with their first pick, but Smith played only three undistinguished seasons in Kansas City before leaving the NFL for good in 1974. The Chiefs fared no better in the later rounds, and hardly any picks from their 1970 draft became starters, much less standouts. It was still a strong team, but poor drafting was to be a primary reason the team's success started to wane after 1972. The Vikings' draft was similarly mediocre, and first-round pick John Ward, a lineman from Oklahoma State, had six unspectacular years in Minnesota. They did find a steal, however, in the tenth round with the selection of tight end Stu Voigt, who would be a solid performer for eleven seasons and play in three Super Bowls.

THE MISSING PLUMBER

The one notable absence from the rematch was Joe Kapp, the Minnesota quarterback who had become a folk hero during the Super Bowl season. In an era of picture-perfect passers like Sonny Jurgensen and Johnny Unitas, Kapp was more admired for his toughness than his athletic skills. "You won't see me ducking out the window when somebody wants to tangle," he once said.[6] Sportswriter Marty Ralbovsky wrote that if "watching Namath was like watching an artist at work, watching Kapp was comparable to watching a plumber fix pipes."[7]

Still, Kapp seemed to inspire something special in his teammates, and his fire played a large part in the Vikings' success. "There are three kinds of quarterbacks," said Minnesota defensive back Dale Hackbart. "There's the brain, like Bart Starr, and the arm, like Joe Namath, and the leader, like Joe Kapp."[8] As teammate Karl Kassulke simply put it, "Joe Kapp is one tough son of a bitch."[9] When he was named the team's MVP after the 1969 season, Kapp refused the award, saying that all the players deserved the honor. He truly seemed to live up to the team's motto, "Forty for Sixty"—forty men playing together for sixty minutes.

But Kapp, whose esprit de corps apparently had financial limits, was now no longer one of the forty. Prior to the 1969 season, he became one of the few NFL players to play out his option, meaning he simply allowed his contract to expire without signing a new one. The unusual move made Kapp one of the NFL's few free agents for the 1970 season. Minnesota, apparently figuring it had enough pieces to win a championship even without its star plumber, never did sign Kapp, and most other teams shied away as well.

Minnesota was no stranger to quarterback problems, and in fact, one such controversy threatened the franchise right from the start. When the Vikings began as an expansion team in 1961, the franchise's two most dominant personalities were head coach Norm Van Brocklin and rookie quarterback Fran Tarkenton. "We had had our differences," said Tarkenton. "We're both strong personalities; both stubborn cases in our own ways."[10]

Van Brocklin, "The Dutchman," was a foul-mouthed, chain-smoking former quarterback who took over the Vikings the season after leading the Eagles to the 1960 NFL championship. He made the Hall of Fame as a pocket passer, and he wanted his young quarterback to play that way as well. But at just barely six feet tall and 190 pounds, Tarkenton felt better on the run, especially given the Vikings' sketchy offensive line. Simply as a way of surviving, he began to "scramble," and while his constant running and weaving left defenders dizzy, it also drove Van Brocklin crazy. On top of everything else, the coach wanted the reserved Tarkenton, the son of a Methodist minister, to be more aggressive. "[He's just] like a preacher's son," Van Brocklin complained of his quarterback, "too damned nice."[11]

Van Brocklin and Tarkenton lasted six stormy years together, and departed within a day of each other after the 1966 season. Tarkenton demanded and eventually got a trade (to the Giants), while after a year's layoff Van Brocklin resurfaced as coach of the Falcons.

To keep the franchise from coming apart at the seams, Minnesota looked to the Canadian Football League. Joe Kapp came from British Columbia, where he had led the BC Lions to the first Grey Cup title in team history.[12] A far more significant move was the hiring of Bud Grant as head coach. The former NFL and NBA star had spent ten years coaching in the CFL, winning more than 100 games and 4 Grey Cups. Grant's icy demeanor and conservative approach seemed a perfect fit for Minnesota, and he soon turned the Vikings into consistent winners. Under Grant and Kapp, the team went to the playoffs for the first time in 1968, followed by the Super Bowl season in 1969.

With Kapp still temporarily looking for work as the 1970 season began, the Vikings turned their offense over to Gary Cuozzo, an adequate quarterback playing for his third team in eight seasons. But the Vikings, a team built on Grant's philosophy of ball control, running, and defense, weren't necessarily looking for the spectacular. In 1968 journeyman Earl Morrall had won NFL MVP honors and taken the Colts to the Super Bowl, suggesting that a great team could win with just an above-average quarterback.

"[It] doesn't hamper our offense at all," said Grant of the quarterback change. "If anything, it enlarges it. Gary is a very intelligent man with exceptional retention. I'm perfectly sure Gary will do well."[13] Cuozzo, who had backed up Unitas in Baltimore, knew what it was like to replace a popular quarterback. "I really didn't feel pressure because of Joe's popularity with the squad," he said. "The pressure I felt was on quarterbacking the league champions. I wanted to repeat it."[14]

The Chiefs-Vikings rematch would also give Grant another chance to test his coaching philosophy against his polar opposite, Hank Stram. Few had criticized the Vikings in 1969 when they led the NFL in scoring and beat fourteen of sixteen opponents. But when the Minnesota offense disappeared in the Super Bowl, critics called it stodgy, primitive, and outdated.[15] By contrast, Stram's offense was high-flying, with its multiple sets, men in motion, and moving pass pocket. On the eve of Super Bowl IV, Stram predicted, "This game will match the offense of the future against the offense of the past. The decade of the '60s was the decade of simplicity. The '70s will be the decade of difference. What we do is to create a moment of hesitation, a moment of doubt in the defense."[16]

When Kansas City won the Super Bowl, Stram was hailed as a genius and Grant's philosophy was relegated to the Mesozoic Era of football. Lost in the discussion was the fact that the Chiefs barely outgained the Vikings in total yardage, and scored one of their two touchdowns after a turnover deep in Minnesota territory.

The Vikings' defense was strong even in its early years, and over the course of nine seasons the team developed a dominating unit. The focal point was the defensive line, which featured two future Hall of Famers and perhaps the most durable player in NFL history. Defensive end Jim Marshall began his career in Cleveland, but then joined the Vikings for their 1961 expansion season. He went on to play until 1979, setting NFL longevity records for most consecutive games (282) and most games started (270).[17]

Marshall's rugged lifestyle also seemed to fit in well in Minnesota. In the off-season, he skydived, snowmobiled, and generally lived like a real-life Paul Bunyan. One such adventure almost ended in disaster. Marshall and sixteen others were caught in a Wyoming blizzard, while taking a fifty-five-mile winter hike. Marshall's snowmobile went off a steep cliff and almost rolled on top of him, but his companions managed to pull him to safety. When the blizzard forced them to spend the night huddled near a tree, the group kept warm by burning the only thing it had—money. "Money didn't mean anything at this stage," Marshall said. "You can't beat nature with money. We would have burned everything we had if necessary."[18] Marshall credited his football training for helping him survive until help arrived.

Despite his success on the football field, and his life off of it, Marshall was better known for one event that took place on October 25, 1964. In a game against the San Francisco 49ers, Marshall recovered a fumble but somehow got confused and ran sixty-six yards in the wrong direction. When he reached the end zone, Marshall threw the ball away, celebrating what he believed to be a touchdown. Since the ball went out of bounds, and in the wrong end zone, the resulting score was a safety for the 49ers, not a Vikings' touchdown.

"That is something I would rather forget, although it's not going to happen," Marshall later said. "In the years I spent playing football, trying to play the best I could play, to have that all overshadowed by one play . . . it's not the ideal situation."[19] Marshall redeemed himself later in the game, forcing a fumble which was recovered by Carl Eller, who returned it for the game-winning touchdown in a 27–22 Vikings victory.

Aside from Marshall, the most interesting Vikings' player was team captain Bill Brown. Brown was an undersized, 5-foot-11 running back who earned the nickname "Boom-Boom" for his straight-ahead, reckless running style. He wasn't the most talented player in the league, but may have been the most determined.

"I hated to see him come around the corner," said Cowboys' defensive back Herb Adderley. "He ran with his shoulder about two feet off the ground and when he hit you, he punished you. Trying to tackle him was like to trying to tackle a rolled up rug."[20]

Brown's personality and passion for the game fit the Vikings' philosophy perfectly, and he became a fan favorite. When his time as a starter ended, Brown volunteered for special teams and spent the tail end of his fourteen-year career as a wedge buster on the Vikings' kickoff team.

"He was incredible," said Fran Tarkenton, who played with Brown later in the '70s. "He went from a genuine superstar to playing little more than special teams, and he never complained. There's never been one like him."[21]

It was that kind of toughness that defined the Vikings, especially on defense. Jim Marshall, defensive end Carl Eller, and defensive tackle Alan Page were the core of a unit that came to be known as the "Purple People Eaters," after a popular song of the 1950s. That nucleus helped propel the Vikings to nine NFC Central titles in ten years starting in 1970, and put Eller and Page in the Hall of Fame. Page was especially dominant, and in 1971 was named NFL MVP, one of only two defensive players ever to win the award.[22] Much of the Vikings' defensive success was due the fact that the team stayed together so long. Marshall played until 1979, while Eller and Page stayed with the Vikings through 1978. Another Hall of Famer, safety Paul Krause, anchored Minnesota's defensive secondary from 1968 to 1979. He ended his career with an NFL-record eighty-one interceptions.

Despite Minnesota's superior defense, the Chiefs had easily handled them in Super Bowl IV, and the Kansas City players came into the game with a quiet confidence. Maybe Minnesota wanted to turn the game into a grudge match, but for their part, the Chiefs looked at it as business as usual. "It's important we win because it's the first game," said running back Mike Garrett, "not because it's Minnesota. If you lose your first game playing in our division, it's like cutting your own throat."[23]

"I think we've graduated to the right tempo," added Stram. "This is a mature team. They know what to do."[24]

Even though they were playing at Metropolitan Stadium in Bloomington, Minnesota, the Vikings would not enjoy their preferred home-field advantage. Vikings players felt that bitter cold intimidated opponents, as did the fact that many of them wore short sleeves even under the most brutal conditions. Head Coach Bud Grant played up the psychological edge and refused to allow heating devices on the Vikings sidelines.[25] In Minnesota's two home playoff wins during the 1969 season, the temperatures were a mere ten and eight degrees. For the 3 p.m. kickoff this September Sunday, it would be a much more reasonable seventy degrees in Minnesota, aided by a thirteen mile per hour breeze.

"I KEECK A TOUCHDOWN!"

The rematch started much like the Super Bowl, with defenses dominating in a scoreless first quarter. Cuozzo and the Vikings finally put together a drive in the second quarter, which led to a 20-yard field goal by Fred Cox and a 3–0 lead. Cox would go on to hit one more field goal and all three of his extra points.[26]

In 1970 most of the kickers in the NFL were of the old-fashioned, straight-ahead variety like Cox, and side-winding "soccer-style" kickers were still very much a novelty. In fact, only five teams had unconventional kickers—Jan Stenerud with the Chiefs, Garo Yepremian with the Dolphins, Horst Muhlmann with the Bengals, and the Gogolak brothers, Pete with the Giants and Charlie with the Patriots. These kickers came in for quite a bit of ridicule from other players, not only for their unconventional style and slight frames, but the fact that most of them were from foreign countries. Stenerud (Norway), Muhlmann (Germany), Yepremian (Cyprus) and the Gogolaks (Hungary) had never even seen a football until they emigrated to the United States, which prompted Lions' defensive tackle Alex Karras to complain that these kickers would come into a game, kick a field goal, then exclaim, "I keeck a touchdown!"[27]

In reality, kicking a football like a soccer ball was much more efficient and accurate. Stenerud proved that when he hit 77 percent of his field goals in 1969; Yepremian would lead the NFL in 1970 at 76 percent. In addition, coming from the side added a lot more power—Stenerud, who would eventually make the Hall of Fame, had kicked a record 48-yarder against Minnesota in Super Bowl IV.[28] That opened a lot of eyes in the NFL at a time when a 50-yard field goal was a rarity, and straight-ahead kickers were struggling to hit 50 percent of their attempts.[29] By the end of the decade, soccer kickers were the norm rather than the exception.

Defensively, the Vikings seemed much more prepared for the Chiefs' multiple offense, especially in handling the running game. Kansas City had rushed for 151 yards in Super Bowl IV, but in the rematch it could manage only one first down running, and finished the day with 63 yards on twenty-one attempts. Mike Garrett also coughed up a fumble for the Chiefs in the second quarter, which Marshall recovered and began to run back (the right direction, it should be noted). When he encountered trouble halfway to the end zone, Marshall lateraled to Roy Winston, who finished the 36-yard touchdown run for a 10–0 Minnesota lead.

With the running game shut down, Chiefs quarterback Len Dawson was forced to throw. He found some initial results with a 59-yard touchdown to Otis Taylor, who had slipped behind Kassulke, but Minnesota clamped down on the Chiefs' offense the rest of the game, holding Kansas City to a harmless Stenerud field goal. Kassulke got his revenge on Stram with an interception off a deflected pass, and Krause added another interception—one of four turnovers the Vikings forced on the afternoon. They also sacked Dawson twice.

"We didn't stop to think every time they shifted into one of their formations," said Krause. "When they went into a certain set, we just tried to ruin it for them with blitzes or by jamming the blocking."[30]

Cuozzo also threw two interceptions but otherwise directed the Minnesota offense with efficiency. After Taylor's score, Cuozzo retaliated, leading the Vikings on a 97-yard drive that culminated with a 1-yard Dave Osborn run, and a 17–7 halftime lead. Cuozzo was helped a great deal by a running game that produced 132 yards; double what the Vikings had accomplished against Kansas City in the Super Bowl. Bill Brown rammed for 55 yards, while Oscar Reed added 35. After the Chiefs cut the deficit to a touchdown, it was Reed who essentially put the game away with another 1-yard score in the fourth quarter to make it 24–10. A late Cox field goal made the final score 27–10, although the statistics were not as lopsided as the score. On the day, Minnesota outgained the Chiefs in total yardage by only 220–218. "Every game is decided really by four or five big plays," said Stram. "The difference in this game was the fumble recovery that they turned into a touchdown."[31]

"Man, was I proud," admitted Joe Kapp, who watched the game with relatives in California.[32] "Kapp?" said Mick Tinglehoff, the Vikings' center, "We'd like to have Joe back, sure. But Cuozzo's our quarterback."[33] Paul Krause shared the opinion. "Everybody looks to Cuozzo as the leader now," he said. "He proved it. If Kapp comes back, he'll have to beat Gary out."[34] For his part, Cuozzo tried to take the win in stride. "Scared? No, I wasn't scared," he said afterward. "Up for the game, but not scared. Scared isn't a word for a football player."[35]

Schedule-makers had put the Chiefs on the road for three straight weeks to open the season, and after Minnesota, the team would have to go to Baltimore and Denver. Kansas City lost to the Broncos, but beat the Colts 44–24 behind safety Johnny Robinson, who intercepted three passes and returned a fumble for a touchdown. On October 11, they rebounded with a 23–10 home win over Boston, a game that marked the season debut of none other than Joe Kapp.

Desperate for a quarterback, the lowly Patriots signed Kapp to a five-year deal in September that made him the highest paid player in the league.[36]

As if reliving his Super Bowl IV nightmare, Kapp completed just two of eleven passes against the Chiefs for a total of 16 yards. When Boston hosted Minnesota on December 13, the Vikings also roughed up their former teammate, intercepting Kapp three times in a 35–14 win.

The Vikings used their emotional win over the Chiefs as a springboard to another championship season. They captured the NFC Central title with a 12-2 record, finishing two games ahead of the Detroit Lions (who also qualified for the playoffs as the NFC wild card team). Minnesota's defense was outstanding all season, permitting only 143 points, the fewest in the NFL. On offense, Cuozzo struggled after the opening day win, in part because of a mid-season ankle injury. He completed less than 50 percent of his passes, threw more interceptions (10) than touchdown passes (7), and finished near the bottom of NFL quarterback rankings. Dave Osborn led the team with 681 yards rushing but averaged only 3.3 yards per carry, while Bill Brown and Oscar Reed averaged 3.2 and 3.1 yards, respectively, in limited roles. It appeared that if the Vikings were going to make a return trip to the Super Bowl, defense, and perhaps their frozen home-field advantage, was going to have to carry them.

★ 4 ★

WEEK ONE:
New York Jets at Cleveland Browns

"THE SHOW IS THE THING"

Technically, the 1970 season did not open with the Chiefs-Vikings game or with any other games that Sunday. Play actually began on Friday night, September 18, when the Rams beat the Cardinals, 34–13 in Los Angeles. The following night, the Bears beat the Giants in New York, 24–16. It was not unusual for the NFL to play on Friday nights and Saturdays, and there would be seven such games in 1970. These games were often required because of scheduling conflicts, most particularly with college football or professional baseball. In an era of multi-purpose, multi-user stadiums, the NFL had to share, just like everyone else. In the Giants' case, Yankee Stadium had to be prepped for a three-game baseball series between the Yankees and Washington Senators that began on September 21.

Football on days other than Sunday had been a tradition as old as the NFL itself, especially on Thanksgiving—the Lions began playing annually in 1934 and the Cowboys started in 1966. The AFL had also played a game on Thanksgiving each of its ten seasons. The NFL had experimented with occasional games on Monday nights to take advantage of captive audiences and attractive matchups. The first Monday night game was played on September 28, 1964, when Detroit set a home attendance record (59,203) against the Packers.[1] The success of that game prompted the NFL to stage a limited number of Monday night games from 1966–1969, and the AFL added some Monday games in 1968.

A permanent Monday night schedule was a marriage of convenience between the NFL and ABC. ABC had been left out in the cold during the last round of contract negotiations in 1964, despite offering the NFL more than $26 million over two years. "I couldn't get it through my mind," says Ed Scherick, then ABC's vice president in charge of programming. "Do you realize our whole blasted *network* had cost only $15 million in 1951?"[2] It was a clear signal, said *Sports Illustrated*'s William Johnson, that "whatever pro football did in the future, the decisions would have to be made in terms of the economic needs of television."[3]

ABC needed *Monday Night Football* more than the other networks did. CBS had the NFL/NFC games, and a strong Monday lineup that included top-rated shows *Here's Lucy* and *The Doris Day Show*. NBC had the former AFL/AFC contract and, like CBS, passed on the opportunity. Despite a last-minute offer from billionaire Howard Hughes and his sports network,[4] ABC won the thirteen-game contract for $8.6 million.

"We were worried that we'd lose a whole load of affiliates to Hughes on Monday," said ABC producer Roone Arledge. "We didn't delude ourselves. We simply couldn't risk the competition."[5] In reality, ABC also had serious doubts about *Monday Night Football*, but NFL commissioner Pete Rozelle used the Hughes offer as a wedge to get Arledge and ABC to commit.[6]

Arledge had made a name for himself at ABC with his work on college football, the Olympics, and the *Wide World of Sports*. Since *Wide World of Sports* focused on lesser-known sports such as sailing and weightlifting, Arledge had to find a different way to gain an audience for the series. By personalizing the athletes and giving audiences an extremely close up look at them, Arledge shifted the emphasis of television sports from the competition to what *Wide World of Sports*'s opening theme would famously describe as "the human drama of athletic competition."

"What we set out to do," Arledge later explained, "was get the audience involved emotionally. If they didn't give a damn about the game, they might still enjoy the program."[7] It was an approach Arledge had also used with some success when ABC had televised AFL games from 1960–1965.

Arledge wanted to employ that same philosophy with *Monday Night Football*, but with a slight twist. He believed *MNF* could become more than a game—it could become an event. Coverage of pro football on television had traditionally focused on the action and the outcome of the game; Arledge wanted to add show-biz. It was part of what the *New York Times* called his sports credo: the game was no longer the thing—the show was the thing.

To make it work, Arledge needed football broadcasters who could be more than just announcers. He wanted a broadcast booth that had star power, and to get it he had to break a few television rules. First, he added a third man to the broadcast booth, a revolutionary idea at a time when every game was handled by two people—the play-by-play person and a game analyst. Next, Arledge ignored the rule that required announcers to be approved by the league. He wanted someone caustic, controversial, and colorful in his *MNF* booth—someone he knew would never gain the approval of the stodgy NFL. The man he had in mind was Howard Cosell.

Cosell got into broadcasting by accident. While working as a lawyer in New York in the 1950s, he was asked to host a Little League Baseball radio program, an opportunity that ultimately caused him to change careers. In the 1960s Cosell rose to prominence as a boxing announcer and general sports reporter on ABC television, which may have been a surprise to everyone but him. "Some men are endowed with greatness," he admitted, showcasing the egomania and bombast that earned him legions of critics.[8] Among other things, those critics called him "sport's answer to Martha Mitchell,"[9] "all wrong for television . . . overeducated, odd in appearance,"[10] and "someone who can no more keep his mouth shut than a porcupine can sing opera."[11] But others respected his willingness to tackle tough subjects and his journalistic integrity, both of which were evidenced in his public support for Muhammad Ali when the boxer was blacklisted for refusing induction into the U.S. military.

Arledge figured Cosell would be the perfect lightning rod to quick-charge his *MNF* broadcast booth. To join him, Arledge lined up play-by-play man Keith Jackson and analyst and former quarterback Don Meredith, a complete novice at football broadcasting. Meredith had failed in his efforts to lead the Cowboys to a Super Bowl and, tired of constant criticism from fans and the media, had retired in 1969 at the relatively young age of thirty-one. Unsure about what to do with his future, Meredith hesitated when ABC executives approached him because he also had an offer to work weekends on CBS. His good friend and former teammate, Pete Gent, told him, "Don, on Monday nights you're going to be the only game on. If you're good, you're going to make a fortune."[12]

Meredith signed with ABC, which used an exhibition game between Detroit and Kansas City as a practice run. By his own admission, Meredith was terrible and unprepared. According to Arledge, Meredith said, "Look, fellas, this really isn't my bag, and I don't even know that much about football. I think I'll just leave."[13] Cosell eventually calmed down Meredith and persuaded him to give it another shot, so Arledge's three-man experiment was in place when the regular season opened in Cleveland, even if one part had serious doubts.

The first *Monday Night Football* game was a complete success from every standpoint. Jackson was professional, but Meredith and Cosell produced instant chemistry. "Dandy Don" was "fresh, undisciplined, honest, witty [and] homey."[14] And just as Arledge had hoped, Cosell became the conduit through which everything flowed—a man whom audiences could love or hate, but could not ignore. Millions of football fans tuned in to watch the game, but they stayed tuned for Howard Cosell.

"Then the mail came in," said Arledge. "Sacks and sacks of it. In Howard Cosell, they found the man they loved to hate."[15] *Newsweek* called him "the master of the verbal cheap shot. Wretched prattle . . . towering ignorance of football."[16] Someone asked Arledge if he was worried about the controversy. "Worried?" he said. "That's exactly what I'm looking for!"[17]

"Maybe I am abrasive," said Cosell. "But it is not entirely my fault that some people react the way they do. I am simply trying to bring the tenets of good journalism to television. It is difficult because sportscasting is a bottle that was put to sea many years ago and has been lost."[18]

History has vindicated both Arledge and *Monday Night Football*. The show became a ratings winner for ABC, which paid $8.6 million that first season for the rights to the games. Its success eventually translated into an eight-year, $15.5 billion dollar contract signed by ESPN in 2011. The program also made celebrities out of Meredith and Cosell, especially Cosell who was both cheered and vilified at every *MNF* event. [19] "It was a carnival," said broadcaster and former Giants star Frank Gifford, who replaced Jackson as the play-by-play man in 1971. "Every city we went to, Don had a great name for it. He called it 'Mother Love's Traveling Freak Show.'"[20]

Interest in *MNF* became so great that ABC even received death threats from angry fans whose teams were not selected for the weekly halftime highlights segment. Cosell narrated the segment, which in the days before ESPN, was often the only time audiences could see highlights of their favorite teams. "We used to tell people that Howard was in charge of picking the teams that were featured," recalled producer Don Ohlmeyer. "Howard had nothing to do with it, but we figured if there were death threats we would prefer they be directed at Howard."[21]

Even though Cosell's egomania eventually became disruptive, he helped make the program exactly what Arledge envisioned—an event. *Monday Night Football* was the closest thing to the Super Bowl in terms of must-see sports television. Bowling leagues, bingo parlors, and poker games either shut down or moved to a different night. *Variety* reported a significant decline in Monday night movie attendance, while restaurant and bar business fell off some 25 percent.[22] Herb Rushing, owner of two steakhouses in California, noted, "Monday's the worst night of the week, period. It's been terrible the past few months but since the NFL telecasts began it's atrocious."[23]

During the fall, Monday night meant *Monday Night Football*, and by the time it left ABC in 2006, *MNF* was the longest-running prime-time entertainment show in history. "Even people who didn't like football, watched *Monday Night Football*," said announcer Al Michaels, who sat in the *MNF* booth for twenty years, starting in 1986. "It was an institution."[24]

It didn't last forever, of course. Meredith left for a few years before returning in the late 1970s, and there were many other cast changes as well. The 1980s saw Cosell's departure and the rise of more viewing options on cable television, both of which cut into *MNF*'s popularity. ABC stayed with the game until 2006, before handing the program over to sister-network ESPN.

It doesn't get the huge ratings anymore, and it's certainly not the cultural force it was in the 1970s, but *Monday Night Football* is still alive and kicking in 2013. It deserves a lot of credit for changing the way football is telecast, and it pioneered many innovations beyond the three-man broadcast booth. "This was the first time that a big sports event was cast the same way you would cast a Western, with a good guy and a bad guy," said former NBC Universal Sports and Olympics Chairman Dick Ebersol.[25]

STADIUM STRUGGLES

ABC's first Monday night game took place in one of the NFL's oldest stadiums. Cleveland's Municipal Stadium opened in 1931 as a multi-purpose facility with seating for more than eighty thousand fans, depending on the activity.[26] Its primary tenants were the Cleveland Indians, and during the team's pennant-winning seasons in 1948 and 1954, games would often draw more than seventy thousand fans. During the World Championship season of 1948, the Indians drew 2.62 million fans, a baseball record that lasted until the Dodgers broke it in 1962.[27] The NFL's Cleveland Rams began playing in the stadium in 1936, and then the Browns took over in 1946, when the Rams left Cleveland for Los Angeles.

By 1970, continuous use of the stadium by the Indians, Browns, college football teams, and rock bands made it seem old and out of date. Because it was built with pillars, views were obstructed for many fans, and its proximity to Lake Erie led to bitter cold winds during the winter and swarms of insects during the summer. For all of these reasons, along with its cavernous size and the general poor play of the Indians, Cleveland Stadium became known as the "Mistake on the Lake."

Browns' owner Art Modell was a shrewd businessman who knew all about the problems with his home stadium. Modell was also aware that several NFL teams were designing new, modern facilities, including two teams in his own division. In 1970 the Pittsburgh Steelers opened Three Rivers Stadium, while the Cincinnati Bengals moved to Riverfront Stadium. With the Houston Oilers playing in the indoor comfort of the Astrodome, which was only five years old, Modell felt he was falling behind his chief rivals.

Modell was unique among NFL owners in that he did not come from a patrician background and was not a "gentleman" sportsman with family money to fall back on. He worked in advertising and television in New York and borrowed heavily to buy the Browns in 1961. The team was his main source of income, and he was constantly looking for ways to keep the Browns profitable, which was one of the reasons he decided to let the Browns host the first Monday night game.[28] "No one else wanted the game because they thought it would die at the gate," he said. "But I was willing to take a chance. All I said was, 'Give me the Jets,' because I figured having the New York market would give the game a jump."[29]

Modell also took some business risks regarding Cleveland Stadium, which he eventually purchased, becoming the Indians' landlord. Over the next twenty-five years, Modell worked to get improvements to the facility, but he ran into several problems. The Indians left in the 1990s to build a new baseball-only stadium, and Modell's debt forced him to get financial help from the city for any renovations. By the mid-1990s, Modell tried to work two angles: getting the city to pass a special tax to fund renovations, while secretly meeting with Baltimore officials about moving the team. Not waiting on the outcome of the vote, on November 7, 1995, Modell announced he was moving the Browns to Baltimore. The deal was one of the most lucrative in NFL history—a rent-free, $200 million stadium which would open in 1998, and permission to charge as much as $80 million in one-time seat license fees to fans wishing to buy season tickets. "I had no choice" but to accept it, said Modell. "What is required, and what we have here, is far beyond the capacity of the community in Cleveland."[30]

Cleveland voters went ahead and approved the tax, then filed suit to try and keep the team from moving. Even though the suit failed, the city did retain the rights to the team name, history, and colors, which they resurrected when the NFL awarded Cleveland an expansion franchise in 1999. That inaugural season the team played in a brand-new Cleveland Browns Stadium, a $290 million facility built with money from several government and private sources. Modell's team had to change its name to the Baltimore Ravens.

For his part, Modell became the most vilified man in northeast Ohio the moment he agreed to move the Browns to Baltimore. Even NBA star LeBron James, when he announced his intention to leave his hometown Cleveland Cavaliers for the Miami Heat in 2010, could not dislodge Modell as public enemy number one. After LeBron's announcement, the *Cleveland Plain-Dealer* asked area fans about their biggest sports disappointment. While 29 percent named LeBron's departure, 64 percent still said it was the Browns leaving Cleveland.[31]

"I'm not waiting around for LeBron to take me off the hook," Modell said. "I'm not on any hook. I did what I thought was right for the players, coaches and employees in my organization. I have no regrets."[32]

A TALE OF TWO CITIES

None of this—the state of Cleveland's stadium or the traveling circus known as *Monday Night Football*—affected the Browns or Jets as they prepared for the season opener. Joe Namath remained the face of the Jets, but more and more his off-field activities were a distraction. In 1970 he played the starring role in a movie called *CC and Company*, which also featured Ann-Margret. The biker movie was an attempt to cash in on the popularity of *Easy Rider*, but Namath was certainly no Dennis Hopper. *Sports Illustrated* seemed to speak for fans everywhere with the cover of its August 17 issue, which featured Namath working on yet another movie, *The Last Rebel*, and the heading, "Back to Work, Joe Namath!"

When Namath wasn't making movies, he was running afoul of Commissioner Pete Rozelle. Shortly after the Jets' Super Bowl win in 1969, Namath and some associates opened a Manhattan bar called Bachelors III, and it didn't take long for the establishment to get the reputation as a hangout for gamblers and other bad characters. The NFL had always taken gambling, or even the hint of gambling, seriously, so Rozelle acted quickly and ordered Namath to sell his interest in the place.[33] Namath refused to back down, and at a teary June 6, 1969, press conference he announced his retirement, even though he had not been personally connected to any wrongdoing. "I'm not selling, I'm quitting," Namath sobbed. When Namath's college coach, Bear Bryant, later called to try and talk him out of it, Namath said, "No sir, coach. I know I'm right. I know I've got to do this."[34]

Cooler heads ultimately prevailed and Namath eventually sold his part of the bar and ended his retirement, but he let the Jets twist in the wind for six weeks before deciding to return to football.[35] "Turmoil follows Joe Namath everywhere," wrote sportswriter Dave Anderson, "as if it were an invisible member of his entourage. Because of it, Joe Namath never has a quiet crisis. The headlines are always big."[36]

Namath continued to be involved in film projects, television and newspaper advertising, and a chain of quick-lunch restaurants. The Jets, on the other hand, believed that Namath needed to spend his time worrying about quarterbacking and not his next television or film role. The team had won the AFL East in 1969 with a 10-4 record, but quickly dropped out of the playoffs with a first-round home loss to Kansas City. Namath and the offense took much of the blame for the 13–6 loss to the Chiefs—New York failed to score a single touchdown, despite at one point having a first and goal from the Kansas City 1-yard line. To beef up the offense, the Jets drafted tight end

Rich Caster in the second round of the 1970 draft, and Caster provided some immediate help. He ended up making the Pro Bowl three times during a thirteen-year career, eight years of which he spent with the Jets.[37]

The rest of New York's draft was for defense. Even though the Jets still had several capable defenders, many of them were on the downhill side of thirty, including linebacker Larry Grantham, who began playing with the team in 1960 when it was still the New York Titans. Defensive lineman Verlon Biggs and safety Jim Hudson were in their last seasons with the Jets, and Randy Beverly, a hero with two Super Bowl interceptions against the Colts, was already with the Patriots.

Unfortunately, the draft would not provide much help, in 1970 or in the future. Number one pick, defensive back Steve Tannen of Florida intercepted just twelve passes in his five years with the Jets, and draft picks Dennis Onkotz (third round, linebacker), John Ebersole (fourth round, linebacker), and Terry Stewart (sixth round, defensive back) never really panned out. Much like the Chiefs, the Jets would begin a long descent into mediocrity during the 1970s because of poor drafting.

The blue-collar Browns were the exact opposite of Namath and the glamorous Jets. While the New York players were almost household names, particularly the moonlighting quarterback, the Browns were virtually anonymous, except for Leroy Kelly, the two-time NFL rushing leader. Kelly had taken over for Browns Hall of Famer Jim Brown at running back in 1966, and somehow managed to replace the irreplaceable. He eventually made the Hall of Fame, and was one of the main reasons the Browns had advanced to two straight NFL Championship games, even though both ended in losses (34–0 to Baltimore in 1968 and 27–7 to Minnesota in 1969).

"Jim Brown used to say that anyone could run outside, but it took a great one to run inside," said Browns coach Blanton Collier. "Kelly can do that because he has good speed, balance and is quick to sense interior openings and get through."[38]

The problem for Collier was surrounding Kelly with other offensive weapons. Quarterback Bill Nelsen finished in the top half of NFL quarterbacks in 1969, but no one ever confused him with Namath in terms of leadership or ability. The Browns did have a game-breaker in wide receiver Paul Warfield, who as recently as 1968 had caught fifty passes for more than 1,000 yards and twelve touchdowns. But in a stunning move after the 1969 season, Modell traded the twenty-seven-year-old star, who was in the prime of his career, to the Miami Dolphins for a first-round draft pick.

"The people there were really upset to see Paul Warfield go," said running back Ron Johnson, whom Modell also traded. "Some of them took out ads in the newspapers saying they were giving up their season tickets."[39]

Johnson went to the Giants in exchange for receiver Homer Jones, who came to Cleveland as Warfield's replacement. The Browns' other wide receiver, Gary Collins, was a productive player over the course of his career, but as it turned out, neither he nor Jones had much left in the tank. Jones would retire after just one season in Cleveland, while Collins would last only two more years. In 1970 it appeared that the Browns offense would have to rely more than ever on Leroy Kelly.

These issues caused Cleveland to go after offensive players in the 1970 draft. The additional first-round pick the team acquired from Miami in the Warfield trade was the third overall draft pick—thanks to Miami's poor 3-10-1 record in 1969. In a clear statement about their confidence in Nelsen, the Browns used that pick to take Purdue quarterback Mike Phipps, then with their second first-round pick took University of Texas offensive tackle Bob McKay. As it turned out, neither player solved Cleveland's offensive problems. Phipps did play a dozen years in the league, but only seven with the Browns, and he finished his career hitting less than 50 percent of his passes and with twice as many interceptions as touchdowns. McKay played six undistinguished seasons in Cleveland.

The only help the Browns got in the draft came from their second-round pick—defensive lineman Jerry Sherk, who made the Pro Bowl four times in a twelve-year career. Sherk was a much-needed shot of youth into a unit that suddenly seemed very old. Defensive back Erich Barnes and future Hall of Famer guard Gene Hickerson both started their careers in 1958; long-time Browns lineman Dick Schafrath started in 1959. Many of the team's defenders were holdovers from the team's last NFL title in 1964.

NAMATH'S BROWNOUT

An all-time Cleveland record crowd of 85,703 jammed into the old stadium to be a part of history. Not only was Joe Namath in town for the first *Monday*

Night Football game ever but the Browns were also making their AFC debut. "You know everyone's going to be trying to knock our blocks off," said linebacker Jim Houston. "We're the Establishment moving in."[40]

Shortly after 9 p.m. (EST), ABC's telecast hit the air with these words from Keith Jackson: "From Municipal Stadium in Cleveland, Ohio, two powers in professional football meet for the first time ever as members of the new American Football Conference of the National Football League."[41]

The first *MNF* score came on the Browns' first possession of the game. After the Jets took the kickoff and failed to move, Nelsen led a drive that culminated with an 8-yard touchdown pass to Collins. The second time the Browns got the ball, Nelsen was even more successful, driving 82 yards in ten plays before Bo Scott went over from 2 yards out, giving the Browns a 14–0 lead. The Jets were starting two rookie defensive backs, Tannen and Earlie Thomas, and their inexperience had led to two costly pass interference penalties on the drive. The Browns seemed in complete control after the first quarter.

An Emerson Boozer run sliced the lead to 14–7 at the half, but then came one of those magical plays that seem to happen so often on Monday night. The Browns' Homer Jones took the opening kickoff of the second half and raced 94 yards for a touchdown, increasing their lead to 21–14.

The Jets rallied in the fourth quarter, trailing only 24–21 with less than three minutes to play, and got the ball back by forcing a Browns' punt. The stage seemed set for another Namath comeback, until Billy Andrews made a diving interception deep in Jets territory, got up, and ran 25 yards for a clinching touchdown.

The first game in Monday night history was a wild 31–21 Cleveland victory. After the game, an ecstatic Modell answered those who criticized both his move to the AFC and hosting *Monday Night Football*. "I don't know if I made the right move," he said smugly. "Did you hear the crowd? Did you hear the din? They loved it."[42]

Somehow, the Jets managed to lose the game despite outgaining the Browns in total yards, 454–221, which included a 300-yard passing night from Namath and 108 yards rushing from Matt Snell. But the knock on Namath was always inconsistency—he seemed to manage to make a bad decision or throw an interception at the worst possible time, and on this night, it killed the Jets. The Browns forced four New York turnovers—one recovered fumble and three Namath interceptions, including Andrews' winning return. "We met a fine team and got licked," said Jets' coach Weeb Ewbank. "We can't do what we did and expect to win."[43]

Despite the loss, the Jets fully expected to make the playoffs for a third straight season. Their division, the AFC East, was one of the weaker divisions in the new NFL realignment. Buffalo and Boston were rebuilding, and would go on to win only three and two games, respectively, in 1970. The Miami Dolphins had won only three games the previous year and had never had a winning season in their four years of existence. The Jets, and most of the sportswriters around the country, figured the Cleveland loss would only be a small bump in the road.

"The Jets will be better once their rookies get some experience," wrote Chuck Heaton in the *Cleveland Plain-Dealer* the day after the game. "The way the two teams battled, it's just possible there could be a rematch with the American Football Conference honors at stake."[44]

But the Jets were in for some unhappy surprises that season. The Dolphins, who had hired Baltimore Colts coach Don Shula in the off-season, would be much, much stronger than anyone had guessed. They came to New York on October 10 and beat the Jets, 20–6, another game in which Namath threw three interceptions. After that defeat, the Jets record stood at 1-3, with their biggest obstacle of the season still looming. Realignment had put the Colts with the Jets in the AFC East, and on October 29, Baltimore would come to New York for the first of two games that season. As Namath and his team would discover, the Colts had very long memories, reaching all the way back to Super Bowl III.

The Browns also had playoff expectations, which were helped by an early season schedule that saw the team play four of their first five games at home. After a 34–31 loss in San Francisco, rookie quarterback Phipps replaced an injured Nelsen and led the Browns to a 15–7 win over the Steelers. That set the stage for a grudge match on October 11—the Browns and Bengals in the first-ever "Ohio Super Bowl." Bengals coach Paul Brown would be returning to Cleveland for the first time since Modell fired him in 1963.

After Cleveland's dramatic win over the Jets, week one of the 1970 NFL season was in the books—a week in which NFL and former AFL teams played in the regular season for the first time. The old NFL teams had a 3-1 advantage in head-to-head competition with former AFL teams, including the Vikings' win over the Chiefs and Cleveland's defeat of the Jets. The only AFL win that week came with the Oilers' 19–7 win over Pittsburgh, but now both teams were part of the AFC Central. One could also discount the Colts' 16–14 win in San Diego because both teams were now in the AFC. In that game, Baltimore rookie Jim O'Brien kicked three field goals, including the game-winner with less than a minute to play. He would make a much bigger kick under similar circumstances four months later.

WEEK TWO:
Pittsburgh Steelers at Denver Broncos

DENVER IS BURNING

As the Denver Broncos prepared to host the Pittsburgh Steelers in week two of the NFL season, they did so sitting on top of the AFC West. Oakland, Kansas City, and San Diego had all lost their opening week games, leaving Denver alone in first place with a record of 1-0. The Broncos had opened the season in Buffalo by beating the Bills, 25–10, holding O. J. Simpson to just 52 yards on eighteen carries. Denver allowed only 149 total yards and sacked Buffalo quarterbacks five times.

To say that the Broncos sitting in first place was a novelty, even if it was just for one week, would be an understatement for a team that had never had a winning record in its ten-year history. Denver was an original AFL franchise and had struggled to win games right from the outset. The team's only non-losing season (7-7) in 1962 was celebrated chiefly for another reason. That was the year Coach Jack Faulkner took over the team and made wholesale changes, especially to the Denver uniforms. He changed the color scheme from brown and mustard yellow to orange, blue, and white, and more important, he ditched the team's awful vertical-striped socks. The brown and yellow stripes had made Denver the laughingstock of the league, a situation Faulkner addressed by gathering up the offending hose and holding a public bonfire. "No way I was going to put that on the players," said Faulkner. "I got sick of looking at them. Before our first preseason game I brought out a big tub and burned the socks and some of the other stuff."[1]

The bonfire may have made the players and fans feel better, but it did not help on the field. Faulkner won just four games total in the two seasons following 1962, before giving way to Mac Speedie and then to Ray Malavasi. Denver went through four head coaches in seven seasons, but in 1967 the team believed it had finally ended its coaching carousel when it hired Lou Saban.

Saban was a sound coach who had won two AFL titles with the Bills in 1964 and 1965. His 1964 Buffalo team may have been the best in the history of the AFL, winning thirteen of fifteen games and holding high-powered San Diego to just a single touchdown in a 20–7 win for the AFL Championship. The following season, the Bills shut out the Chargers, 23–0, in San Diego to claim their second consecutive league title under Saban.

But for all his success as a coach, Saban never could seem to stay in one place very long. Denver was already his third AFL coaching stop in just seven years, and sandwiched in between had been an unsuccessful one-year stint at the University of Maryland. Part of the problem was Saban's autocratic style, which had caused several clashes with team players and owners. "He was old school," said Denver running back Floyd Little. "And he loved it. He hollered and screamed at me as much as anyone else."[2] Once during his tenure with the Bills, Saban jumped on a table at halftime and challenged anyone on the team to a fight. "Good thing nobody accepted," he said afterward. "If you're asking me if I made some wrong turns, I probably have. But I can't look back and I don't."[3]

Now in his fourth season in Denver, Saban had not brought the success Broncos' management expected when he was hired in 1967. The team had finished in fourth place in the AFL West every season under Saban, and the best he could manage in terms of a record was a 5-8-1 mark in 1969. Saban believed that defense and a power running game could win championships, which he had already proven twice in Buffalo, but he didn't have the horses in Denver (so to speak) to make his system work. Floyd Little would go on to a Hall of Fame career, but in 1967, with only 381 yards, he was Denver's leading rusher. The defense also had some notable performers, including lineman Rich "Tombstone" Jackson, a three-time Pro Bowler so named because his pass rush often buried quarterbacks. But the Broncos gave up more than four hundred points in each of Saban's first two seasons and in 1968 and 1969 only escaped last place in the AFL West because of the newly added Cincinnati Bengals expansion team.

Another sore spot was at quarterback, where Denver had struggled to find a marquee name to compete with other AFL quarterbacks such as Daryle Lamonica in Oakland, Len Dawson in Kansas City, and Joe Namath in New York.[4] In 1970 the Broncos' main starters were Steve Tensi, who had played three undistinguished seasons with the Broncos, and Pete Liske, who came to Denver from Canada. Liske had been named the CFL's Most Outstanding Player in 1967 after throwing forty touchdown passes for Calgary, but he never got close to that success in the NFL.

Despite their history, the Broncos had developed a strong following in the Rocky Mountains. When the AFL began play in 1960, Colorado was still somewhat virgin territory for professional sports, with the exception of a few failed hockey and basketball franchises and the minor league baseball Denver Bears. The Broncos played their first nine seasons at Bears Stadium, which was obviously configured more for baseball than football, and still drew respectable crowds. In their last season there, the Broncos averaged better than forty thousand fans for their seven home games, with a high of more than fifty thousand for a November game against Oakland. But true to form, Denver had a losing home record that year and in the game against the Raiders, the Broncos were blown out, 43–7. The team moved to Mile High Stadium in 1969 and the crowds got bigger, even as the losses continued; the Broncos averaged nearly forty-seven thousand per home game that year. The 1969 season marked the last time a Broncos home game failed to sell out, and as of 2013 the streak is at forty-three years and counting.

A seminal moment for the franchise came in 1965 when the Broncos were seriously thinking of leaving town. Other AFL owners and NBC, which had just picked up the rights to televise AFL games, believed the Broncos were a detriment to the league and wanted the team to abandon Denver. Pressure mounted as interested groups in Atlanta and other cities began offering millions for the team to relocate. Alarmed, Broncos' fans decided the team was worth saving and began buying more tickets. The team sold nearly eighteen thousand season tickets, the third highest total in the AFL that season. "Fantastic," said Denver assistant general manager Paul Manasseh. "I've been in sports a long time and I've never seen anything like this."[5]

So, five years later, as 50,705 fans filed in for the home opener against Pittsburgh, optimism was running high. Not only had the season opening win over Buffalo given the fans some reason for hope, they were further encouraged by the fact that their visitors had an even more checkered past than the Broncos.

OFF TRACK

Of the many adjectives used to describe the Pittsburgh Steelers in their thirty-seven seasons of play up until 1970, two stick out: colorful and woeful. The color came from owner Art Rooney, an outgoing native of Pittsburgh's Northside neighborhood who had played football, baseball, and boxed during the 1920s. Rooney also had an affection for playing the horses, and he was very good at it, visiting a variety of tracks across the country during racing season. During some of the worst times of the Depression, Rooney was making a nice living just at the track. His 1937 winnings, for example, totaled nearly $400,000. Losses cut that figure down substantially, but writer Bob Considine still figured, "He is definitely $200,000 ahead."[6]

In 1933 Rooney used his track winnings to help finance a franchise in the NFL, which he originally named the Pirates after the city's baseball team. If Rooney hoped the name would help his team emulate the baseball team's success, he was sadly mistaken, as his football club began with nine consecutive non-winning seasons. A name change to the Steelers in 1941 didn't help either, and the team had only six winning seasons between 1932 and 1969.[7]

"They are daily getting worse," one sports columnist noted in 1935, an observation that could have applied to any number of Rooney's Pittsburgh teams. "It takes high-powered football players to stay in this big show and the Pirates, up until the present time, do not have enough of them."[8]

Rooney and the Steelers may have touched bottom in 1969 when the team went 1-13, the most losses in franchise history, but two men who made their debut that season would soon help turn things around. Chuck Noll became head coach of the Steelers on January 27, 1969, after spending several seasons as an assistant in both the NFL and AFL. Future Hall of Fame defensive tackle Joe Greene was the team's first-round draft choice that year and was named the 1969 NFL Defensive Rookie of the Year. That same draft produced future stars L. C. Greenwood and Jon Kolb, as well as a solid backup in quarterback Terry Hanratty.

The Steelers' 1-13 record in 1969 was matched by the Bears, so the teams held a coin flip to determine who would get the overall number one draft pick in 1970. Pittsburgh won, and selected quarterback Terry Bradshaw of Louisiana Tech, a small-town country boy who also happened to have one of the strongest arms in football. "When they called me and told me they'd drafted me No. 1, I just couldn't believe it," said Bradshaw. "I mean, all along I wanted to go with a loser. I wanted to go someplace like Pittsburgh or Chicago where if I made it they would make it with me."[9] In addition to Bradshaw, the Steelers also drafted a future Hall of Fame defensive back in Mel Blount and a gifted receiver in Ron Shanklin. In just two drafts, Pittsburgh had seemingly added more talent than it had in the previous thirty years.

But in 1970 that talent was still inexperienced, and when Pittsburgh lost its season opener to Houston, 19–7, it marked the team's fourteenth consecutive defeat. Like most rookies, Bradshaw had a steep learning curve and did not play well in his NFL debut, completing only four of sixteen passes for 70 yards and an interception. He was also forced out of the end zone while attempting to pass in the third quarter, giving the Oilers an embarrassing safety. Hanratty fared only a bit better—completing six of fourteen with a touchdown. Heading into the Denver game, Pittsburgh was very unsettled at the quarterback position.

GLIMPSES OF GREATNESS

The Steelers came to Denver as new members of the AFC Central, since Rooney had decided to move over from the NFL along with the Colts and the Browns. In addition to the $3 million moving incentive, Rooney figured he needed to keep the geographical rivalry with Cleveland, where games with the Steelers often drew in excess of eighty thousand fans. "When it finally came down to it, I couldn't have done it unless [Browns owner Art] Modell had come, too," Rooney said.[10]

The first meeting between the Steelers and Broncos kicked off on a chilly, forty-nine degree afternoon at Mile High Stadium, and it soon became apparent why each team had struggled in recent years. Denver's problem was turnovers—any time the Broncos mounted a serious threat they seemed to fumble or throw an interception. By the end of the day, Steve Tensi had thrown two interceptions and the team had given up two fumbles. When Denver did hold on to the ball, it got the only score of the first quarter, a short 1-yard run by Willis Crenshaw.

The Steelers, on the other hand, could do nothing on the ground and would finish the game with only 18 yards total on twenty-eight carries. Preston Pearson, Dick Hoak, and John "Frenchy" Fuqua were Pittsburgh's three starting running backs. In the 1970 season, Fuqua would have the NFL's best rushing day, burning the Eagles for 218 yards in the season finale, and Pearson would go on to have a solid career in Dallas, but on this day they could do nothing. Pearson rushed thirteen times for 8 yards, while Fuqua carried only once for 3 yards. Hoak did manage a 4-yard touchdown run that tied the game at seven in the second quarter, but that was about it for the Steelers' running game.

That Pittsburgh was able to move the ball at all was due to Terry Bradshaw, who had briefly been knocked out of the game, but soon returned to action. Bradshaw's statistics were not that impressive—thirteen of twenty-six for 211 yards and an interception—but they were a vast improvement over his debut against Houston and showed flashes of the skill that had made him the top draft pick. Six of Bradshaw's completions went to Shanklin, who wound up with 123 yards receiving. By year's end, Shanklin would have thirty receptions and four touchdowns in a commendable rookie campaign.

A Floyd Little fumble at the Denver 6-yard line set up a Gene Mingo field goal that gave Pittsburgh a 10–7 halftime lead. Pittsburgh got close to the Broncos end zone early in the third quarter, but again Denver stiffened and forced a Mingo field goal. From that point on, the game belonged to the Broncos' defense, and especially safety Paul Martha. In his first season with the Broncos after six years in Pittsburgh, Martha had ten tackles, an interception, and recovered a fumble. "I told myself I wasn't going to get too high for this game," he said afterward, "but I guess I did and I enjoyed every minute of it."[11] In the third quarter, the Broncos cut the lead to 13–9 when Dave Washington tackled Bradshaw in the end zone for a safety.

The ensuing free kick gave Denver excellent field position, and Saban decided to open things up. Floyd Little had been fairly well contained by the Pittsburgh defense and would finish the day as Denver's leading ball carrier with just 54 yards in twenty-four attempts. Momentarily abandoning the ground game, Tensi hooked up with Billy Van Heusen, the Broncos' regular punter who also doubled as a wide receiver, for a 38-yard score that turned out to be the game-winning touchdown. With less than two minutes left and Denver leading 16–13, Pittsburgh's Mingo missed a 27-yard field goal attempt that would have tied the game.

The defeat ran the Steelers' losing streak to fifteen, which became sixteen when the team lost the following week in Cleveland. "Despite recent records to the contrary, we do think things are getting better for the Pittsburgh Steelers," said Noll. "Naturally, we have great hopes for Terry."[12]

But Bradshaw, who came to Pittsburgh as a cocksure, confident extrovert, began to press too hard and play hesitantly as his rookie season turned into a nightmare. He finished the year with six touchdown passes compared to a league-leading twenty-four interceptions. "The pressures kept building up," Bradshaw said after the season ended. "Fans, writers, everything. I felt I had to retaliate, but instead I kept digging myself a bigger hole."[13]

Bradshaw's growing pains included booing from his home fans and periodic benching by Noll, but it was obvious that he had the talent to succeed in the NFL, and so did the Steelers. Despite finishing 1970 with a 5-9 record, at one point the team won four of five games and seemed to have turned the corner. Noll used succeeding drafts to surround Bradshaw with future Hall of Fame talent, including running back Franco Harris and receivers Lynn Swann and John Stallworth. By 1974, the Steelers had put all the pieces in place and they won the first of their four Super Bowls, becoming the "Team of the '70s." After the first Super Bowl win, a dominating 16–6 defeat of the Vikings, the game ball went to the man who had waited forty-two years for a championship. "That's the greatest man who ever lived," said Bradshaw of Art Rooney in the crowded locker room. "Winning this for him was the big thing."[14]

Denver's win gave the team a 2-0 start, which eventually mushroomed into a 4-1 record and a solid grip on first place in the AFC West. But the Broncos simply didn't have enough offensive weapons to stay competitive with Kansas City and Oakland through the long season. Little had a nice year, running for more than 900 yards, but he accounted for only three rushing scores all season. Liske would eventually get more snaps than Tensi, but the two quarterbacks would combine for nineteen interceptions compared to ten touchdown passes and neither completed more than 50 percent of his passes. Denver would finish the season eighteenth out of twenty-six teams in total offense. The Broncos collapsed to 5-8-1 and another fourth place finish.

Saban switched to Steve Ramsey and Don Horn at quarterback the following year, but the team won just two of its first nine games in 1971 before Saban resigned.

"Lou Saban should be credited as the individual who first brought respectability to the Denver Broncos," said Pat Bowlen, who would buy the team in 1984.[15] It was an interesting comment considering that Saban compiled a record of 24-51-3 in his four-plus seasons in Denver. The Broncos would not completely earn respectability, and reward the devotion of their long-suffering fans, until 1977 when new coach Red Miller led the team to its first Super Bowl appearance. By then, many of the Broncos who had played in the 1960s and early 1970s were gone, but certainly not forgotten.

"Something that all of the guys that I played with are most proud of is being part of the building blocks to get the Broncos to where they ultimately won the Super Bowls and become a contender every year," said Van Heusen. "That's just a source of pride for everybody that played when I played."[16]

$$\star \ 6 \ \star$$

WEEK THREE:
San Diego Chargers at Los Angeles Rams

CHARGING THROUGH THE AFL

San Diego followed its last-second loss to the Colts on opening weekend with another home game against Oakland. Down 27–13 in the fourth quarter, John Hadl threw two touchdown passes—a 65-yarder to Jeff Queen and a 37-yarder to Lance Alworth—to tie the game at 27–27. Hadl and Alworth were holdovers from the glory days in San Diego, when the Chargers dominated the AFL behind the coaching genius of Sid Gillman.

Gillman played at Ohio State in the 1930s, but realizing he was too small to make it in the pros, he quickly turned to coaching. He led the Los Angeles Rams to a conference championship in 1955, but found himself expendable after a 2-10 season four years later. Jumping to the new American Football League, Gillman brought with him the seeds of a revolutionary passing game that continues to sprout and grow today.

"Sid Gillman was the father of modern-day passing" said Al Davis, who served as an assistant under Gillman for three seasons. "It had been thought of as vertical, but Sid also thought of it as horizontal. Sid used the width of the field."[1] Gillman noted that the field was 100 yards long and more than 53 yards wide "and we're going to use every inch of it."[2]

With the Chargers, Gillman had the players to make his offense work, including Alworth, Hadl, and running backs Paul Lowe and Keith Lincoln. Alworth was a special talent at receiver, although he actually played running back at the University of Arkansas. Davis signed him on the field following the 1962 Sugar Bowl, and after switching to receiver, Alworth put Gillman's passing offense in high gear. Following a slow rookie season, Alworth recorded seven consecutive seasons of 1,000 yards or more receiving, averaging more than sixty catches and ten touchdowns each season.

"He runs like a thoroughbred," said Chargers running back Charlie Flowers. That attribute, combined with his frail physique, earned Alworth the nickname, "Bambi."[3] "He made it look like a wide-open game," Chiefs owner Lamar Hunt once observed, "because he was always wide open."[4]

Alworth was named league MVP in 1963 with sixty-one catches, 1,205 receiving yards, and eleven touchdowns. It was not his best season statistically, but that year he led perhaps the best team the AFL ever fielded. The Chargers went 11-3 to win the AFL West, and then destroyed Boston for the league championship, 51–10. Lincoln rushed for 206 yards and a touchdown, Lowe added 94 more, and Alworth caught a touchdown pass. The dominating performance led many to believe the Chargers could have beaten the NFL champion Bears, a team known for its defense, but with little offensive weapons.

"I've argued that for years and years," said Gillman. "We had one of the great teams in pro football history, and I think we would have matched up pretty well with the NFL. We had great speed and talent, and I think at that time, the NFL really underestimated the talent we had."[5]

Even though 1963 was their only AFL championship, the Chargers won five of the first six Western Conference titles under Gillman. They started to slide a bit in 1966, winning about as many games as they lost, but by the time the AFL ended, the Chargers had the most winning seasons (nine) and the most division championships (five) in league history, and were second only to the Chiefs in regular season wins (eighty-seven to eighty-six). Alworth, Gillman, and offensive lineman Ron Mix would all go on to the Hall of Fame.

The end of the AFL also brought an end to the Chargers' dominance. In 1969 Gillman began having health problems that would eventually force his premature retirement from coaching, so he became the team's general manager. Assistant coach Charlie Waller took over the team. The Chargers were wildly inconsistent in 1969, following a four-game winning streak with a four-game losing streak. They bounced back yet again at the end of the season to win four in a row, prompting optimism for the next season. There was no serious concern when the team went 0-1-1 in its first two games of

1970; Hadl had played well in both games, although the Chargers were having difficulty running the ball.

Week three would bring the Chargers to Los Angeles, which would represent a homecoming for both Gillman and the team. Not only had Gillman coached the Rams for five seasons but the Chargers franchise itself had started in Los Angeles. Taking the Rams head on, the Chargers did much better on the field than they did at the gate—winning the first AFL West title in 1960—but only Oakland and Denver drew fewer fans than the Chargers, who averaged less than sixteen thousand fans per game. By contrast, the Rams averaged more than sixty-one thousand fans per game in 1960, even though the team only won four of twelve games.

Chargers owner Barron Hilton lost $900,000 that first season and knew his team couldn't survive with the Rams in town, so he began looking for other cities. Seattle and San Diego were the prime suitors, but Hilton wanted to stay in California and San Diego sportswriter Jack Murphy was making a big push to get a pro football team. Murphy was the leader behind San Diego's Proposition 1, which authorized $27.5 million for the construction of a multi-purpose stadium with fifty-thousand seats. When the proposition passed, it persuaded Hilton to move south.[6] Until the new stadium could be built, the Chargers played in smaller Balboa Stadium, which was expanded to thirty-four thousand seats. The Chargers averaged almost twenty-eight thousand fans their first year in San Diego, then climbed to thirty-seven thousand when the new stadium opened in 1967. By the last year of the AFL, the team averaged more than forty-six thousand fans per game.

"WINNING IS LIVING"

Until the Chargers arrived in 1960, the Rams had Los Angeles to themselves. The team had moved west after winning an NFL title in 1945 as the Cleveland Rams, and it became a consistent winner and box office attraction during the 1950s, winning another NFL championship in 1951 and playing for the title three more times. But the Rams' 2-10 mark in 1959 was an omen of things to come, and between 1960 and 1965 the team never had a winning season, sinking to 1-12-1 in 1962. The turnaround began in 1966 with the arrival of Coach George Allen, a defensive specialist with the Bears who had studied under coaching icon George Halas, and a man destined to become a coaching legend in his own right.

Allen was single-minded, almost slavish, in his devotion to coaching, and he lived by a set of rules that seemed to come straight from Frank Merriwell's playbook:

- "Every day you waste is one you can never make up."
- "Winning is living."
- "There is no detail that is too small."
- "A hundred percent is not enough."[7]

"I've never known a man who concentrated his energies so totally on one goal," said Roman Gabriel, the Rams' quarterback. "He works day and night, weekdays and weekends, fall and spring. He fills every minute of every day with football."[8] Allen sought to change things in Los Angeles by example; he would be the motivator, the cheerleader, he was out doing calisthenics with the players, all in an effort to build team unity. "Allen always has time for [the players]," said Rams' owner Dan Reeves, "[he] talks to them as individuals as well as in meetings, always lets them know he's thinking about them."[9] "You've got to motivate everybody, veterans and rookies alike," said Allen, who considered his players "like members of my family."[10]

Another Allen philosophy was "The Future is Now," meaning he preferred veteran players to untested rookies, and he began trading for many of his former Bears players as soon as he arrived in 1966. That first season he led the Rams to an 8-6 record, which was followed in 1967 with an 11-2-1 record and a division championship, for which Allen was named NFL Coach of the Year. The Rams were similarly strong the next two seasons, going 10-3-1 and 11-3, including an eleven-game win streak to open the 1969 season, but had trouble in the playoffs, losing first-round games both times. The 1970 season was expected to be another successful year, and one in which Allen might get the Rams over the playoff hump.

Allen deserves a great deal of credit for his work with the Rams, but it also helped that the team had a ton of talent, especially on defense. The Rams' four defensive lineman—David "Deacon" Jones, Merlin Olsen, Lamar Lundy, and Rosey Grier—were so effective that they became known as the

"Fearsome Foursome," one of the best nicknames in NFL history. It certainly was one of the catchiest, and it helped promote the quartet in an age when defensive players, and especially lineman, didn't get that much publicity. The group even sang together, and in 1965 appeared on Grier's local television show, *Shindig*.[11]

Grier may have been the television star, but it was Deacon Jones who got the headlines on the field. Virtually ignored by pro scouts (he was a fourteenth-round draft choice in 1961 out of Mississippi Vocational College, now Mississippi Valley State), Jones set about making a name for himself in the NFL. He used the name Deacon because he wanted to stand out from the crowd, and coined the term "sack" when he tackled opposing quarterbacks behind the line of scrimmage. "You take all the offensive linemen and put them in a burlap bag, and then you take a baseball bat and beat on the bag," Jones said. "You're sacking them, you're bagging them. And that's what you're doing with a quarterback."[12] The NFL didn't recognize sacks as an official statistic back then, but by his own count Deacon had 26 in 1967, and finished his career with 173.5. The NFL finally had to outlaw his signature "head slap" technique with which he rang the helmets of offensive linemen across the league. "I came as close to perfection as you can possibly get," he said unashamedly.[13] Los Angeles sportswriter Jim Murray described him as "unstoppable as a flood, and as elusive as a fly in a hot room."[14]

By 1970, half of the Fearsome Foursome had departed—injuries did in both Grier, who retired after 1966, and Lundy, who played through 1969. But the Rams still had Jones and his line mate Merlin Olsen, a quiet performer who didn't get near the attention of the Deacon, but like Jones would also eventually make the Hall of Fame. On offense, the Rams had perhaps the best, if not the biggest, quarterback in the NFL. Roman Gabriel was 6-foot-5 and 245 pounds, which at that time made him as big as some defensive linemen. Gabriel mostly sat on the bench early in his career, but one of the first things Allen did when he arrived was make Gabriel the starter and it paid off handsomely. Gabriel made the Pro Bowl three straight seasons starting in 1967, and in 1969 he was named the league's MVP after throwing for twenty-four touchdowns. He was the Rams' undisputed leader and the team's driving force. "He has attained a certain majesty," said receiver Bernie Casey. "It rubs off on all of us."[15]

The Rams and Chargers had played in a series of preseason games starting in 1967, and in their first meeting, Los Angeles humiliated San Diego, 50–7, in the Chargers' second game in their new stadium.[16] The rivalry was cemented when the Rams returned their starting defense to the field with a 50–0 lead in the fourth quarter.

"We didn't want them to score," said Olsen. "That's why we asked to come back into the game." But he also added, "I wouldn't want to judge the Chargers on this one game."[17] The Chargers got a measure of revenge with a 35–13 exhibition win the following summer, and when the teams met in 1969, the largest crowd ever in San Diego (53,071), including President Richard Nixon, came to watch the Rams win, 24–14.

"CATCH IT, TUCK IT AND RUN IT"

When the teams met for the first time in the regular season on October 3, 1970, more than sixty-nine thousand turned out at the Los Angeles Coliseum. The Rams scored on their first drive on a 17-yard pass from Gabriel to Jack Snow, a former Notre Dame prodigy who never quite lived up to his billing. A first-round selection by the Vikings, Snow was traded to the Rams before the season started and became a capable receiver. He made the Pro Bowl in 1967, but never caught more than fifty-one passes in a season. The 1970 season would turn out to be Snow's best statistical year, with 859 yards receiving and seven touchdown catches.[18]

David Ray kicked a field goal to give the Rams a 10–0 lead after one quarter, and then Los Angeles broke the game wide open. Les Josephson, another workmanlike player for the Rams, scored on a 12-yard run to make it 17–0. Like Snow, Josephson was a steady, capable player, but not really a star, rushing for 800 yards in his best season. He was also as tough as nails, reviving his career after tearing an Achilles tendon in 1968. A broken jaw had kept him out for weeks one and two, but in the San Diego game he responded with a typical lunch-bucket performance—fourteen rushes for 71 yards and three catches for 50 yards—all with his jaw held together with rubber bands. "I can't eat steak yet," he said afterward, "but I had some ravioli the other night and it was great."[19]

Almost immediately, George Allen's defense set up another score, this time by holding the Chargers deep in their own territory and then blocking a Rick Redman punt, which Pat Curran fell on in the end zone for a touchdown. John Hadl threw four interceptions in the first half, three leading to scores, and the Rams built a 30–3 lead, prompting sportswriter Bob Oates to observe, "The two teams used to be in two different leagues and still might be the way this looked."[20] The Rams sacked Hadl and his backup, Marty Domres, ten times while cornerback Kermit Alexander shutout Lance Alworth and picked off two passes. In mop-up action, Domres threw a touchdown pass to Willie Frazier, while Karl Sweetan tossed another touchdown pass to Snow, making the final score 37–10. If there was such a thing as the battle for Los Angeles, or at least southern California, the Rams had won it decisively. "You can't set your sights for any one team in this league," said Deacon Jones, downplaying the rivalry. "That's absurd. San Diego has a good team, but we beat them with a big rush."[21]

That big rush frustrated the Chargers' passing attack in a harbinger of the season that lay ahead for Alworth. With just thirty-five catches for 608 yards and four touchdowns, Alworth would have his poorest showing since his 1962 rookie season. Apparently convinced his great skills had faded, the Chargers traded him to Dallas in the off-season, and the Cowboys turned him into a possession receiver. Instead of bounding down the field after long passes, Bambi had to run the tough routes over the middle. "In San Diego, I used to walk around the house mumbling, 'Watch it, catch it, tuck it and run it,'" said Alworth. "In Dallas, I growled at the cat, made faces in the mirror and kicked the trash can."[22]

An era was clearly ending in San Diego. Lowe and Lincoln were long gone; Hadl would only last two more years before bouncing around with several teams at the end of his career. The Chargers dropped to 5-6-3 in 1970, their first losing season since 1962 but certainly not their last. Gillman briefly returned to coach in 1971 but had to give up the reins again, and the Chargers floundered for most of the decade. In 1978 Don Coryell brought a passing offense reminiscent of Gillman's heyday, but San Diego never could find a defense to match. Even with a Super Bowl appearance after the 1994 season, long-time Chargers' fans would still argue that the 1963 team was the best in franchise history.

After the win over San Diego that moved the Rams to 3-0, Allen admitted, "We've got a good football team."[23] But the following week they flunked their first real test of the season, losing 20–6 to the division rival 49ers. The teams met again November 29 in San Francisco, and this time the Rams turned the tables with a 30–13 win that tied them for first place with the 49ers with three weeks left in the season. "This was the biggest win in the five years I've been with the Rams," said Allen. "We beat [the 49ers] in their own backyard, and that means more, too."[24] But that was the high water mark of the Rams season. The team won two of its final three games, only to watch San Francisco sweep its remaining three opponents and win the division by a game. Los Angeles finished out of playoff running at 9-4-1.

Rams' owner Dan Reeves didn't particularly care for Allen and had actually tried to fire him two years prior. For all intents and purposes, Reeves *did* fire Allen two days after Christmas in 1968, even with the team coming off a 10-3-1 record and playoff appearance.

"I said something like 'Merry Christmas,'" Allen reported of the phone call he received from Reeves. "I'm not sure what he said at first, but then he said something like, 'This is the end. You're fired.'"[25]

When the story hit the newspapers, Allen appeared at a press conference flanked by several of his players—including Jones, Gabriel, and four other starters—who essentially mutinied against Reeves, vowing to quit or retire if Allen didn't get his job back. "George knew how to communicate with people, with the team," Gabriel said later. "Also the individuals within the team. George knew how to get the best out of all of us."[26]

Reeves reluctantly backed down, but his ill feelings for Allen still simmered. He didn't care for Allen's "win at all costs" mentality, which John Hall of the *Los Angeles Times* called a "grimly all-out, no smiles, 24-hour-a-day death march approach to football."[27] That claim included charges of spying on other teams, which distressed Reeves even further when he found out they were true. Reeves himself once admitted, "George Allen takes all the pleasure out of owning a club."[28] Now that the Rams had missed the playoffs, Reeves saw his chance and wasn't going to blow it again; he fired Allen a second time, and this time for good.[29] No players came to his defense. Instead of shedding a tear for Allen, wrote Jeff Meyers, "The public should shed a tear for Allen's successor. New coach Tommy Prothro will be trying to untangle the mess left by George," who had traded away all the team's draft picks to acquire veteran players.[30]

But in truth, Allen had left a solid foundation in place as he went to take over the Redskins. The Rams were consistent winners throughout the 1970s under Prothro and then Chuck Knox, but like Allen they could never get the team over the top. The Rams advanced to several playoffs and even a Super Bowl, but never managed a Super Bowl victory in Los Angeles.[31] The franchise would finally get that championship after the 1999 season, but by then the Rams had abandoned Los Angeles for St. Louis, and the feats of Roman Gabriel and Deacon Jones seemed like ancient history.

WEEK FOUR:
Cincinnati Bengals at Cleveland Browns

"It will be a typical Browns-Bengals game."[1]
—**Former Browns quarterback Otto Graham before the
teams met for only the second time ever**

THE PRODIGAL FATHER

Through his own blood, sweat, and inspiration, the man builds an empire that becomes the envy of everyone in his profession. He dominates the landscape, becoming admired by his followers and feared by his enemies. As time goes by, he becomes a patriarch, and his disciples continue his work and legacy. Then, an outsider appears, takes control, and sends the patriarch into exile. He bides his time; waiting, plotting, scheming for the day when he will get his chance at revenge. Finally, that day arrives.

It may sound like the plot of a prime-time soap opera or even a scene from the Bible, but this story took place in the NFL, and it involved Paul Brown, the Cleveland Browns, and the birth of the Cincinnati Bengals.

By any standard, Paul Brown was a coaching genius and a seminal figure in the development of pro football. In the 1930s and 40s, he won six state championships in Ohio high school football, then won a national championship at Ohio State University, which he turned into a college power. Joining the new All-America Football Conference as coach of the Cleveland Browns in 1946, he dominated that league as well, losing only four games in four years and winning the championship every season. The Browns kept right on winning when they joined the NFL in 1950, with Brown directing them to the NFL title game seven times in eight seasons, and winning three championships.

Brown was a winner, but he was also an innovator. It was Brown who first developed the playbook, called plays from the sidelines, and used practice and game films to learn more about other teams, as well as his own. Many of his assistants, such as Weeb Ewbank, Chuck Noll, and Bill Walsh, took his philosophies to other teams and won Super Bowl championships, and the concepts and strategies he developed are still in use today. Former NFL Commissioner Pete Rozelle once remarked, "He changed the game forever. Whether they know it or not, nearly everyone in the game has been affected by Paul Brown."[2]

But for all his many talents, Brown could be a difficult man. He was extremely strict and regimented (making players dress formally on road trips), and his no-nonsense approach often made him seem cold and unapproachable. When his 1949 Browns lost for the first time after winning twenty-nine straight games, his players expected a sympathetic word from their coach. Instead, Brown told them, "I'm telling you this and it's cold turkey. If those of you who fell down on the job don't bounce back, I'll sell you."[3] And the players knew Brown meant it. When team captain Jim Daniell was pulled over by Cleveland police and flunked a sobriety test shortly before the 1946 AAFC championship game, Brown told him he was finished and immediately released him.

Brown's approach was tolerated, as long as the Browns kept on winning, but in the late 1950s and early 1960s they began to slip. Between 1956 and 1962, the Browns had only one first place finish in the Eastern Conference, and worse yet, won no NFL titles. Brown reportedly had trouble getting along with his players, most particularly star running back Jim Brown, who represented a new breed of expressive athlete and didn't appreciate his coach's uncompromising style. "If I ever coach one day," Jim Brown once told his teammates, "I would do it 180 degrees differently than Paul."[4]

The noose really began to tighten when Art Modell purchased controlling interest in the Browns in 1961. At the time, Modell was a young, brash businessman who wanted to take a hands-on approach to his new investment. He predicted the Browns would win the NFL title that year, but in part because the players were in near-revolt against Brown, the team staggered to a third place finish in the NFL East. Jim Brown denied ever complaining about his coach to Modell, but he was frequently critical of Brown to everyone else, especially regarding how his own talents were being used.

Modell really didn't need an excuse to release Brown, but another third place finish in 1962 sealed his fate, and in January 1963, Modell fired the coach for whom the franchise was named. In Modell's version of events, Brown felt threatened by the new owner's hands-on approach. "He really didn't like my being in the office at 7:30 in the morning," said Modell. "Our relationship cooled."[5] According to Brown, Modell told him, "This team can never be fully mine as long as you are here because whenever anyone thinks of the Browns they think of you. Every time I come to the stadium I feel like I am invading your domain, and from now on there can only be one dominant image."[6]

The bombshell caught Brown completely by surprise, and he had difficulty figuring out what to do next. Since he still owned a small (10 percent) stake in the team, he did some scouting and made draft suggestions, but he was very much a fish out of water. His induction into the Hall of Fame in 1967 only reminded him how much he missed coaching.

"It was terrible," he later recalled. "I had everything a man can want: leisure, enough money, a wonderful family. Yet with all that, I was eating my heart out. Football had been my life. I had a strong desire to become alive again."[7] His exile would last five years.

THE BENGALS ROAR

During that time, Brown had several offers to coach, but turned them all down. "I couldn't go back unless I was in complete charge," he said, so expansion seemed the only way to go.[8] The AFL was looking to add a franchise, since the addition of Miami in 1966 gave it an odd number of teams. The year before, Ohio governor James Rhodes began to push for a second team in the state, and Brown's son, Mike, did a feasibility study on the Cincinnati area.[9] The city was already concerned that the Reds might leave town, so in 1966 it approved construction of multi-purpose Riverfront Stadium, which would open in 1970.[10] When Brown put together a syndicate of fifteen owners willing to pay the expansion fee of $7.75 million, he cleared the last hurdle.[11] On September 26, 1967, the AFL officially welcomed Cincinnati as its tenth franchise, with Paul Brown as part owner, general manager, and head coach. "I came back because this is my life," said Brown. "This is what gives me pleasure. I'm going to have fun."[12]

Brown named the team the Bengals, ostensibly to honor a pro team that played in Cincinnati in the 1930s. Coincidence or not, the "CB" Cincinnati Bengals sounded and looked a lot like the "CB" Cleveland Browns, right down to the dominant orange in their color scheme. "We wondered why we looked so much like the Cleveland Browns," said Bill Bergey, a linebacker in his second season with the Bengals in 1970.[13] According to Mike Brown, "Modell objected to that. Then my dad said, 'Well, who stole whose uniform?'"[14]

Like most expansion teams, the Bengals had to make do with draft picks and other teams' castoffs, but in their inaugural 1968 season Brown showed that he could still coach. The Bengals surprised everyone by winning two of their first three games, and even though they sank back to reality with a 3-11 record, there were several promising signs. Running back Paul Robinson led the AFL in rushing with 1,023 yards and won league Rookie of the Year honors.[15] Tight end Bob Trumpy would make four Pro Bowls in eight seasons. "Patience with this club is an easy virtue," Brown said that first season. "There is no fierce pressure on you to win."[16]

The most promising figure in the Bengals early history was quarterback Greg Cook. A hometown product from Chillicothe, Ohio, and the University of Cincinnati, Cook was the Bengals' first-round draft pick in 1969. While watching game films of Cook in college, Brown allegedly pointed to the screen and said, "That's our guy. That's our draft pick."[17] When the Bengals did draft Cook they wasted no time getting him in the starting lineup, and he took the AFL by storm in 1969, throwing for more than 1,800 yards and fifteen touchdowns and winning league Rookie of the Year honors. The Bengals finished only 4-9-1, but with Cook at the helm they had reason for justifiable optimism. Brown called him "strong like a Gabriel, maybe a little faster. His strength is his quick release and accuracy. He's everything we thought."[18] Former NFL coach Bill Walsh, who was a Bengals assistant that year, said, "Greg Cook could very well have been remembered as the greatest NFL quarterback of all time."[19]

But what Walsh, the Bengals, and even Cook himself didn't know was that Cook had suffered a significant injury in the third game of the 1969 season. Tackled hard by Chiefs defenders, Cook kept playing with what he thought was a bruised shoulder. It turned out to be a torn rotator cuff, similar to the injuries baseball pitchers often suffer. With today's medical advances, treating a rotator cuff is somewhat routine, but in 1970 it was major surgery, and not always successful. Cook never fully recovered from the injury and never again regained his 1969 form, although he kept trying for four more seasons. After his brilliant rookie year, he threw only three more passes in the NFL, and finally retired in 1973.

"I never looked at me as being a victim," Cook later said. "I try to, if I can, avoid that trap. What could have been; it's an unhealthy way of thinking. I had some success, and I thank God for that."[20] But the questions will always remain for the greatest "what if" player in Bengals history. "Regardless of what Greg has told you, it's affected him psychologically for a long period of time, as well it should," said Trumpy. "He got cheated, and it's a scar he carries with him to this day. I don't know what he would have done if he had played 10 or 12 years. I do think my fingers would have been filled with Super Bowl rings."[21]

The new man under center was Virgil Carter, who came to Cincinnati after unhappy stops in Chicago and Buffalo. "I gave the Bears a lot of verbal trouble," he admitted, which may explain why he had only thrown ninety-one passes in two seasons.[22] The other contender for the job was Sam Wyche, another young and untested quarterback. But the Bengals had seen enough of Wyche in two seasons with the team to know that he was not the answer, and although he would play seven years in the NFL, 1970 would be his last season in Cincinnati, at least as a quarterback.[23]

Even without Cook, the Bengals had a roster filled with young talent. Using its first-round selection in 1970, Cincinnati took defensive lineman Mike Reid from Penn State University, who became a two-time Pro Bowl selection.[24] The Bengals hit again in the seventh round with selection of defensive back Lemar Parrish from tiny Lincoln University. Parrish went to the Pro Bowl eight times in a thirteen-year NFL career, including his rookie season with the Bengals. In 1970 he recorded five interceptions, one fumble recovery, 194 yards returning punts, 482 yards returning kickoffs, and scored two touchdowns on kick returns.

ROUND ONE

The Bengals opened the 1970 season at home and used two big plays to beat the Raiders, 31–21. Wyche got the start over Carter and scored two touchdowns, one rushing and another on a 51-yard pass to Essex Johnson. But the real surprise was third-year running back Jess Phillips, who broke loose on a 76-yard scoring rush late in the third quarter to break a 21-all tie. He finished the day with 130 yards against a strong Raider defense.

Wyche and Carter split quarterback duties the following week in Detroit, but neither was effective in the 38–3 loss. The Lions held Phillips to 31 yards and Cincinnati had to get a late field goal from Horst Muhlmann to avoid the shutout. As Carter began getting more comfortable with the Cincinnati offense, he began to get more playing time, and in week three against Houston he hit ten of twenty passes, including a touchdown to Trumpy. However, a late Charley Johnson touchdown pass to Alvin Reed won it for the Oilers, 20–13, and dropped the Bengals to 1-2 on the season.

The Browns would come into week four 2-1 under coach Blanton Collier, the man Art Modell turned to after he fired Paul Brown in 1963. Collier started as an assistant under Brown but left to take the head coaching job at the University of Kentucky, where he was fired in 1962 despite going 41-36-3 in nine seasons. Collier returned to Cleveland at the precise moment Modell was getting ready to sack Brown, and in 1963 became the second head coach in franchise history. Although Collier took the job with Brown's approval, the move did create some hard feelings between the men.

Collier seemed the temperamental opposite of Brown in almost every respect—he was easy-going, reluctant to criticize, and got along very well with Jim Brown and Cleveland's other black players. Although he learned the game under Paul Brown, he did not have his mentor's authoritarian streak and gave his players much more freedom in terms of their decisions on the field. Apparently, the change was just what the Browns needed, for they improved immediately under Collier. Cleveland just missed the playoffs with a 10-4 record in 1963, then came back to win the NFL East in 1964 with a 10-3-1 record.

The '64 Browns were led by quarterback Frank Ryan, who threw twenty-five touchdown passes, and Jim Brown, who piled up 1,446 yards, most in the league. They were heavy underdogs to the Colts in the NFL Championship game, but in one of the greatest upsets in football history, the Browns won the title, shutting out the highest-scoring team in the league, 27–0.

Sportswriter Chuck Heaton, who had covered the Browns since their inception in 1946, called it "what well may be the best performance ever in the sparkling history of this football club."[25] It was the last title for Collier, although the Browns returned to the NFL Championship game three more times. In the seven seasons he had coached the Browns prior to 1970, the team finished first or second in the standings every year.

When the Browns officially became a part of the AFC and were placed in the Central Division, it guaranteed they would play two games every year against the Bengals and Paul Brown. While most pointed to the October 11 meeting in Cleveland, the 1970 preseason schedule provided an added bonus: the teams would meet face-to-face for the first time in an exhibition game on August 29 at Riverfront Stadium in Cincinnati. "That will be the biggest day of my life," said Brown when the game was announced.[26] A more understated Blanton Collier noted, "I know we'll have to be ready for a great effort."[27]

A sellout crowd of 57,112 certainly gave it a great effort, treating the meaningless exhibition like it was a playoff game. The Browns built a 14–0 lead, prompting Collier to remove his starters, but sensing the moment, Brown stayed with his regulars. The Bengals roared back, but by the time Collier put his first-teamers back on the field it was too late. Cincinnati pulled away to win, 31–17.

Paul Brown, who skipped a post-game handshake with Collier, had his first measure of satisfaction. "Thank you," he said when his players presented him with the game ball. "This is one ball I'll keep. I'll promise you that. It'll go in our trophy case."[28] In the other locker room, the Browns were especially disconsolate for losing a pre-season game. It wasn't so much that they had lost, but they had lost for Art Modell. Captain and linebacker Jim Houston said, "We're disappointed we didn't win for Art. We knew how much he wanted to win."[29]

As satisfying as the exhibition win was, Brown and the Bengals knew it really didn't count for much. The first true test would come October 11 in Cleveland, and it would continue the subplots that had already become so familiar—the all-Ohio rivalry, the Bengals' quarterback problems, and the teacher versus student angle of Collier coaching against Brown. But this game would add another feature that would become the game's screaming headline: Paul Brown's return to Cleveland.

ROUNDS TWO AND THREE

Paul Brown had not been to a Browns game since he was fired in 1963, and had only ventured inside the city once. Sportswriters looked at this as yet another burning log on the bonfire of the Browns-Bengals rivalry, which also included Brown's statements after the Bengals' exhibition win in August. But now, with the rematch at hand and the teams playing for real, Brown tried to put on the brakes.

"You newspaper people are always trying to build up this Cincinnati-Cleveland game as some sort of personal grudge match," he said the week of the game. "You people can't realize how much water has gone over the dam since I left."[30] As always, the phlegmatic Collier was tight-lipped. "I believe the Bengals will be fired up," he said, "for a lot of reasons."[31]

Much of the attention focused on how Brown and Collier would get along. Brown's refusal to shake hands after the exhibition game had not gone unnoticed by the media, especially since Collier had walked to midfield just for that purpose. Brown explained that it was "an AFL tradition" not to shake hands, and that "Blanton understands. That's all I care about."[32] Collier singled out Brown before the rematch and the two shared a few innocuous pleasantries. "We just said hello and wished each other luck," explained Collier.[33] They would not shake hands afterward.

A standing-room only crowd of 83,520 filled Cleveland Stadium on a grey, dark afternoon, but they were silenced in the early going. Cincinnati got a Muhlmann field goal and a 2-yard touchdown run by Phillips to take a 10–0 lead. The Browns cut that lead to 10–9 with a safety and short touchdown pass from Bill Nelsen to Leroy Kelly. The teams traded touchdowns after that, and the Bengals led at the half, 17–16. The only scoring in the third quarter came on another Muhlmann field goal, and with just fifteen minutes to play it appeared that Paul Brown might get the sweetest revenge of all, right in his former ballpark.

But the Browns had moved the ball well most of the afternoon, and they began to grind down the Bengals' defense. Kelly opened the fourth quarter with a one-yard touchdown run, which was followed by another long drive and a short touchdown by Bo Scott. Kelly would finish the day with 84 yards rushing, as the Browns piled up 346 total yards. Even suffering from bad knees, Nelsen enjoyed one of his finer days of the season, hitting seventeen of twenty-nine passes for 226 yards and two touchdowns. Cleveland led 30–20 with seven minutes to play.

Carter was also enjoying one of his better days and quickly drove the Bengals downfield. He completed twenty of twenty-eight for 218 yards and a touchdown that came on a 16-yard pass to Speedy Thomas with three minutes to play, which cut the Browns' lead to 30–27. The Browns effectively ran down the clock, however, and held on to win the game by that same score.

Paul Brown had been greeted warmly when he arrived at the game, saying, "There were so many people who said hello to me on the way in. It seemed as if every policeman and everyone else wanted to greet me."[34] But when Cleveland fans realized he was not going to come to midfield to shake Collier's hand, they started booing, and continued as their former coach left the field. Unable to give their owner a win in the preseason, the Browns gave the game ball to a beaming Art Modell after the game.

With the exception of not being able to run the ball (only 54 yards on twenty-one carries), the young Bengals had acquitted themselves well. Unfortunately, it counted as just another loss in the standings, one of six in a row the team suffered after its opening day win over Oakland. However, most of the losses were close and the Bengals were improving. Writing in the *Cleveland Plain-Dealer* the next day, Chuck Heaton noted, "[The Browns] beat a good football team; one that will be even better as the season progresses."[35] He did not know how prophetic his words would be.

What Heaton could not have foreseen was the Browns' impending slide. The win over the Bengals put Cleveland in first place in the AFC Central with a 3-1 record, but Nelsen, Kelly, and Scott were all struggling with injuries, and the team lost four of its next five games. The fourth loss came in a November 15 rematch with the Bengals in Cincinnati, which had finally broken its losing streak with a convincing 43–14 win over the Bills. Before a record Riverfront crowd of 60,007, the Bengals spotted the Browns a 10–0 lead before rallying for a dramatic 14–10 victory. At the end of the game,

Paul Brown "half-danced, half-pranced" off the field with his team, then accepted the game ball in the locker room. "This is the best victory of all," said the man who won three NFL championships and four more in the AAFC. "It made coming back worthwhile."[36]

Brown also couldn't help but stir the pot some more with his former employer. Mike Phipps played the entire game for the Browns in the rematch with the Bengals, and he did not have a good afternoon, finishing eleven of twenty-five with an interception. It was unknown whether Nelsen was healthy enough to play, but Brown chose to believe that Modell wanted Phipps to play to justify his high selection in the draft. "This is the kind of thing that happens when non-football people decide they know how to run a football team," Brown said.[37]

Modell, not one to let the barb pass unnoticed, countered, "How sad it is that a man can be that embittered after so many years."[38]

"Bitter people bore me," Brown had said shortly after his return to the NFL. "They say football passed me by, and I say that time has the answer for everything."[39] The Browns and Bengals would not meet again on the football field until 1971, but Paul Brown and Art Modell would make sure that the rivalry would continue to sizzle in Ohio for 365 days a year.

★ 8 ★

WEEK FIVE:
Baltimore Colts at New York Jets

LASSIE GETS HIS KICKS

The Colts, Steelers, and Browns had all agreed to take three million dollars for jumping from the NFL to the new AFC, but exactly how to align the conference remained a contentious issue. In 1969 and early 1970, league owners conducted a series of meetings over several days before finally deciding the final alignment by drawing names out of a hat. Thus, it appears the Baltimore Colts and New York Jets ended up in the same AFC Eastern Division mainly by chance. Either that or someone in the NFL office had a very twisted sense of humor.

It had been two years since the Colts had suffered their championship loss to the Jets, becoming the first NFL team to lose a Super Bowl. Baltimore had entered Super Bowl III with a 15-1 record and as more than two touchdown favorites. They left the game 16–7 losers and the laughingstock of pro football. "No one knows the despair, the abject humiliation we felt that day," said Colts linebacker Mike Curtis. "The 1968 Baltimore Colts; a perfect football machine. And we lost to somebody we would have beat a thousand times after the Super Bowl. It was humiliation, to be kind."[1]

The loss seemed to put the Colts in a trance and they sleepwalked through their 1969 season, finishing 8-5-1 and missing the playoffs. Don Shula had coached seven successful seasons in Baltimore, but in the eyes of Colts owner Carroll Rosenbloom he had failed when it counted most. Shula had lost two of the biggest upsets in NFL championship history, and in both games the heavily-favored Colts had been embarrassed—27–0 by Cleveland in 1964 and 16–7 by the Jets four years later.

At the same time that Rosenbloom left on an Oriental vacation in February 1970, the Miami Dolphins went into the market for a new coach. The Dolphins made Shula an offer, but there were conflicting reports as to whether Miami had properly asked permission to do so. Rosenbloom returned from vacation and accused the Dolphins of tampering, probably more out of spite than a desire to keep his coach. Commissioner Rozelle ultimately decided to let Shula go to Miami and gave Rosenbloom the Dolphins' first-round draft pick as compensation.

The Colts' players weren't exactly unhappy over Shula's departure. "Maybe everybody hated Shula and that's what he wanted," said Curtis. "Maybe he felt it would translate into making us a close team because we hated him. It was a bad situation."[2]

Into the bad situation stepped Baltimore assistant Don McCafferty, who was Shula's antithesis. While Shula had been intense, hard-driving, and uncompromising, McCafferty was quieter and laid back, and had been known to sit in on the players' poker games and drop a few dollars now and then. "When Shula was here, he'd get upset about a lot of things and start hollering," said defensive end Bubba Smith. "McCafferty is beautiful, man; he doesn't holler at all. Everybody on this team will go out and break his neck for the guy."[3]

Even late in his career, quarterback Johnny Unitas was still the Colts' dominant personality, but many of the other cast members had changed since Super Bowl III. The Colts had used the draft to make some needed upgrades, particularly at wide receiver. Eddie Hinton was the team's number-one draft choice in 1969 and he was joined at receiver by Roy Jefferson, who came to the Colts in a trade with Pittsburgh. Hinton and Jefferson gave Unitas some speed on the outside, which helped open up things on the inside for tight end John Mackey. The 1970 draft brought running back Norm Bulaich in the first round, defensive back Ron Gardin in the sixth, and running back Jack Maitland in the sixteenth, all of whom would make contributions during the season.

The most intriguing draft selection was the third-round pick of receiver Jim O'Brien from the University of Cincinnati, by way of the Air Force Academy. O'Brien originally signed with Air Force but didn't care for the strict discipline, admitting that during his time as a cadet he developed ulcers because he "didn't like someone else telling me what to do."[4] He also looked and acted the part of a renegade, with long, flowing hair that earned him the nickname "Lassie" from his older teammates, many of whom still sported crew cuts. "I've got some strange ideas," O'Brien admitted.[5] He took a tremendous razzing about his hair throughout the season, with many on the Colts promising to give him a haircut, particularly if the team could get to the Super Bowl and win it.[6]

Although O'Brien was drafted as a receiver, he would also handle the Colts' place-kicking duties in 1970. In an age when NFL rosters were limited to only forty players, the Colts, like many other teams, did not want to tie up a roster spot for someone who could only kick.[7] They had used defensive lineman Lou Michaels as their kicker for the past six seasons, with mixed results. A straight-on kicker, Michaels missed two short field goals in Super Bowl III, and then made only 45 percent of his kicks the following season, prompting the Colts to release the popular twelve-year veteran. When O'Brien missed three of four field goal attempts in a preseason game, some Colts told him, "Lou's probably sitting by his phone right now waiting for a call to tell him to come back."[8] But the Colts kept O'Brien, who was also a straight-ahead kicker, figuring his youth and receiving ability were worth the gamble. O'Brien would catch exactly one pass the entire season—good for twenty-eight yards.

STRIKE TWO

A new coach and new kicker were not the only off-season issues the Colts had to face. Tight end John Mackey was president of the NFL Players Association (NFLPA), which for the first time was very close to calling a strike and shutting down the season. The NFLPA was formed in 1956, but had been largely ignored and ineffectual until the rise of militancy and sports unionism in the 1960s.[9] In 1968 NFL players had staged a brief strike over pension benefits, forcing owners to accept a collective bargaining agreement and minimum player salary of $10,000 per year.

Efforts to ratify a new bargaining agreement in early 1970 stalled, and in June the NFLPA filed an unfair labor practice charge against the owners. In July, Commissioner Rozelle tried to calm the situation by delaying the opening of training camps by a week, but both sides seemed determined to fight. At the end of July, the Chiefs had to receive permission from the NFL to play the annual exhibition game matching the league champs against a team of college all-stars. Kansas City won the game, 24–3, after only a week of practice.[10] Following the July 31 game, the lockout resumed and when players did not report to camp, the threat of losing the entire season seemed very real. "I think there is a possibility that the season is over now," said Eagles owner Leonard Tose.[11]

Tensions escalated even further when owners opened their training camps, but only for veteran players. "We knew that would happen," said Chiefs' player representative Jim Tyrer. "The owners are trying to weaken the players and bust the Players Association."[12] But even with strong support of the players, one of Mackey's own teammates crossed the picket line and reported to Colts training camp. Mike Curtis was a brutally honest player both on the field and off, and his ferocious, straight-ahead style had earned him two nicknames—"Mad Dog" and "The Animal."

Curtis was also an old-fashioned, lunch-pail type of player who believed in a day's work for a day's pay. "I have one job," he said, "This game. I have to prepare myself. And to prepare properly, I have to be here."[13] Curtis's stand was complicated by the fact that for road games he roomed with the Colts' player representative, Bill Curry, but there were apparently no hard feelings between the two. "What Mike is more than anything else is a pure football player," said Curry. "Totally dedicated to football and obsessed by winning. Excellence is more important to him than acceptance."[14]

With the season teetering on the brink of collapse, federal mediators stepped in and helped the two sides hammer out an agreement. On August 3, a new collective bargaining agreement was signed that raised the minimum player salary to $13,000, but more important, it significantly increased owner contributions to player pensions and insurance.[15] "We're a team, an association, a family," said Tyrer. "We pro players are unified on what we're fighting for."[16] The players had stared down the owners in a big-money game of poker and called their bluff. It would not be the last time players would walk away from the table with a big pot of money, or the last time union unrest would threaten an NFL season.[17]

The Colts' first game in the AFC took place in San Diego, and it could not have started much worse. Veteran running back Tom Matte, who had been the focal point of the Colts' running attack for the better part of a decade, went down with a knee injury and was lost for the season after just twelve carries for 43 yards. The Colts had to replace the man who led the NFL in combined rushing and receiving yards in 1969, which is why drafting Bulaich now seemed like such a blessing. The rookie added another 43 yards on ten carries, but it was the long-haired rookie O'Brien who had the biggest day, kicking three field goals, including the game-winner with less than a minute to play in a 16–14 Baltimore victory.

The Colts came home and entertained the Chiefs in the second Monday night game of the season, if "entertained" is the right word. Kansas City intercepted Unitas and Earl Morrall five times, sacked them seven more times, and collected seven turnovers in a 44–24 beating. "We stunk out the joint. It was a real team effort," said McCafferty, who had to be talked into watching the game films by his coaching staff. "There's no use looking up a dead horse's butt."[18]

"The tendency is not to figure out how good the Colts are," wrote Baltimore sportswriter Sam Lacy after the game, "but to ponder whether they are as bad as they looked."[19] In the first two weeks of the season, Baltimore had played two teams from the old AFL and found both to be better than advertised. "I remember going back to my teammates," said Curry, "and telling them, 'I think these guys want to humiliate us.'"[20] Baltimore rebounded to beat Houston and Boston on the road. A late touchdown pass from Unitas to Jefferson put away the Patriots, 14–6, in week three, and the two hooked up again late in the game to beat the Oilers, 24–20, in week four.

The first place Colts had a 3-1 record heading into their meeting with the Jets, who stood only 1-3 after a loss to the Dolphins, primarily because of injuries, poor defense, and turnovers. In week three, New York had somehow blown a two-touchdown lead to winless Buffalo in a 34–31 loss. Even worse, running back Matt Snell, who was leading the AFC in rushing at the time, ruptured an Achilles tendon during the game and would miss the rest of the season. In the 20–6 loss to Miami, Namath threw three interceptions, his sixth in four games, giving the Jets nine turnovers for the season. The Jets even got a scare from the lowly Patriots before eventually winning, 31–21.

Statistics, records, and division standings were not on the Colts' minds heading into the October 10 game at Shea Stadium. "I could beat the Jets a thousand times by a hundred points and it would never make up for that Super Bowl," said Curtis. "But this being the first game coming to play the Jets, I just wanted to kill them."[21]

"We knew what was going to happen," added Curry. "Everybody on the team knew what was going to happen, and I imagine they knew it too. We were going to kick their ass."[22]

LOGAN'S RUNS

Game day was a sunny, somewhat chilly fifty-one degrees for kickoff. The Colts had developed the disappointing habit of moving the ball well, and then having to settle for field goals rather than touchdowns. True to form, O'Brien made it 3–0 with a 28-yarder in the first quarter. Without Snell, the Jets unveiled their game plan right from the start—throw, throw, and then throw some more. The strategy may have been sound, but as he had done so far in 1970, Namath struggled with the execution, throwing an interception on his first pass attempt of the day, which safety Jerry Logan returned 31 yards for a touchdown. "Maybe he was off a little bit," said Logan. "It wasn't really his fault, though. Joe had to wait, wait, wait a lot of times."[23]

Down 10–0, the Jets fell into a deeper hole before the first quarter ended when Unitas hit Tom Mitchell with an 11-yard touchdown pass. Then Jim Turner kicked a field goal to put the Jets on the board, 17–3 before time expired. After the fireworks of the first quarter, the second was much tamer. Two promising Jets' drives were killed by interceptions deep in Colts' territory, from Curtis and then Logan again. O'Brien kicked another field goal, while the Jets tackled Jack Maitland in the end zone for a safety. Baltimore led at halftime, 20–5.

Namath continued having trouble finding guys in the right-colored jerseys and threw yet another interception in the third quarter, this one returned for a touchdown by Bob Grant. O'Brien missed the point after, but at 26–5, the Colts were more than comfortably ahead. Undeterred, Namath kept firing and finally made some headway. He threw a 17-yard touchdown to Eddie Bell, and his passing set up a short touchdown run by Emerson Boozer to cut the lead to 26–19 heading into the final period. The Jets would get no closer and after the teams traded field goals in the fourth quarter, the Colts had their satisfaction, 29–22.

The game was a disaster for Namath in more ways than one. With no running game to help him (only 37 yards on seventeen carries), Namath threw the ball sixty-two times against Baltimore, completing thirty-four for 361 yards. But he had been intercepted an incredible six times, two of which were run back for touchdowns.[24] In a game where the Colts' offense had struggled, scoring only one offensive touchdown, the turnovers were undoubtedly the key to the game. Worse yet, Namath broke his wrist in the fourth quarter after a hard hit by Billy Ray Smith. He stayed in the game and threw five more passes with what was believed to be a jammed wrist, but once the injury was diagnosed Namath would need an operation and his season officially ended. "If he was playing any other position, he'd be able to play," said a Jets spokesman after Namath's surgery.[25]

Their margin of victory was smaller than expected, but the Colts were happy just to survive Namath's air raid. "The longest day I ever spent on a football field," said Bubba Smith. "Namath threw sixty-two passes and I know I was rushing hard on every damn one of them."[26] After his performance in Super Bowl III, Namath had earned a grudging respect from the Colts, and despite the interceptions the Baltimore players were still impressed. "I know we intercepted six of his passes," said Mackey, "but he keeps coming at you all the time, and that's the sign of a man."[27]

Unitas threw three interceptions of his own, and the Colts offense also suffered a fumble and a safety, so without the play of the defense, Baltimore's grand plans for revenge might have come to nothing. Jim Duncan, Mike Curtis, and Bob Grant all had one interception, but the real hero was Jerry Logan, who picked off three passes, including the one he returned for a touchdown. In his account of the game, Milt Richman of United Press International compared Logan to Baltimore Orioles' third baseman Brooks Robinson, who had just completed a sensational World Series as the Orioles beat the Cincinnati Reds in five games. "There was one small difference, though," Richman wrote. "Robinson gets a car for what he did [winning the Series MVP]. Jerry Logan got a [game] ball."[28]

"We're all for the Birds," said Logan afterward. "We all appreciated what they did in the Series and I'm sure they got a kick out of what we did today."[29]

The teams met again in Baltimore on the last weekend of the regular season—this time without Snell and Namath. Jets' star receiver Don Maynard was also hurt and struggling (he had just thirty-one catches and no touch-downs all season), and the team simply didn't have enough weapons to compete. Backup quarterback Al Woodall didn't play badly in Namath's place, but the Colts still won easily, 35–20.

The Jets finished the year with a 4-10 record, marking a dark turning point for the Jets franchise. Just two years after their 1968 Super Bowl championship, the team collapsed under age and injuries. Namath was plagued by injuries for the remainder of his career, and the Jets would not have another winning season until 1981.

The Colts had clinched the AFC East and home-field advantage the week before their second meeting with the Jets, so they rested many of their starters, including Unitas. Backup quarterback Earl Morrall stepped in and gained his own personal measure of satisfaction with four touchdown passes. Morrall had not forgotten, nor would sportswriters and fans let him forget, the nightmare he had suffered in Super Bowl III, when he had thrown three interceptions in the first half. "Sweet revenge," Morrall said after the second Jets game.[30] He was to get a much bigger win just a few weeks later.

The Colts' other grudge match games came against former coach Don Shula and the Miami Dolphins. When the teams met for the first time on November 1 in Baltimore, the Colts won easily, 35–0. The players weren't into revenge as much as owner Carroll Rosenbloom, who was still steaming that Shula had out-maneuvered him to get the Dolphins coaching job. Before the game he explained, "I have not talked to [Dolphins owner Joe] Robbie or Shula since this happened. I will not talk to Robbie or Shula ever again. One stole something from me. The other allowed himself to be stolen."[31]

Not even the dominating win seemed to cool Rosenbloom's anger. After the game, he characterized the Dolphins as a poorly coached team with good material "which was put together by [Colts] talent scout Joe Thomas and former coach George Wilson."[32] Rosenbloom had much less to say when the teams next met November 22 in Miami and the Dolphins won, 34–17.

The loss in Miami came in the midst of a three-game losing streak, in which the Colts tied lowly Buffalo and then had to rally furiously to beat the Bears, 21–20. Fans started to boo the team at home, and sportswriters began to question whether the Colts had the talent and desire to make it back to the Super Bowl.

"Late November and December is a time for patching up, not ripping apart," wrote Larry Felser in *The Sporting News*. "From here, Baltimore doesn't look like a strong bet at playoff time."[33] Another sportswriter said the Colts "did not roll through the American Conference like a threshing machine, leaving pretzeled bodies in their path. They barely won games in which they were heavily favored, resembling overworked tractors."[34] The Colts understandably snapped back, including taking some shots at their normally supportive fans. According to reports, Tom Matte, Bill Curry, Bob Grant, and Fred Miller were the most vocal, referring to fans as "childish" and "bush."[35]

In their first year in the AFC, the Colts had the best record in the conference and home-field advantage throughout the playoffs. But unless they could exorcise the demons of Super Bowl III, their season would be considered a complete failure.

★ 9 ★

WEEK SIX:
Dallas Cowboys at Kansas City Chiefs

"NEXT YEAR'S CHAMPIONS"

As week six of the 1970 NFL season approached, the Kansas City Chiefs were right in the thick of the competitive AFC West, trailing the first place Broncos by one game. Denver had run out to a 4-1 record, including a decisive 26–13 beating of the Chiefs on October 4. The normally potent Kansas City offense had been held to 33 yards passing, primarily because the Broncos sacked Len Dawson seven times. Kansas City rebounded to beat Joe Kapp and the Patriots, 23–10, but so far in the early season the Chiefs had been maddeningly inconsistent, which was reflected in their 3-2 record. They needed a home win over Dallas to stay headed in the right direction.

Inconsistency was not a problem for the Dallas Cowboys who, under Tom Landry, had become one of the most consistent winners in the NFL since 1966. For Dallas, the issue was winning in the playoffs, which they chronically had failed to do for four straight years, despite having some of the best talent in the league. First came two straight losses to the Green Bay Packers in the NFL Championship. The Cowboys went toe-to-toe with the Packer dynasty but lost each game in heartbreaking fashion; giving up a last-second touchdown in the 1967 Ice Bowl was particularly hard for the players to accept.

"All of this created problems, serious problems" said receiver Lance Rentzel, who caught a fourth-quarter touchdown pass in the Ice Bowl that was the go-ahead score until the Green Bay comeback. "Once that set in, once the cancer started to work, the whole organization began to contend with its image."[1]

The Cowboys showed no ill effects in the regular season, going 12-2 in 1968 and 11-2-1 in 1969. But in the playoffs, the team played hesitantly, as if waiting for something bad to happen; and it usually did, part of what Rentzel called a "self-fulfilling prophecy."[2] In the 1968 playoffs, the Cowboys lost 31–20 in the mud of Cleveland Stadium, and then laid another egg the following year in a playoff rematch, 38–14. "With all their talent, if you come out and stick it to Dallas early, something happens," said Browns' lineman Jack Gregory.[3] Dallas tight end Pettis Norman didn't exactly disagree. "In the locker room after a game in which we had expected so much of ourselves, it was just total devastation," he said. "It was a low point."[4] Sportswriters mockingly called the Cowboys "Next Year's Champions."

Landry approached the problem in his usual methodical way, which may have only made things worse. Before the season started, he sent each player a lengthy questionnaire and then followed with computer evaluations of player performance. Playing time would be determined only by which players received the highest grades after each game. "No one on this team has his position made," he announced in training camp.[5]

"Landry had the idea that maybe the team was not serious or dedicated enough," said Rentzel. "He made it clear he wanted it to be all business."[6] To that, sportswriter Marty Ralbovsky remarked, "One could envision Lombardi approaching the same problem by promising each of his players hard kicks in soft places."[7]

Part of Landry's problem was a change in leadership. Quarterback Don Meredith, who had suffered both physically and mentally in getting the Cowboys to the doorstep of the Super Bowl, had retired after the 1968 season and was replaced by Craig Morton. Morton was a four-year veteran who had shown flashes of stardom, but like Meredith he enjoyed the nightlife and was not necessarily a dedicated athlete. The Cowboys also had to replace their all-time leading rusher after the 1968 season. Walt Garrison would take over for Don Perkins, who had retired after eight seasons and 6,217 yards, which at the time made him the fifth leading runner in NFL history.

The other spot in the Cowboys' backfield should have belonged to Calvin Hill, who burst onto the scene in 1969 and won Rookie of the Year honors. Hill was leading the NFL in rushing midway through his first season, until he sustained a series of nagging injuries that hampered him for the rest of the year. Concerned about Hill's health, the Cowboys used their first-round pick in the 1970 draft to select running back Duane Thomas of West Texas State (now West Texas A&M). The Cowboys knew Thomas had a history of disruptive behavior, but they also had him rated as the best back in the draft. "Does that mean he's better than Calvin Hill?" Landry asked his chief scout, Red Hickey. "If he comes here," said Hickey, "he'll be your half-back. Get him if you think you can handle him." Landry replied, "Then, I'll think I'll try to handle him."[8]

Thomas was another gem in what had become a crown of successful Dallas drafts. When the Cowboys entered the league in 1960, drafting was still an inexact science, and many players were taken simply because of some publicity they may have received in a college football magazine. Landry and general manager Tex Schramm introduced computerization to the drafting process. As Dallas scouts fanned across the country looking at prospects, they graded each player and entered the data into the Cowboys' computer.

This system gave the Cowboys a distinct advantage over other teams, and helped turn Dallas from expansion team into league power in just a few short years. In 1964 alone, the team drafted three future Hall of Famers: quarterback Roger Staubach, receiver Bob Hayes, and defensive back Mel Renfro. The Cowboys also prided themselves on being able to find hidden talent in the lower rounds of the draft and from small schools. Staubach went in the tenth round in 1965, while defensive tackle Jethro Pugh of Elizabeth City State was an eleventh-round pick.[9] Hall of Fame offensive tackle Rayfield Wright, from Fort Valley State, came in the seventh round of the 1967 draft.

The 1970 draft was another successful one for the Cowboys. In addition to Thomas, Dallas added seven more rookies who would contribute to the team's success. Third-round picks Charlie Waters, a safety from Clemson, and Steve Kiner, a linebacker from University of Tennessee, would see significant playing time during the year, and by year's end Waters would be the only rookie starter on the Cowboys' intimidating "Doomsday Defense." Center John Fitzgerald (fourth round), defensive end Pat Toomay (sixth round), and defensive back Mark Washington (thirteenth round), became starters in future years. Free agent safety Cliff Harris saw extensive playing time until he had to leave for army duty in October.[10]

While Thomas sat out the early part of 1970, a healthy Calvin Hill returned to his old form. He rushed for 117 yards in a 17–7 win over Philadelphia on opening day, and then went for 117 more in a week-four shutout of the Falcons, 13–0. Thomas got his first significant action of the season after Hill got hurt the following week in Minnesota. He rushed for 79 yards on thirteen carries, but his effort made little difference in a 54–13 loss, the worst in Dallas history. With Hill now sidelined, Thomas would make his first start of the season in Kansas City.

The loss in Minnesota suggested that Dallas still had not overcome playoff scars from the past few seasons. The offense had struggled mightily the first five weeks—averaging less than 16 points a game, thanks in large part to inconsistency at quarterback. Morton was hurt in the early part of the season, and even after he returned, he was bothered by a shoulder injury suffered the previous year. Roger Staubach filled in for Morton when needed, but it was only his second season and he was still more of a runner than a passer. Staubach, who was suffering from bursitis, also got hurt in the Vikings game and did not even suit up in Kansas City. With its passing attack grounded, Dallas stayed on the run in 1970, and by season's end led the NFL in rushing at 164 yards per game.

THE BATTLE FOR DALLAS

The Chiefs-Cowboys game was the culmination of an inner-city feud that began more than a decade earlier. The team was hastily put in Dallas in 1960 to meet the challenge of the AFL and Dallas Texans owner Lamar Hunt. It was originally called the Rangers in honor of the state's famed law enforcement group, but later changed its name to the Cowboys. "They [the NFL] hadn't shown any serious interest in expanding before our announcement," said Hunt. "It was apparent they had identified the strong points of the AFL and were trying to cut the legs out from under us."[11] The battle for Dallas was on.

In many respects, it was a strange battlefield. The NFL had experimented with a franchise in Dallas, but the 1952 Texans were a miserable failure, both at the gate and on the field. "We were primarily a dog and pony show," remembered Hall of Famer Art Donovan, "[We were] following geek shows and carnivals, and playing exhibitions in out-of-the-way hamlets all across the country just to pick up a fan or two."[12] With fans in Dallas more interested in high school and college games, the largest crowd the Texans could draw for the four games they played at the Cotton Bowl was 17,499 on opening day. By midseason, the franchise was broke, forcing the NFL to step in and move the base of operations from Dallas to Hershey, Pennsylvania. The Texans played their last five games on the road, went 1-11 on the season, and still have the distinction of being the last NFL team to go bankrupt. Apparently unafraid of repeating history, Hunt named his AFL team the Dallas Texans.

So now, eight years later, Dallas had not one, but two professional teams, and they were strikingly similar to one another. Both were financed by the sons of Texas oil barons, both had young, inexperienced head coaches, and both were starting absolutely from scratch. And while both teams would play their home games in the Cotton Bowl, they appealed to different segments of the city.

"The Cowboys appealed to the country-clubbers, the establishment, the patrician elite," said sportswriter and author John Eisenberg, who grew up in Dallas in the 1960s. "The Texans attracted the young, the disenfranchised, and the hip. The team was an underdog."[13]

In the early going, the Texans appeared to have the upper hand in terms of attendance, primarily because they were more competitive. The Texans drew an estimated forty-two thousand fans to their home debut, a 17–0 win over the Chargers, en route to an 8-6 record and second place finish in the AFL West. By contrast, the Cowboys did not win a single game, and only managed a tie with the New York Giants, going 0-11-1 in the 1960 season. It appeared the Texans had gained a foothold in their battle with the Cowboys, until critics pointed out that thousands of Texans tickets had been giveaways or part of a free promotion.

"We got people in there for free, but not nearly to the extent that they did," said Schramm. "We concentrated on building a team and did not go into the marketing and giving tickets away. We had to establish ourselves with a little bit more integrity because we were in the National Football League."[14] For that first season, the Texans had an announced average of about twenty-four thousand fans per game, which was about three thousand more than the Cowboys.

The teams also feuded bitterly for college talent. Back when the AFL and NFL held separate drafts, the Cowboys and Texans both selected Bob

Lilly, E. J. Holub, Don Meredith, and Roger Staubach (Lilly and Meredith signed with the Cowboys, while Holub went with the Texans). Quarterback and 1963 Heisman Trophy winner Staubach was a special case—after graduating from the Naval Academy, he had to spend four years in the service before he could play for either team. The Cowboys (tenth round) and Texans (sixteenth round) both took a chance on him in the 1964 draft. Hunt badly wanted the drawing power of a Heisman Trophy winner, so he offered Staubach a $10,000 bonus and $500 per month. Before Staubach signed with the Chiefs he checked with the Cowboys, and when they offered him the same deal, the future Hall of Famer took it.

"They were in the NFL and not in the AFL," said Staubach, "and they drafted me higher than Kansas City. "I didn't want to get in a bidding war. I just wanted to get it behind me, and I felt Dallas was the right thing."[15]

The one place the Texans desperately wanted to challenge the Cowboys was on the field. Hunt's team was extremely competitive during its three years in Dallas, winning twenty-four games over that span and an AFL championship in 1962. Over the same three years, the Cowboys won only nine games and never finished higher than fifth in their conference. Following the 1960 season, Hunt shrewdly suggested that the teams play an exhibition game for charity. The Cowboys, realizing they had nothing to gain and everything to lose, politely declined, and the two teams would never play during the time they shared the city of Dallas. "They surely would have had a chance," said Landry when asked about the possibility of a matchup. "I suspect that they were the better team, [but] they never had a chance to prove it."[16]

By 1962, it had become clear that Dallas could not support both of its pro teams. Even after winning the AFL title, the Texans could not significantly increase their attendance, and Hunt was losing about a million dollars a year. "I didn't think that winning the championship was going to have a big impact," he admitted. "If we had stayed it was going to be a long, hard battle and probably a long time before anyone won."[17] Dallas also had the credibility of the NFL behind it, and even though the Cowboys were not yet winning, established stars such as Jim Brown, Bobby Layne, and Paul Hornung were visiting the Cotton Bowl every season.

With that in mind, Hunt decided to move his team to Kansas City, although he had also flirted with several other cities, including New Orleans and Miami. On May 22, 1963, with a guarantee of thirty-five thousand season ticket sales at their new home, the Dallas Texans officially became the Kansas City Chiefs.

"I was crying like a baby when I drove out of town, just thinking about the fact that we were having to leave," said Texans/Chiefs coach Hank Stram. "Lamar explained the economics to me and I understood. [But] I felt like Dallas was our town."[18]

The Chiefs finally got their exhibition game with the Cowboys in August 1970. Although it came almost a decade too late, the trip back to the Cotton Bowl had to be a rewarding one for Lamar Hunt's franchise. The former Texans were returning to Dallas as Super Bowl champions, having conquered the Vikings in January, and they got a large measure of satisfaction by not only beating the Cowboys but also shutting them out, 13–0. There was no reason to think the October 25 rematch in Kansas City's Municipal Stadium would have a different outcome, especially with Dallas coming off its terrible beating in Minnesota.

A ROOKIE RIDES HIGH

Despite a bad elbow, Calvin Hill tried to play against the Chiefs, but he was severely limited in his abilities and ended up rushing for only 8 yards on two carries. With Walt Garrison also sidelined, Dallas was forced to go with a backfield of Duane Thomas and Dan Reeves. Reeves was another one of the Cowboys' success stories—an undrafted free agent quarterback from South Carolina who didn't even have a position when he signed with the team in 1965.

"I knew I wouldn't get a chance at quarterback, because the Cowboys had drafted Craig Morton and Jerry Rhome," said Reeves, whom the Cowboys tried at defensive back, receiver, and running back. "They drafted four or five running backs, too, so it never occurred to me that I would get to run."[19]

When injuries had forced Dallas to play Reeves at running back in 1966, he responded with 757 yards, good for sixth-best in the NFL, and added versatility to the Cowboys backfield. He returned kicks, threw halfback passes, was second on the team with forty-one catches, and led the explosive Cowboys' offense with sixteen touchdowns. Reeves also had a penchant for making big plays—he scored a touchdown in the Cowboys' 34–27 loss to Green Bay in the 1966 NFL Championship, and then the next season threw a touchdown pass to Rentzel in the Ice Bowl.

Reeves suffered a major knee injury in 1968 that ended his season and slowed him for the rest of his career. But the Cowboys had also recognized something else about him—his ability to understand the game—and in 1970 they took the unusual step of making Reeves a player/coach to help with the running backs.[20] "I learn all the assignments on every play," he said, "so I know what everyone is going to do. It helps me set up blocks, and I think that is my major asset as a runner."[21] The Chiefs game would be Reeves' first serious action of the 1970 season. With Hill, Thomas, and Garrison already in the Cowboys backfield, Reeves had played sparingly in the first five games, rushing exactly one time for 0 yards.

Dallas had continued to bring Thomas along slowly. He sat on the bench for the first two games, and then carried only once in the Cowboys' 20–7 loss in St. Louis. But Hill's injuries forced Thomas into action, and he seemed to respond with the brilliance of a natural runner. In a downpour against Atlanta, Thomas sloshed for 29 yards on only six carries, and then added 79 yards on thirteen carries against the Vikings. He wasn't necessarily piling up yards, but he was averaging more than 5 yards per carry. By the time his season ended, that average would sit at 5.3, putting Thomas in first place in the entire NFL.

The other addition to the Cowboys lineup was receiver Bob Hayes, the Olympic sprinter who had struck terror into opposing defenses since his 1965 rookie season. Hayes's blinding speed—which carried him to a gold medal and world record 10.05 seconds in the 100-meter dash in the 1964 Olympics—has been credited for the invention of the zone defense. No one could cover Hayes man-on-man, and in his first five years in the NFL he had averaged more than ten touchdown catches and nearly 20 yards per catch a season. As early as his second year, Hayes had already drawn raves from *Sports Illustrated* writer Tex Maule, who said he was "on his way to becoming the finest deep receiver ever to play the game. Hayes has exceptionally sure hands and a real football sense, differing in this respect from most track men who have switched sports."[22]

But Landry's new emphasis on accountability often left Hayes the odd man out, since Landry wanted his receivers to block as well as catch passes.

Hayes didn't put as much effort into blocking as he did with his pass routes, and consequently he had played only two games and caught two touchdowns so far in 1970. "Bob just wasn't meeting the requirements for what an end does or should do," explained Landry.[23] Hayes reacted predictably. "I'm unhappy and they know it," he said after sitting out the season opener. "If I can't play regularly I'd rather leave. I don't like playing on the second team when I know I'm the best."[24] Whether Landry saw an improvement in Hayes's blocking or he felt the struggling Cowboys' offense needed a lift, he told Hayes he would play against the Chiefs. But it was just another indication that all was not well in Dallas.

The Chiefs lineup had a familiar look, but the team made a significant move in October, trading running back Mike Garrett to San Diego. Garrett had put the Chiefs in a difficult position, announcing that he would give up pro football after the season to attempt a baseball career. Kansas City felt it had a promising young runner in Ed Podolak, so one of the most exciting and versatile players in Kansas City history went west for a second-round draft pick. As it turned out, Garrett never made it in pro baseball, but played three more years in the NFL and even managed another thousand-yard rushing season in 1972. Podolak was very similar to Reeves in terms of his versatility, and the next season he would set an NFL playoff record for a single game with 350 all-purpose yards.[25]

The game kicked off under sunny, ideal conditions for late October. Podolak got the first touchdown with a 5-yard run in the first quarter. The Chiefs tried to take advantage of Podolak's versatility throughout the afternoon, but by game's end they had little to show for it. He would finish the day with only 18 yards rushing on seven attempts, although he did catch two passes for 74 yards. Two Mike Clark field goals brought the Cowboys within one in the second quarter, and a 1-yard Thomas touchdown gave Dallas a 13–10 lead.

Unable to run (they would finish with only 53 yards on eighteen carries), the Chiefs went to the air and found similar trouble. Dawson would not complete half of his passes, going seventeen of thirty-eight with two interceptions, both picked off by Mel Renfro, a consistent All-Pro at cornerback who led the NFL with ten interceptions in 1969. The Cowboys had another All-Pro at safety in Cornell Green, and a budding star in rookie safety

Charlie Waters, so with opposing teams obviously reluctant to throw at Renfro, the issue was finding a cornerback who could shut down the other side. In the past few seasons, Dallas had tried Dick Daniels, Warren Livingston, and Otto Brown with little success, and problems at that cornerback spot had taken much of the blame for previous playoff losses to Green Bay and Cleveland.

In an effort to solve the problem, the Cowboys had traded two backup linemen to the Packers in exchange for cornerback Herb Adderley, during the 1970 preseason. Adderley was on the downside of a twelve-year career, but he had been a five-time Pro Bowl performer, and, more importantly, won five NFL titles under Lombardi in Green Bay. "Herb walked into his first meeting and held up his finger with a championship ring on it and said, 'I'll help you get one of these,'" said defensive tackle Jethro Pugh. "He brought a real swagger that was missing after the Cleveland games."[26] He also helped shut down his side of the field, making it almost as dangerous for quarterbacks as throwing to Renfro's side.

The Cowboys went back to the ground in the second half, and Thomas continued his productive afternoon. Midway through the third quarter, he took off on a weaving, twisting 47-yard touchdown right up the middle, in which he seemed to magically run through the entire Kansas City defense. The game would serve as Thomas's coming-out party in the NFL. He wound up with 134 yards on twenty carries and two touchdowns, and by the end of the season would finish eighth in the league with 803 yards, despite sitting on the bench for the first four games.

"I just had visions of Jim Brown coming back to life," said Cowboys' defensive tackle Bob Lilly, referring to the Hall of Fame Cleveland running back. "Duane had the same moves. You think you have him and he just wiggles out of it. He could go off tackle as good as I ever saw."[27]

The Thomas score was the Cowboys' longest rushing touchdown so far in the season and it helped loosen up the Kansas City defense. A bit later, with Dallas facing third and 23 from its own 11-yard line, Morton noticed Chiefs safety Johnny Robinson cheating up toward the line of scrimmage. He audibled to a deep post to Hayes, who streaked down the middle of the field for an 89-yard touchdown. The two lightning strikes gave the Cowboys a 27–10 lead and effectively ended the game. The Dallas defense allowed only two Jan Stenerud field goals the rest of the way, in a 27–16 victory. "We had a great game plan," noted Morton. "We used a lot of formations and were changing up a lot of them, keeping them off balance."[28]

It was an impressive road win for the Cowboys, one Morton called "the biggest one we've had since I've been here," and for the moment it quieted their growing number of critics.[29] "That 'choke' business is so old I don't even bother to read about it anymore," said Landry. "Think positive. That's the way we want things around here."[30] But aside from Thomas and the two long touchdowns, there was very little that was positive about the Dallas offense. Reeves had played an efficient game, carrying sixteen times for 56 yards and catching two passes for 16 more. But Morton still looked uncertain, and, by extension, so did the Dallas passing game. Morton finished the day seven of fourteen passing, but take away the long bomb to Hayes and he had a pedestrian 71 yards. Hayes caught only one other pass for 11 yards, and Rentzel caught three for 44.

The Cowboys' passing attack would spring to life the following week at home against Philadelphia, as Rentzel caught two touchdown passes of 86 and 56 yards, while Hayes added a 40-yard scoring catch. Dallas squeaked by the Eagles, 21–17, and with a record of 5-2 it led the NFC East at the halfway point of the season. Based on past history, the smart money figured the Cowboys would cruise through the rest of their schedule and take the division title. Those predictions would eventually turn out to be correct, but not before the team sank to perhaps the lowest depths of its ten-year history.

After the loss to Dallas, the Chiefs hosted Oakland and seemed to have the victory well in hand, but the bad blood that always seemed to exist when the Chiefs and Raiders played boiled over near the end of the game. With Kansas City ahead and trying to run out the clock, the Raiders' Ben Davidson made what looked like a late hit on Dawson. When a fight broke out, Kansas City's Otis Taylor was penalized and ejected, so the Chiefs had to punt the ball back to Oakland. With just seconds to play, George Blanda kicked a 48-yard field goal and the game ended, 17–17. "When Oakland takes a shot at him like that, it's up to us to protect him," said Taylor.[31]

The Chiefs rallied from the deflating tie and had a chance to take the AFC West by winning their last two games of the season. Still unable to run the ball, Kansas City lost 20-6 in Oakland and 31–13 in San Diego. The loss to the Chargers was particularly galling, as San Diego won only five games all season. Mike Garrett rubbed it in a bit more by scoring twice and picking up 135 yards rushing and receiving. At 7-5-2, the Chiefs finished a game behind Oakland in the standings and would miss the playoffs for the first time in three seasons. As of 2013, fans in Kansas City are still waiting for a second Super Bowl title.

★ 10 ★

WEEK SEVEN:
New York Giants at New York Jets

WHO OWNS NEW YORK?

The ascendancy of the Jets in football came at an interesting time in New York sports history. For decades, the Yankees in baseball and the Giants in football, but particularly the Yankees, had dominated the city and national sports scenes. Between 1921 and 1964, the Yankees created the greatest dynasty in professional sports history, winning twenty-nine American League championships and twenty World Series titles.[1] In the 1930s they became the first team to win four World Series in a row, then a few years later won five straight. Their stars became legends whose names are still revered today: Ruth, Gehrig, DiMaggio, and Mantle.

The Yankees were not a colorful club like the "Gashouse Gang" Cardinals of the 1930s or the "Boys of Summer" Brooklyn Dodgers of the 1950s. Instead, they won games with cold, mechanical efficiency, and even their iconic pinstriped uniforms gave them the air of a successful company looking for its next corporate takeover. They were the "lordly" Yankees, and they towered above baseball for nearly half a century.

"The Yankees and Yankees fans were different from us," recalled Larry King, a Dodgers fan and longtime broadcaster who grew up in Brooklyn. "Yankees fans didn't scream; they clapped like at the opera. There was always a feeling, 'If you puh-leeze, this is the Yankees.' And you knew they weren't going to lose."[2]

To a certain extent, the Giants were pro football's version of the Yankees. Going back almost to the founding of the NFL itself, their tradition was just as deep as the Yankees, as was their success. Between 1927 and 1963, the team won fourteen division or conference titles and four NFL championships. And just like the Yankees, their players had been mythologized in the game's history. Giants' running back Kyle Rote, who won an NFL title in 1956 and played in the 1958 championship—"The Greatest Game Ever Played"—observed, "I think a lot of us automatically associated ourselves with the Yankees and their success."[3] It's doubtful that the '58 game was the best in NFL history, but it was played at Yankee Stadium, broadcast on national television, and went to overtime before the Colts beat the Giants, 23–17.

Playing in the nation's media capital, the Giants cashed in on their success through personal appearances, interviews, and most especially, advertising. Handsome Frank Gifford was the face of the franchise, and more than anyone else he epitomized the attraction of the Giants team in New York and across the nation. "The advertisers and television executives could feel it too," Gifford said. "Television ratings began to climb. Athletes who once labored in a lunch-pail league were now the stars of prime-time television shows and graced the cover of weekly magazines."[4] New York made household names out of players who previously had been ignored, like linebacker Sam Huff, who was featured on the cover of *Time* magazine in 1959, then in 1960 became the subject of a CBS documentary called *The Violent World of Sam Huff*.

Both the Yankees and Giants faced new challenges in the early 1960s. The Yankees had the city to themselves when the Dodgers and Giants moved to California in 1958, until the National League expanded in 1962 with the addition of the New York Mets. Playing in the dilapidated Polo Grounds, the former home of the New York baseball Giants, the sad-sack Mets set an all-time record with 120 losses in their inaugural season, but still managed to attract nearly a million fans. The Yankees, still winning pennants and World Series, could not figure out the Mets' popularity. They never understood that fans came out to see the Mets because they represented everything the Yankees were not—entertainingly flawed, colorful, and fun to watch. The Mets team was so bad, wrote New York columnist Jimmy Breslin in 1964, "That it has stepped out of sports and has become, along with the Guggenheim Museum, a driving force in the city's culture."[5] The Mets kept losing, but the fans kept coming, and by the end of the decade the team was outdrawing the Yankees by more than a million fans a year.

At roughly the same time that the Mets appeared, the Yankee dynasty began to crumble. The team fired manager Casey Stengel after a 1960 World Series loss to the Pirates, and the Mets capitalized by hiring the popular seventy-year-old "Perfesser."[6] The Yankees won World Series titles in 1961 and 1962, and returned to the Series in 1963 and 1964, but after that the winning suddenly stopped.[7] They finished twenty-five games out of first place in 1965, and would have only one winning season the rest of the decade. In 1969 the Mets, who had started to draft quality players, capped off an improbable season with a World Series win over the favored Orioles. Suddenly, a team that had never finished higher than ninth place was the best team in baseball, and more important, the best team in New York.

An eerily similar fate befell the Giants. The team continued its dominance between 1958 and 1963, winning five Eastern Conference titles. Even though the Giants lost all five NFL title games—two to Baltimore, two to Lombardi's Packers, and one to the Bears—there was no reason to think that they would be anything but an NFL contender in the ensuing years. But the team did not age gracefully and suddenly the glamorous stars of the 1950s were old men in the 1960s. The bottom dropped out in 1964 when New York sank to 2-10-2 and last place in the Eastern Conference; it got even worse in 1966 when the team again finished last and managed to win only one game.

Coach Allie Sherman figured the problem was at quarterback, where the Giants were struggling to find a replacement for retired Hall of Famer Y. A. Tittle. (One of the team's passing leaders in 1966 was none other than Earl Morrall.) Fran Tarkenton had become disenchanted with the Vikings and coach Norm Van Brocklin, so in 1967 Minnesota shipped him to the Giants. Tarkenton was certainly an upgrade over anything the Giants had, but that wasn't saying much. "Tarkenton arrived in New York at the right time," Joe King opined in *The Sporting News*. "He will take the heat off a non-descript team without a single star except himself."[8]

Tarkenton came to New York for a staggering price: two number-one draft picks and two number-two picks over the course of the next three years, making him "the most expensive player in the history of the organization" according to sources from the Giants organization.[9] Tarkenton played well his first three seasons in New York, finishing near the top of NFL passing leaders each year, but the best the Giants could do were 7-7 records in 1967 and 1968. The team could never surround Tarkenton with players to match his talent, in part because it gave up so many draft picks to get him.

The Giants' rapid descent to the depths of the NFL coincided with the rise of the New York Jets. Like the Mets, the team began in New York in the early 1960s and played their home games at the Polo Grounds. Originally named the Titans, their problem was not so much on the field as it was at the box office and in the newspapers. Legendary former quarterback Sammy Baugh coached the Titans to respectable 7-7 marks in their first two seasons, but it came at a time when the Giants were at the height of their popularity.

"The sportswriters made fun of us, and that made it even worse," said receiver Don Maynard, who was cut from the Giants and latched on with the Titans. "The Giants had New York all to themselves and we were treated like intruders, or worse, clowns."[10] Poor attendance made it impossible for owner Harry Wismer to make any money, and Titan paychecks began to bounce—if the players got them at all. Three games into the 1962 season, the checks stopped coming altogether and players wanted to go on strike. "The league rule clearly states that paychecks have to be delivered within 24 hours after a game," said Titans' guard and co-captain Bob Mischak. "Our paychecks are now 194 hours overdue."[11]

"Personally, I didn't think there would be a New York Titan team after that [third] season," said Maynard. "I remember shaking hands with my teammates wondering if I'd ever see them again."[12] But in 1963, talent agent and music impresario Sonny Werblin took the team off Wismer's hands and infused some much needed cash and energy. He paid only $1 million to get the team out of bankruptcy court. "I figured any sports franchise in New York was worth $1 million," said Werblin, who at the time had estimated stock holdings in the Music Corporation of America worth more than $11 million.[13]

The bold, brash, and forward-thinking Werblin embodied his new team and the rest of the AFL. He immediately changed the team name to the Jets, moved them out of the dumpy Polo Grounds and into brand-new Shea Stadium, and signed rookie quarterback Joe Namath to a record $427,000 contract. He also found a new coach in Weeb Ewbank, who had won two NFL titles in Baltimore, including the classic 1958 championship game. "I was sold on the fact that the new owners were taking football seriously," said

Maynard.[14] In just two short years, the former Titans had money, attention, and credibility.

The team actually regressed a bit in the standings, going 5-8-1 in both 1964 and 1965. Then the climb began—in 1966 the Jets finished 6-6-2 and third place in the AFL East, and the following season they finished in second place at 8-5-1. Then came the transcendent 1968 season, capped off with the win over the Colts in Super Bowl III on January 12, 1969. Almost nine months later, on October 16, the Mets won the World Series in five games over the Orioles.

The Mets and Jets were both champions in the same year, both playing at Shea Stadium, and both beating heavily favored teams from Baltimore.[15] Mets' pitcher Tom Seaver said, "God is living in New York City and he's a Mets fan."[16] If divine intervention couldn't explain it, maybe the stars were aligned just right. Astrologer Jonathan Booth was about the only person on the planet to pick the Jets to beat the Colts in the Super Bowl. Booth had never seen a football game in his life, but ten days before the kickoff he announced, "The Jets have ten aspects going for them; the Colts only six. That could be it."[17]

While the Mets and the Jets were hip, and Shea Stadium was the place to be, Yankee Stadium and its tenants were looking older than ever. In 1969 the Yankees finished twenty-eight and a half games behind the Orioles in the American League East with a record of 80-81. The best Yankees player at the stadium that year was probably Mickey Mantle, the former star who came back for "Mickey Mantle Day" on June 8 to see his number seven retired and a plaque in his honor unveiled in deep center field, near the monuments of Ruth, Gehrig, and manager Miller Huggins. That same season, the Giants went 6-8, the sixth straight year they had failed to produce a winning record, and an embarrassing preseason loss to the Jets may have been what cost coach Allie Sherman his job.

"GOODBYE, ALLIE"

The first meeting between the Jets and the Giants took place August 17, 1969, at the Yale Bowl in Connecticut before 70,874 fans. Even though the Jets were the defending Super Bowl champions, there was still a sense of NFL, and even Giant, superiority. Before the game, sportswriter George Vecsey of the *New*

York Times asked an interesting question: "Right now, they are the champions of the world," he wrote of the Jets. "Does that make them the champions of New York?"[18] Ewbank admitted before the game that the Jets were not approaching it like an ordinary preseason game, a point Namath made clear when his pregame quote appeared in the newspapers: "I don't think too many people are going to take the Giants seriously anymore."[19]

Just as he did when he guaranteed a Super Bowl win over the Colts, Namath went out and backed up his words, hitting fourteen of sixteen passes for three touchdowns. The Jets blew to a quick 24–0 lead and easily won the preseason battle of New York, 37–14. "Did we prove anything?" asked Jets running back Matt Snell. "I mean to the fans, the old NFL fans, they will cop out, they'll find a way to rationalize not how we won, but how the Giants lost."[20] Jets linebacker Larry Grantham said, "I would not have missed this game for anything in the world. It was as important to me as the Super Bowl. In New York for several years people [have] perceived the Jets as minor league."[21]

As for the Giants, "Being number two in New York isn't important to us," said Tarkenton, who threw a pair of touchdown passes during the game. "Being number one in our division is important to us."[22] Rookie defensive end Fred Dryer was probably closer to the truth when he said, "It was emblematic of an old, tired Model T against a Corvette."[23] After the game, Giants fans serenaded Sherman with choruses of "Goodbye, Allie," sung to the tune of "Goodnight, Ladies." Sherman was fired a few weeks after the Giants finished a winless preseason.

The new coach was former Giants' fullback Alex Webster—a link to the glory days of the 1950s and a man who had played in the 1958 NFL championship game. Unlike Sherman and Van Brocklin, Webster not only tolerated Tarkenton's scrambling, he encouraged it, partly as an offensive weapon and partly as a means of injecting some life into a moribund team. "The idea is to take Tarkenton out of the pocket more often so that he can keep defenses guessing; shake up their rush," said the new coach.[24]

In reality, the running game was much more of a concern than Tarkenton's passing. Tarkenton had a good year in 1969, throwing twenty-three touchdowns against only eight interceptions, but the Giants' rushing attack had been woeful. Joe Morrison led with the team with 387 yards, which put him twenty-eighth in the NFL. That's what prompted New York to part with receiver Homer Jones, sending him to Cleveland in exchange for second-year running back Ron Johnson. At first, it looked like a lopsided trade, as Jones had piled up three 1,000-yard receiving seasons in four years with the Giants, while Johnson got little opportunity to run behind Leroy Kelly in Cleveland. A year later, the trade still looked lopsided, but in the Giants' favor.

Trading for Johnson was part of Webster's general housecleaning that saw the Giants bring in eighteen new players in 1970. Most were retreads from other teams and would last only a season or two, and even the draft picks didn't stick around very long. Number one pick, linebacker Jim Files from Oklahoma, never lived up to his billing and lasted only four seasons. *The Sporting News* said the player turnover "was a little extreme," but the newcomers brought a sense of freshness, and new hope, that had been missing for the better part of a decade.[25] "It was a team made up of a lot of new, first-year players; it was not an old Giants team," said Johnson. "We all just sort of meshed together."[26]

THE KIDS ARE ALRIGHT

Both the Yankees and Giants would turn to youngsters in 1970 to try and reverse their fortunes and steal back the headlines from their cross-town rivals. The Yankees newcomer was catcher Thurman Munson, who would go on to win American League Rookie of the Year honors after hitting .302, with seven home runs and fifty-seven runs batted in. Led by Munson, the Yankees won 93 games—a total that would usually be good enough to win a pennant, but the Orioles steamrolled to a division title, winning 108 games and ultimately the World Series. Over in the National League East, the Mets could not repeat the miracle of 1969 and finished at 83-79, six games behind the division-winning Pittsburgh Pirates.

In the early part of 1970, the Giants' youngsters were not making too much difference. The team dropped its first three games, blowing leads against the Bears and Cowboys, and then lost 14–10 to New Orleans after the Saints blocked a punt and ran it back for a score. New Orleans would go on to win only two games all season, and at that point it seemed like the Giants were headed in the same direction. New York blew another lead in week four against Philadelphia, who rallied from a 17–0 hole to tie the game in the fourth quarter, but Johnson broke loose on a 34-yard touchdown run late in the game to give the Giants their first win, 30–23. After three average performances, Johnson busted out with 142 yards and two touchdowns against the Eagles.

Johnson added 86 more yards the following week against the Patriots, but this time it was the defense that stepped up, holding Boston to 155 total yards in a 16–0 shutout. When the Giants hosted the high-flying and once-beaten Cardinals the following week, it was Tarkenton's turn to shine. He threw only eighteen passes, but five of them went for touchdowns in a relatively easy 35–17 win. After starting the season 0-3, New York had won three straight games to even its record and create some momentum for its game with the Jets.

"Everybody, everything was clicking and we had it going," said running back Tucker Frederickson. "We had a chemistry that you could never describe on paper. I don't think we were as good as we played, but we certainly had it going."[27] With Johnson's emergence, Frederickson adjusted to a new role as blocker and spot runner. He had been the main weapon in the Giants' backfield since his rookie season in 1965, but injuries would force him out of the NFL after 1971.

A GIANT STEP

The game with the Jets took place November 1 in Shea Stadium, which technically made it a road game for the Giants and allowed the NFL to lift its blackout policy in New York.[28] The NFL rule at the time was no live broadcast within seventy-five miles of the game site, but the Giants successfully argued that their fans should get to see the game, and so the largest television crowd in New York City up to that time was able to see the first-ever regular season meeting between the teams. Around 67 percent of people watching television in New York City were tuned in to the game, which also attracted a record crowd of 63,903 to Shea Stadium.

Without the injured Namath, Snell, or Emerson Boozer, the Jets managed to surprise the Giants in the early going. Backup quarterback Al Woodall seemed completely unfazed by the situation, completing his first seven passes, including an 8-yard touchdown to George Nock, as the Jets took a 7–3 halftime lead. Webster tried to light a fire under his team with a blistering halftime talk, and the Giants seemed more inspired in the third quarter, even when four straight smashes from the Jets' 1-yard line failed to produce a touchdown. After the fourth attempt, Tarkenton got into a scuffle with Jets' linebacker Larry Grantham and the mini-fight seemed to arouse the Giants. "I don't remember what I did, but I was mad," said Tarkenton. "It's not a nice game; it's pretty nasty sometimes."[29] The Jets took over on downs at the 1, but then Files broke through to tackle Chuck Mercein in the end zone for a safety, which cut the Jets' lead to 10–5.

After the free kick, Tarkenton hit Johnson for a 50-yard gain, and then found Bob Tucker for a 9-yard score, putting the Giants ahead, 12–10. The Giants quickly intercepted Woodall, and Tarkenton threw an 11-yard touchdown strike to Clifton McNeil. In a span of less than two minutes, the Giants had scored a pair of touchdowns and they went on to win, 22–10. "It was a very special game to win," admitted Webster, "even though they didn't have their big guns."[30] Giants' owner Wellington Mara was a little more forthcoming when he said, "You have to be champion in your neighborhood before you can think of conquering the world."[31]

Playing without their main offensive weapons, the Jets acquitted themselves well. Woodall finished twelve of sixteen for 164 yards and one touchdown, but his two interceptions were costly. Nock and Lee White filled in with a combined 87 yards rushing. "Our kids played a great game," said Ewbank. "Woodall was terrific. [But] him replacing Joe [Namath] is like putting another horse in for Man O' War."[32] Tarkenton finished eleven of twenty-two for 153 yards and two scores; he also kept his scrambling under control, rushing four times for only 17 yards. Johnson led the Giants with 69 yards, but it took him twenty-five carries to get there.

The teams would not meet again in the regular season until 1974, so the Giants could claim the championship of New York for at least another four years.[33] That may have meant something to the Jets, who were in the midst of a six-game losing streak and would finish the season at 4–10, but the Giants were entertaining thoughts of a division title. Those feelings became even stronger the following week when New York rallied to beat the Cowboys, 23–20, at Yankee Stadium. Johnson rushed for 140 yards and scored two touchdowns in the second half to give the Giants their fifth straight win.

Their most dramatic win may have come November 15 in Washington, where the Giants trailed the Redskins 33–14 at the end of the third quarter. But in the final fifteen minutes of the game, Johnson scored twice and

Tarkenton threw a touchdown pass to Frederickson as the Giants stormed back to win, 35–33. "I remember we just went crazy after that game," said Johnson. "We had a lot of new players and we all bonded together so well. It took us a couple of games to get bonded, but after that, we felt we could beat anybody. It was just a real great feeling."[34]

Two more wins in weeks eleven and twelve put the Giants at 9-4 and on the doorstep of the playoffs, and they could walk through with a win over the Rams in the final weekend of the season. Having just won nine of ten games and with home-field advantage, New York figured to have all the momentum. Unfortunately, in an indication of how the league was so evenly matched and unpredictable in 1970, the Rams humbled the Giants, 31–3, to ruin New York's playoff hopes. Tarkenton had one of his worst days of the season, hitting only thirteen of thirty-three passes with an interception, and the Rams' defense held Johnson to only 43 yards rushing. "[Hall of Fame defensive tackle] Merlin [Olsen] was a stud and he wasn't supposed to play, so we felt pretty good that we were going to beat them," Frederickson said. "He played the whole game and killed us, so there went our playoff hopes."[35]

Still, the Giants had an encouraging 9-5 season, which saw the breakout of Ron Johnson. He made the Pro Bowl and first-team All Pro that season, leading the league in touches (total yards from scrimmage and rushing attempts); he was also second in rushing yards (1,027), rushing yards per game (73.4), and all-purpose yards (1,654). With Tarkenton and Johnson, the Giants appeared to have a backfield combination that would keep them competitive for years to come, but it didn't work out that way. As he had in Minnesota, Tarkenton became disenchanted with Giants' coaches and the front office, and he demanded another trade, which he got in 1972, ironically going back to the Vikings. Johnson played until 1975, hitting a personal best 1,182 yards rushing in 1972, but without a solid quarterback the Giants floundered throughout the rest of the '70s.

The 1970 season was the high-water mark for the Giants until the arrival of Bill Parcells in 1983. They sank to two wins in 1973, fired Webster in 1974, and did not have a winning record the rest of the decade. But on a glorious 1970 November afternoon, they reclaimed their status as kings of New York and, if only briefly, brought back visions of their proud and storied past.

★ 11 ★

WEEK EIGHT:
Detroit Lions at New Orleans Saints

MARCHING OUT

Like most years in the NFL, the headlines for the first part of 1970 went to the quarterbacks, running backs, and receivers. Quarterback John Brodie was in his fourteenth, and possibly best, season in the NFL, which would see him win the league's MVP award. At age thirty-five, Brodie would finish first in the NFL in passing yards (2,941), passing touchdowns (twenty-four), and passer rating (93.8).[1] Behind Brodie, the 49ers won the NFC Western Division title with a 10-3-1 record, and they seemed capable of winning the first NFL championship in the twenty-five-year history of the franchise.

"We have a real good shot at it this year," said running back Ken Willard. "I'm tired of hearing about how we have all the personnel and still can't win. That's never been true. We didn't have the kind of people we have now and we've never been as deep as we are."[2] Brodie said, "We've got a great many fellows on this team who are winners but haven't won as pros. The veterans are hungry and the young ones are enthusiastic."[3] Brodie and the other NFL quarterbacks rolled on, but in week eight of the season the headlines belonged almost exclusively to kickers—one played right across the San Francisco Bay from Brodie, and another would set a record that still stands today.

The NFL Sunday of November 8 started with what looked like a mismatch between the Saints and Lions in New Orleans. Detroit was cruising to a playoff berth, while the Saints were chasing yet another season of futility. After the team dropped to 1-5-1, it fired head coach Tom Fears, who reacted with a touch of humor. "The funny thing is," he observed, "that our record when I was fired was better than our record [0-6-1] at the same stage last year."[4] J. D. Roberts replaced Fears on an interim basis and began his coaching career against Detroit.

Fears had coached the Saints since they were created as part of the merger. The city had tried for years to get a team but was hurt by its segregationist policies. "New Orleans isn't ready for a black man to wear a coat and tie and sit at a desk," said Saints' running back Ernie Wheelwright on his frustration of finding an off-season job. "One of my black teammates pumped gas. Imagine a man playing for the NFL and pumping gas!"[5] When the 1965 AFL All-Star game was held in New Orleans, mistreatment of black players led to a boycott and the game was moved to Houston.

"The city wanted an NFL team, but it was not going to get it unless it desegregated," said Chargers' lineman Ron Mix, who played in the '65 All-Star game.[6] Another change took place in Washington, where Congress had to approve legislation that would allow the NFL-AFL merger to take place. Led by U.S. Senator Russell Long and Congressman Hale Boggs, both of Louisiana, the legislation passed and the merger became official. "Congressman Boggs, I don't know how I can thank you enough for this," said Commissioner Pete Rozelle. "This is a terrific thing you've done." Boggs replied, "What do you mean, you don't know how to thank me? New Orleans gets an immediate franchise in the NFL."[7] Thus, the Saints were officially born, and began play in 1967.

There were high hopes for the team right from the outset. New Orleans had acquired the great Green Bay backfield of the Lombardi era in Paul Hornung and Jimmy Taylor; the Packers figured an injured Hornung didn't have much left and let him go in the expansion draft, while Taylor's constant squabbling with the team over money earned him a ticket out of town. "He didn't seem much interested in keeping me," Taylor said of Lombardi. "It didn't make much difference to me, because I knew how much I was worth and I figured I'd get it somewhere."[8] It was a homecoming for Taylor, who grew up in Baton Rouge and starred at nearby Louisiana State University.

Other veteran imports included the Bears' great defensive end Doug Atkins, and quarterback Gary Cuozzo, who had spent the previous four seasons backing up Johnny Unitas in Baltimore. "After last year, I decided I would have to do something if I didn't want to spend the rest of my pro life on the bench," said Cuozzo, who requested and received a trade.[9] Looking at the roster *Sports Illustrated* said the Saints "must be rated the best of all the expansion clubs."[10] Optimism rose to giddiness when on the very first play in franchise history, Saints' receiver John Gilliam returned the opening kick-off of the 1967 season 94 yards for a touchdown against the Rams.

But the Saints quickly returned to earth. Hornung's injuries forced him to retire before ever playing a game, and an aging Taylor was limited to 390 yards rushing and two touchdowns in his final year. Cuozzo split time at quarterback with another veteran import, Billy Kilmer, and lasted only one season with the Saints before heading off to Minnesota. The highlight of the 3-11 season may have come in New York, where during a Saints' brawl with the Giants, owner John Mecom leaped off the sidelines and decked an opposing player with one punch.

The Cowboys and Vikings had both risen from expansion to become competitive in six years, but they built through the draft. The Saints strategy of building with aging veterans and castoffs had backfired and set the franchise on a course of mediocrity that would last decades. Just a few years after its 1967 cover story, *Sports Illustrated* sang a different tune: "Throughout their history the Saints have been plagued by an unstable organization. Under impetuous John Mecom, there has been a constantly revolving—nay spinning—door for front-office executives and head coaches."[11]

The Saints had opened the 1970 season by winning only one of their first seven games. The team did play well at times, beating a good Giants team and tying the 49ers in San Francisco, but in other games it wasn't even competitive. New Orleans lost by twenty-six at Minnesota, eighteen in Atlanta, and thirteen at home to the Rams. In the game against Los Angeles, four people were injured when an antique cannon misfired prematurely during a halftime show recreation of the Battle of New Orleans. Then the Saints blew a fourteen-point lead and lost, 30–17. At another game, a "Kilmer for Mayor" sign appeared in the stands. The quarterback was flattered at first, but "then I realized the mayor is the only person in New Orleans who is booed more than me."[12]

THE ROAR RETURNS

If pedigree counted for anything, the Lions would have beaten the Saints in a walk. Detroit began playing in 1930, won its first NFL title in 1935, and became a dominant team in the 1950s, winning three more championships. The last came in 1957 when the Lions and 49ers tied for the Western Conference title and met in a special playoff game in San Francisco. Detroit trailed 27–7 in the second half before rallying for a dramatic 31–27 win. The following week, the Lions did even better, swamping Cleveland in the NFL championship game, 59–14. "The big thing about them was they never quit," said head coach George Wilson.[13] "I guess this is the fightingest team I ever saw."[14] The win gave the Lions their third NFL title in six years.

But since 1957 the well of Lions' success had pretty much dried up.[15] Wilson coached the team in 1957 only because Buddy Parker quit during the preseason. "I have a situation here I cannot handle," Parker told a Detroit booster club meeting. "This is the worst team in training camp I have ever seen. The material is all right, but the team is dead. I don't want to get involved in another losing season, so I'm leaving Detroit football. I'm leaving tonight."[16] Maybe Parker knew something because despite some close finishes, the Lions never seriously threatened for a championship throughout the 1960s, primarily because of Lombardi's Packers. Detroit went 11-3 in 1962, a record that would have won the Western Conference most seasons, but the Lions still finished two games behind Green Bay's 13-1 mark.

Joe Schmidt was a linebacker on the great Lions' teams of the 1950s, and he took over the coaching duties in 1967 hoping to revive the glory days. Schmidt knew defense, and he retooled the Lions around veterans Alex Karras and Dick LeBeau. At defensive tackle, Karras was a thirteen-year veteran who played his last season in 1970, but he still had plenty left. He was often a headache for Schmidt and other Lions' coaches, spouting off in the newspapers and threatening to hold out every season. Schmidt got so fed up that he removed Karras as captain before the season began. But Karras could still be dominating, as could safety LeBeau, who would intercept nine passes in 1970 and eventually make the Hall of Fame.

Another defender destined for the Hall of Fame was Lem Barney, who was a special talent right from the moment he first lined up at cornerback. The "Supernatural" as *The Sporting News* called him, Barney returned three interceptions for touchdowns his rookie year in 1967, including one against Bart Starr in his first NFL game.[17] Barney led the league that year in interceptions with ten and easily won Rookie of the Year. Primarily on the strength of its defense, Detroit went 9-4-1 in 1969 and seemed destined for even better things. "At the end of last year, we could have knocked with anybody," said Schmidt before the 1970 season. "I'm talking about the big boys, the Super Bowl teams and everybody. We've come so close now. We're in reach of a divisional championship."[18]

But to win, the Lions would have to improve on offense, and return of a healthy Mel Farr at running back was a big help. Farr would have one of his best seasons in 1970, making the Pro Bowl on the strength of 717 yards rushing and nine touchdowns, as Detroit finished second in the NFL in scoring, rushing, and total offense. Tight end Charlie Sanders also had a Pro Bowl season, catching forty passes good for six touchdowns, but the key to the Lions' offense was at quarterback, or more appropriately, quarterbacks. Veteran Bill Munson and third-year man Greg Landry split time evenly at the position, leading Schmidt to declare, "Our quarterback situation is the best since the Bobby Layne days."[19] A little dramatic, perhaps, given that Layne was a Detroit legend for leading the Lions to two NFL titles in the 1950s. But with the two-headed tandem of Munson and Landry, the Detroit offense was much improved, scoring twenty touchdowns in the first six games of 1970, compared to twenty-six touchdowns in all of 1969. "None of our plays is any different than in the past," said Munson. "We've been able to get the ball into the end zone, where we weren't able to before."[20]

The Lions came to New Orleans with a 5-2 record, their only blemishes being a loss at home to Minnesota and a puzzling, 31–10 blowout in Washington in which Sonny Jurgensen picked apart the Detroit defense. Otherwise, the Lions looked strong in almost every phase of the game, and they certainly had their best team since 1957. "I think we've got a great young team and the only way someone will beat us is if we beat ourselves," said Sanders.[21] In a *Sports Illustrated* interview, Karras said, "In the 12 years I've played for Detroit I've never felt this way before. We've always had an excuse. Now we don't have one. The gun is loaded. No more blanks."[22]

SAINT DEMPSEY

The Lions and Saints kicked off under overcast skies with temperatures near seventy and a ten mile an hour wind blowing from the north. That seemingly mild breeze would figure prominently in the outcome of the game.

Defensively, the Saints played one of their better games of the season, limiting the Lions in the first half to a 10-yard score by Mel Farr. Unfortunately for New Orleans, its offense fared no better and could manage only a pair of Tom Dempsey field goals before halftime. Dempsey was born with deformities to both his right foot and hand, and as a result he needed permission from the league to kick with a special squared-off shoe that many claimed gave him extra power. "That guy is going to hit one 90 yards one day," marveled Chargers coach Sid Gillman.[23] Dempsey admitted that his kicks "take off a lot faster and higher because of that," but also said it made accuracy more difficult.[24] Through the first seven weeks, Dempsey had hit only five of fifteen on field goal attempts, and would finish the year at eighteen of thirty-four, a 53 percent success rate that was not uncommon for straight-ahead kickers. "Your 'money' kicks are inside the 40 and it's been a disappointing year for me so far," he said.[25]

But Dempsey had also kicked with a leg injury all season, which had finally healed going into the Lions game. He felt so good, he was disappointed that Roberts did not let him try a 55-yarder, but chose instead to punt. "We didn't let him kick that shorter one," Roberts said. "He was upset and I said, 'Well, if you think you can get a high trajectory on it we'll kick a long one a little later.'"[26]

Dempsey kicked a much shorter field goal when the Saints got to the Lions' 1-yard line in the third quarter but could not get in. It came after a Munson touchdown pass to Charlie Sanders, and made the score 14–9 Detroit after three quarters. New Orleans finally made it into the end zone with about seven minutes to play, and a four-yard touchdown run by Tom Barrington put the Saints ahead, 16–14. The Lions had spent most of the day trying to give away the game, as they fumbled three times and suffered three Munson interceptions, but now they began to move down the field and run down the clock. They reached the New Orleans 11-yard line and Erroll Mann kicked an 18-yard field goal to give Detroit a 17–16 lead with just eleven seconds left. It appeared to be yet another loss for the Saints and their fans, who had seen this same script play out too many times before.

Al Dodd took the ensuing kickoff to the Saints' 27-yard line, and then made a spectacular catch of a Kilmer sideline pass, putting the ball on the 45-yard line with two seconds left. Remembering Dempsey's earlier frustration at not getting to try a long field goal, Roberts figured his odds were better with a kick rather than a desperation heave, especially since Dempsey had that wind at his back. Holder Joe Scarpati set up an extra yard back at his own 37-yard line, which would make Dempsey's attempt from the unheard of distance of 63 yards. The Lions, who were laughing as the Saints lined up, said it sounded like a rifle shot when Dempsey connected. Scarpati concurred, adding, "He really got into it. It was a cannon."[27] When the ball just limped over the crossbar the Saints had an incredible, 19–17 win and Dempsey had an NFL record.[28] "It's like winning the Masters with a 390-yard hole-in-one on the last hole," said Lions coach Joe Schmidt.[29] Detroit linebacker Wayne Walker said, "Tom Dempsey didn't kick that field goal; God kicked it."[30]

The crowd of 66,910 at Tulane Stadium went crazy, as did the Saints. "I jumped the fence behind our bench, ran into the stands and began shaking hands," said defensive back Doug Wyatt. "And someone stole my helmet."[31] Off the field on their shoulders the Saints carried their hero, who acknowledged that he had routinely made 65-yard kicks in practice. "I knew I could kick the ball that far," said Dempsey, "but whether I could kick it straight that far kept running through my mind." He paused and added, "It was the greatest thing I ever felt in my life."[32]

After his first NFL win as a coach, Roberts said, "I just hope everyone can get down off the clouds."[33] Unfortunately, there was nothing but storm clouds for the Saints the rest of the season. The win over Detroit marked their last of the year and they finished at 2-11-1. Roberts won just five more games in his two-plus seasons in New Orleans before giving way to yet another new coach in 1973. The Saints won only forty-two games during the '70s, and the '80s started no better. New Orleans went 1-15 in 1980, and their suffering fans began coming to games with paper bags on their heads inscribed with the words, "Aints."

The fans never gave up hope, even in the darkest of years, and that certainly applied to 2005 when Hurricane Katrina devastated the New Orleans area, dislocating thousands and causing an estimated $80 billion in damages right before the season began. It was a disaster of unparalleled proportions and even though the Saints had to play all their games on the road, they were the glue that held the city together. "The anchor of all this was the

Saints," said television reporter Chris Meyers. "They were a football team that in the past had been as unreliable as the weather, but this was not the same old city and these were not the same old Saints. You could count on them this time—you could believe."[34] The Saints returned to New Orleans in 2006 and turned a 3-13 record into 10-6 and an appearance in the NFC championship game. Three years later, they ended forty-two years of voodoo curses by winning Super Bowl XLIV.

The loss to New Orleans seemed to stun the Lions, and they suffered another last-minute defeat the following week in a 24–20 loss in Minnesota when the Vikings' Clint Jones scored the winning touchdown with only 1:23 to play. It was Detroit's second loss to the Vikings in three weeks and it all but ended the Lions' hopes of winning the NFL Central. Even more daunting was the schedule, as Detroit would have to play division-leading teams for the next four weeks. It seemed the team would now truly discover if the gun was loaded or if it was going to shoot blanks for one more season.

Bud Adams (*left*) and Lamar Hunt were two of the founding fathers of the AFL. Both were sons of Texas oil tycoons, and their big bankrolls helped the league stay afloat in its early years. *Courtesy of Murray Olderman*

After the merger, the NFL and AFL held a common draft and stopped bidding against each other for college talent. Tommy Nobis, a linebacker from the University of Texas, was one of the last of the big-money rookies who signed before the merger took place. *Photo by Mark Kauffman/Getty Images*

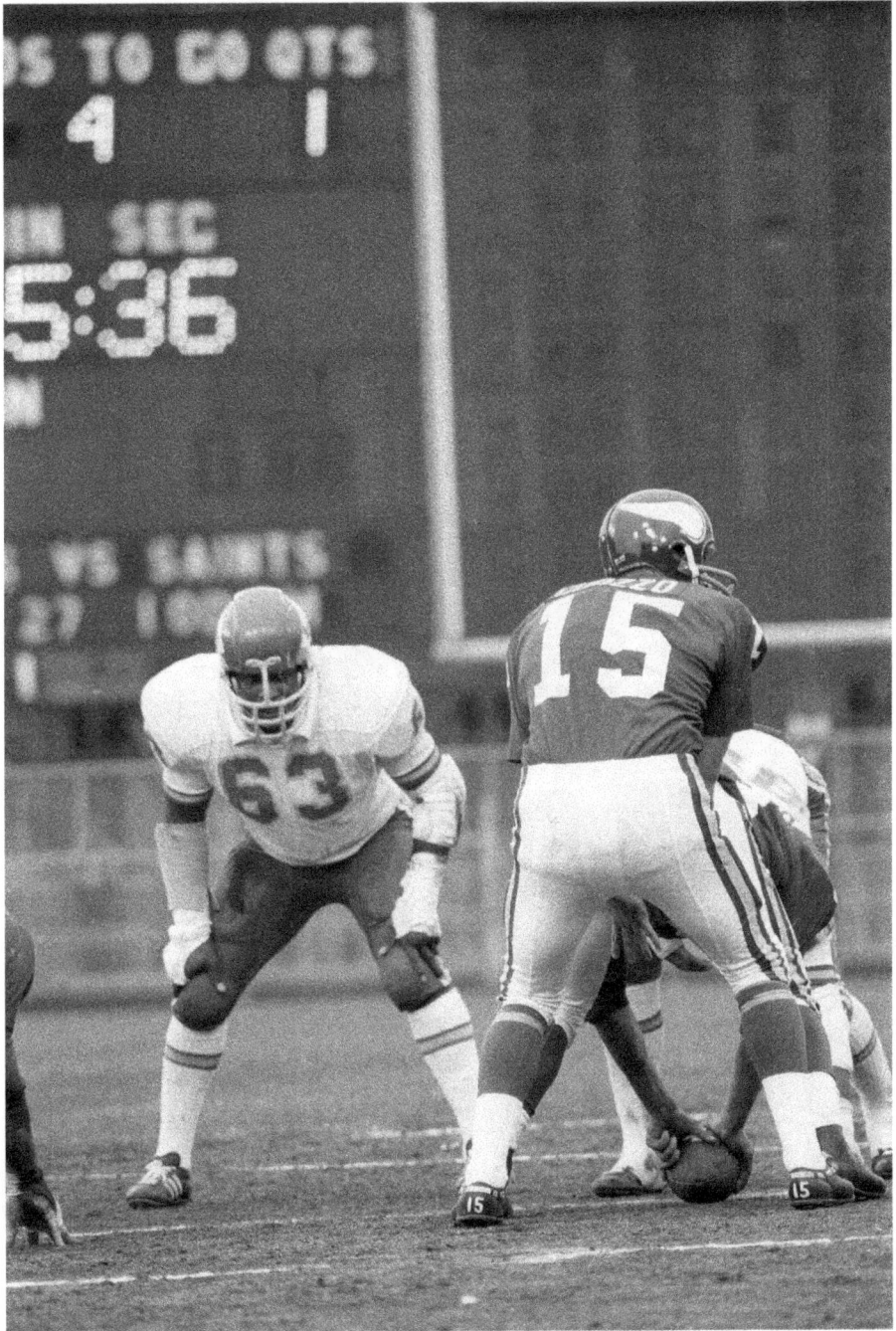

When Kansas City and Minnesota opened the 1970 season in a Super Bowl rematch, Willie Lanier (63) and the Chiefs faced Gary Cuozzo (15) under center, not Joe Kapp. *Photo by Heinz Kluetmeier/Getty Images*

Left to Right: Don Meredith, Roone Arledge, and Howard Cosell prepare to launch a cultural institution—the first *Monday Night Football* game on ABC.
Photo from ABC Photo Archives/Getty Images

This newspaper promo that ran the week of the first regular season matchup between Cleveland and Cincinnati made sure everyone knew it was "Paul Brown's" Bengals. *Courtesy of WCPO-TV, Cincinnati*

Legendary coach Paul Brown was the focal point of two NFL franchises and the Browns-Bengals feud. *Photo by Tony Tomsic/Getty Images*

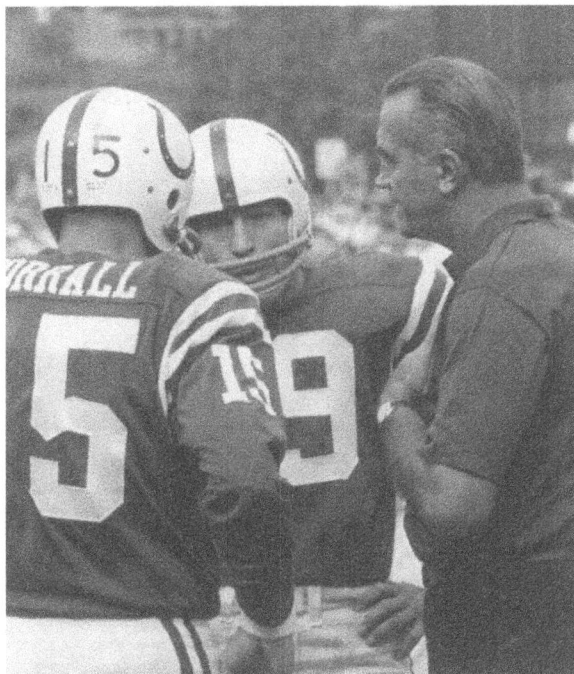

New coach Don McCafferty (*far right*) and the Colts would need both backup quarterback Earl Morrall (*left*) and starter Johnny Unitas during the 1970 season. *Courtesy of the Indianapolis Colts*

Joe Namath's 1970 season ended when he broke his wrist October 18 against the Colts. Even with his hand in a cast, Namath couldn't help but draw a crowd. *Photo from* New York Daily News *Archive/Getty Images*

The Cowboys-Chiefs game in week six matched Tom Landry against Hank Stram— two innovative coaches who pioneered the multiple offense. *Courtesy of Murray Olderman*

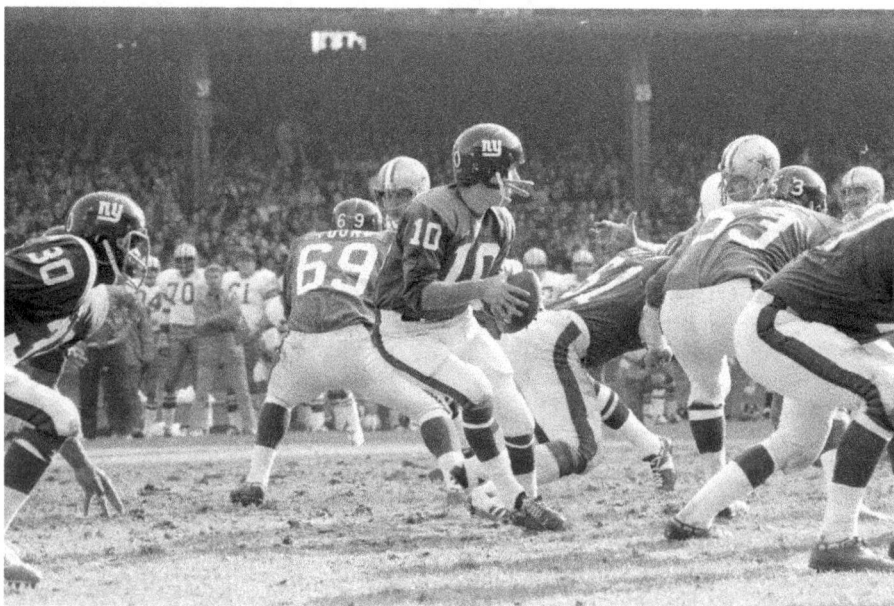

Quarterback Fran Tarkenton (10) and running back Ron Johnson (30) led a resurgent Giants team that was in the playoff chase until the final Sunday. Number 69 is tackle Willie Young and 53 is center Greg Larson. *Photo from* New York Daily News *Archive/Getty Images*

Despite deformities to his hand and kicking foot, the Saints' Tom Dempsey put his name in the NFL record book in week eight against Detroit. *Photo by Al Messerschmidt/Getty Images*

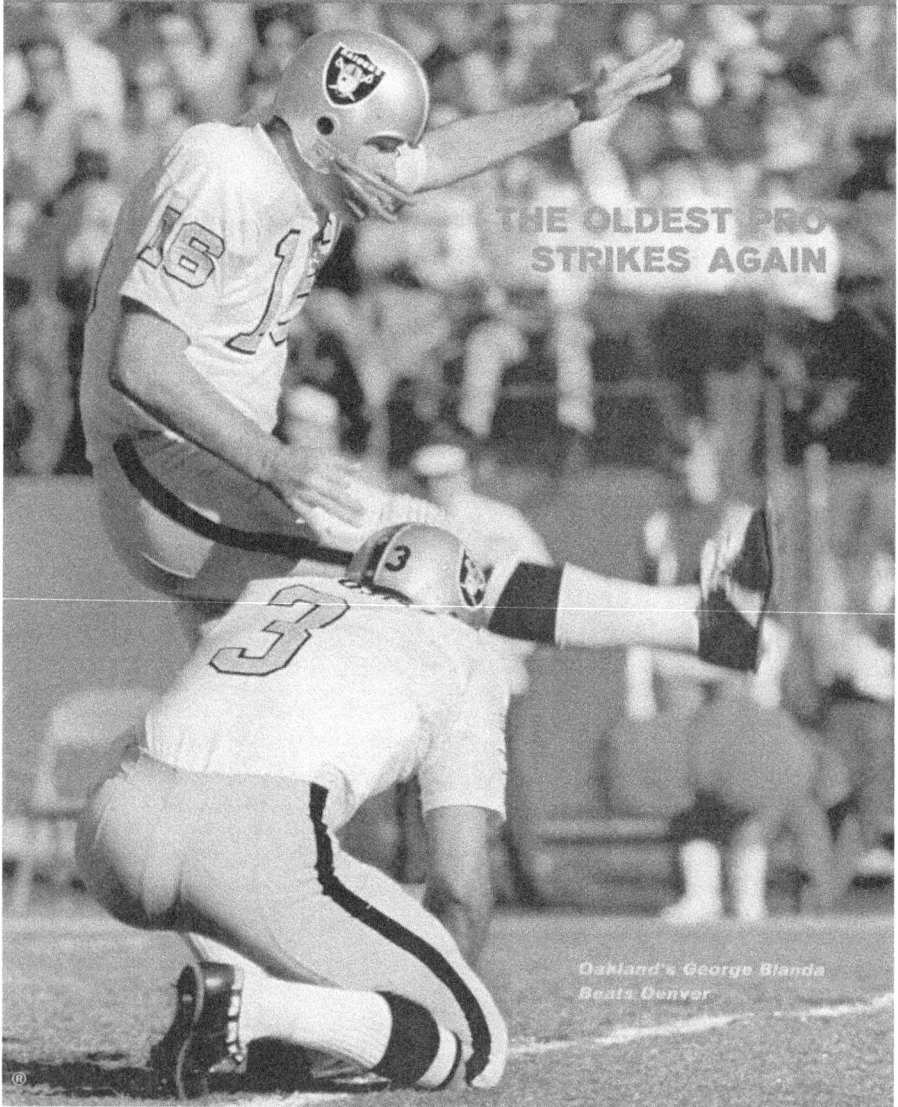

George Blanda's late-game heroics made him a folk hero and a *Sports Illustrated* cover boy. The Raiders' starting quarterback Daryle Lamonica (3) is the holder.
Photo by George Long/Getty Images

Vince Lombardi (*left*) and quarterback Sonny Jurgensen had revived the woeful Redskins, but Lombardi's death in September put a pall over Washington's 1970 season. *Photo by Paul Fine/Getty Images*

Baltimore had a relatively easy time with Cincinnati in the first round of the AFC playoffs, allowing Earl Morrall (15) to get some mop-up duty for Johnny Unitas. Number 45 for the Colts is running back Jerry Hill, and 50 is center Bill Curry. Bill Bergey (66) is the Bengals' linebacker. Baltimore won, 17–0. *Courtesy of the Indianapolis Colts*

San Francisco hoped quarterback John Brodie (12) would lead the 49ers to their first-ever championship in 1970. Brodie was having his best statistical season and would be named the NFL's Most Valuable Player. *Photo by George Long/Getty Images*

With the score tied, 13–13, and just nine seconds to play in Super Bowl V, Colts' kicker Jim O'Brien sends the winning field goal on its way. The Cowboys' Mark Washington (46), who had earlier blocked an O'Brien extra point, is too late this time. Earl Morrall (15) is the holder and Tom Nowatzke (34) scored the Colts' only touchdown of the day. Dallas coach Tom Landry is the man in the hat on the far sideline, just to the right of Washington.

Photo by Focus on Sports/Getty Images

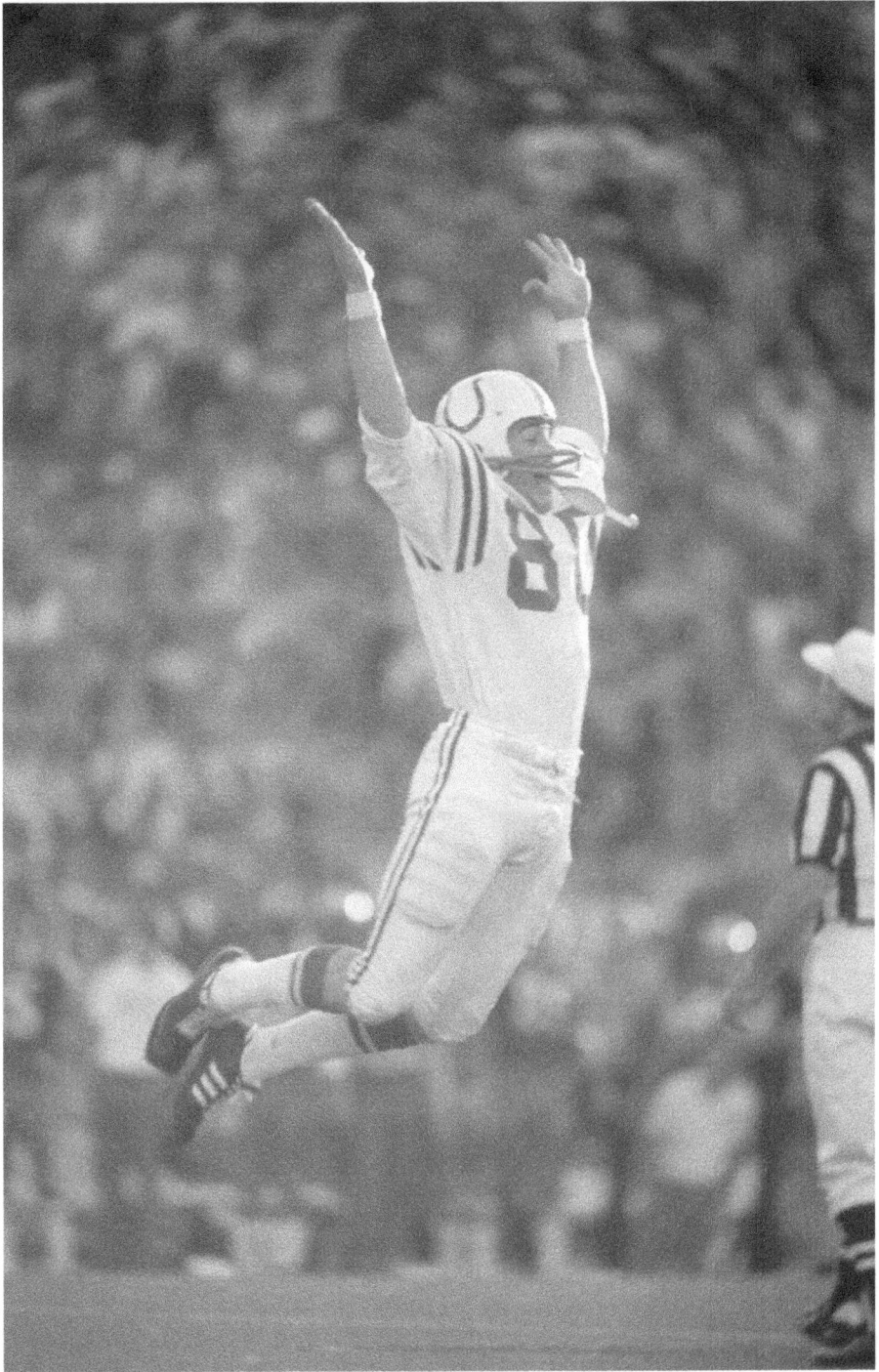

O'Brien celebrates the first game-winning kick in Super Bowl history. *Photo by Tony Tomsic/Getty Images*

To the victors go the spoils: each member of the Colts earned $15,000 and this ring for the Super Bowl victory. *Courtesy of Jostens*

There are actually two Super Bowl V trophies. The original was "hijacked" by former Colts' owner Carroll Rosenbloom, who kept the trophy when he took over ownership of the Los Angeles Rams. This replica was commissioned for the Colts, but when the team moved to Indianapolis in 1984 the trophy stayed behind. It is now on display at the Sports Legends Museum at Camden Yards in Baltimore. *Courtesy of the Sports Legends Museum*

★ 12 ★

WEEK EIGHT:
Cleveland Browns at Oakland Raiders

FATHER TIME

About the same time Dempsey was becoming a hero in New Orleans, the Raiders and Browns were set to kick off in Oakland, and the home team's season was still very much in doubt. Oakland came into 1970 as the three-time defending AFL West champions, and it had won at least twelve games in each of those years. But the Raiders stumbled out of the gate, losing two and tying one in their first three games, prompting one Oakland sports-writer to say that the season should be "swept under the rug immediately."[1] The problem was not so much with the offense and quarterback Daryle Lamonica but with the fact that the normally stout Raider defense suddenly started having trouble, giving up thirty-one points and 364 yards in a loss to Cincinnati, and then 344 yards and twenty-seven points in a tie with San Diego. Wins over Denver and Washington put the Raiders at 2-2-1, a game and a half behind the first-place Broncos.

The sluggish start was somewhat reminiscent of the team's bumpy begin-nings in the old AFL. Oakland was the last of the original eight teams to enter the league, and did so at the very last minute. Only when the Minneapolis expansion group switched from the AFL to the NFL, and Chargers owner Barron Hilton threatened to pull out of the league if another team wasn't added in California, did the Raiders come to Oakland. A group of local busi-nessmen hastily agreed to run the franchise, and there were several problems right from the start. The team had difficulty finding a place to play before settling on tiny Frank Youell Field, which could seat only around eighteen thousand. The Raiders lost around half a million dollars their first season of

125

play in 1960 and survived only when Bills owner Ralph Wilson floated them a $400,000 loan. The patchwork operation showed on the field, as well. After a decent 6-8 record in their first season, the Raiders went 2-12 and 1-13 in 1961 and 1962. Their coaches those first three seasons were Eddie Erdelatz, Red Conkright, and Marty Feldman—hardly a Hall of Fame list.

The turning point came on January 15, 1963, when the team hired Chargers' assistant coach Al Davis as its new head coach and general manager. At thirty-three, Davis began what became a lifelong obsession of making the Raiders into one of the dominant organizations not just in pro football but in all of sports. Almost instantly, the team's fortunes began to change through Davis's desire, innovations, and the sheer force of his personality.

"He has become not only the face of the Raiders, but also their heart and soul," wrote Patrick Patterson in the *San Francisco Examiner*. "He changed the color scheme from the black, white, and gold to the now ubiquitous silver and black because he wanted them to have a tougher image. It is his renegade spirit and desire for domination that became the essence of the Raider mystique. There is no other sporting franchise that is so intertwined with its owner."[2]

His football philosophy was simple—"Just Win, Baby"—and he looked for players who matched his combative, confrontational nature. With players like Ben Davidson, Ken Stabler, and Jack Tatum, the Raiders of the late 1960s and early 1970s developed a renegade reputation that perfectly matched the persona of their leader. "When I played for the Oakland Raiders they were the team people loved to hate," said Stabler. "I don't know if it was a reflection of the cast of characters we had there or if it all started with Al Davis."[3]

Perhaps no player more symbolized the Raiders than defensive end Ben Davidson. Called "Big Ben" for his 6-foot-8, 275-pound frame, Davidson developed a reputation as one of the nastiest—many would say dirtiest—players in the AFL. He regularly placed high in the league in roughing penalties, and in week seven had instigated a bench-clearing brawl in Kansas City. Davidson had been released by Lombardi and the Packers, but he seemed to fit in perfectly with the Raiders, right down to his handlebar moustache. "They say I'm a wild man, an animal, a bloodthirsty savage," said Davidson. "[But] there are times when I just won't put up with an offensive guy holding me. He's using an illegal tactic to put my job in jeopardy. Kick him. Next time he'll think twice."[4]

Davis had no second thoughts about bringing in players like Davidson, and the Raiders quickly became winners, intimidating opponents along the way. Oakland won ten games in 1963, and had seventeen winning seasons in eighteen years. When Davis became AFL commissioner in 1966, he turned over coaching duties to John Rauch, who took the team to Super Bowl II, but Davis was still the guiding force behind the franchise. He was the pugnacious genius who seemed to be one step ahead of everyone else. "Davis always acts like he's got some kind of secret information nobody else knows about," said an AFL coach in 1965, "and much of the time that's true. He's always ready to make a deal, although you'd better look out when you deal with him."[5]

Noting Davis's penchant for cutting corners and his desire to win at all costs, other coaches were less flattering. Former Chargers coach Harland Svare is said to have once approached a light fixture in the visitors' locker room at Oakland, yelling, "Damn you, Al Davis, I know you're up there."[6] Asked if he had indeed bugged the locker room, Davis would say only, "The thing wasn't in the light fixture, I'll tell you that." He went on to add, "I don't care what the other coaches think of me personally as long as they respect what we do on the field."[7]

It was Davis who in 1967 traded for an aging kicker and quarterback named George Blanda. The Houston Oilers had little use for a forty-year-old, sometimes-quarterback and sometimes-kicker, and they got rid of him for almost nothing. Blanda rewarded Davis and the Raiders by leading the AFL in scoring in 1967 with 116 points and helping the team to the Super Bowl. He scored more than one hundred points each of the next two seasons, and entering 1970 he was still a valuable performer at two positions. By mid-season, he became a legend and kept America on the edge of its seat for four consecutive weeks.

It started October 25 against the Steelers, while the Raiders were still struggling. After throwing an early touchdown pass against Pittsburgh, Lamonica went down with an injury. Into the game came Blanda, the soon-to-be hero to America's geriatric set. Blanda would throw three touchdown passes, including one to Raymond Chester on his first play of the game, and

kick a field goal in the Raiders' 31–14 win. "I guess the Steelers didn't realize we like people to blitz us," he said.[8] After the game, Blanda's younger
brother John told him, "George, we've always said you're the third-best quarterback in the family, but the way you're developing we may have to move
you up a notch."[9]

The next week in Kansas City, the Chiefs appeared to wrap up a 17–14
win by making a late first down to run out the clock. But a fight erupted at
the end of the play, which cost the Chiefs yardage and forced a punt. The
Raiders were then able to get in position for Blanda to kick a 48-yard field
goal into the wind, which, with time running out, helped the Raiders escape
with an improbable 17–17 tie. "They get a stupid penalty and all of a sudden
we get a tie, and we're in first place," said Blanda. "How does a tie feel? It
feels fantastic."[10]

That led to the November 8 game at the Oakland Coliseum against the
Browns—a 4-3 team that was every bit as desperate as the Raiders. Blanda
kicked two field goals to help Oakland build a 13–0 lead, but in the third
quarter, Bo Scott burned the Raider defense on a 63-yard scoring run. Early
in the fourth, the Browns added a field goal, and the Raiders were down 20–
13 with time running out.

By now, Blanda was in at quarterback for Lamonica, who left because of
a shoulder injury. It took awhile for him to get moving, but he packed a lot
into the last 1:32 of the game—hitting Warren Wells with a game-tying
touchdown and then kicking the game-winning field goal from 52 yards out
with just three seconds to play. "I put a little more rear end into the kick than
usual," Blanda admitted after the game.[11] "I knew it was good the moment I
kicked it."[12] Raiders' radio announcer Bill King wasn't so sure: "Snap, spot it,
it's kicked. That's got a chance! That is good! It's good! Holy Toledo! The
place has gone wild. Whee-e-e! I don't believe it! I don't believe it! There are
three seconds left in the game. Well, if you can hear me, this place has gone
wild. The Oakland Raiders 23, the Cleveland Browns 20. George Blanda has
just been elected king of the world!"[13]

His heroics made him the talk of the nation: late night comedians mentioned him in their jokes and *Time* magazine chronicled his exploits. It was
with the over-forty crowd that Blanda really struck a chord. A forty-three-
year-old football player, the oldest in the NFL and one who had entered the

league in 1949, was not only still out there playing, he was beating kids half his age. "George Blanda has restored dignity and virility to every man over 40 years of age," wrote Jim Scott in *The Sporting News*. "Those of us with graying hair now feel that if a 43-year old can win where the 20-year-olds can't, we can also give up our slippered ease by the fireside."[14] Humorist Erma Bombeck added that after the Browns game her husband "kicked his tonic bottle 32 feet into the air," and jogged, not walked, to take out the garbage.[15]

The attention was ironic, considering that a decade earlier Blanda had dropped out of professional football. Drafted by the Chicago Bears in 1949, Blanda played very little in his early NFL career. He threw just twenty-three passes his first three seasons, and by 1959 decided ten years of warming the bench were enough, especially when the Bears wanted him to quit quarter-backing and kick exclusively. So he retired, and not under happy circum-stances. "That's kind of water under the bridge, past history," he said in a 1970 interview. "I'd rather not go into it. At that time, we mutually decided I should retire and I remained out a year."[16]

He probably would have stayed retired if not for the new American Football League. The Houston Oilers would let him play quarterback and kick, so he came back to professional football in 1960. "When the AFL was formed, there was a great need for veteran quarterbacks who were fairly good football players," noted Blanda. "I really started to blossom as a quar-terback in my first year of the AFL."[17] Perhaps because Houston let him launch more rockets than NASA, Blanda threw twenty-four touchdown passes his first season, then thirty-six the next, leading the Oilers to the first two AFL championships and just barely missing a third.[18] When the AFL finished its last season of play in 1969, Blanda was the league's second all-time leading scorer (behind Gino Cappelletti of Boston) and its sixth lead-ing passer. All told, Blanda established more than twenty AFL offensive records.

THE LEGEND GROWS

Blanda built not one, but three, reputations in the AFL. Primarily, he was known for his longevity. The 1970 season was his twenty-first in profes-sional football—he played until the age of forty-eight, setting records for oldest player and most years played (twenty-six), and he became the only player in league history to play in parts of four decades.[19] "Really, this has been my life," he said during the 1970 season. "I hope I never have to give it up. I'd like to play until I'm 65. I know that's impossible. Maybe I'm an oddball, but I really enjoy the game and I enjoy the practicing."[20] Blanda added that being able to play both quarterback and kicker probably added years to his career.

Blanda's second reputation was his ability to come off the bench and play exceptionally well in any circumstance, especially after he joined the Raiders and backed up Lamonica. He threw only fifty-five passes in 1970 but actually had a higher completion percentage and quarterback rating than the starter. If one projects Blanda's statistics over the course of the full season, he would have thrown for forty-two touchdowns and more than 3,000 yards. "George is actually playing the game in his head on the sidelines," said Raiders' guard Gene Upshaw. "He knows what will work and what won't. When he comes in he has in his mind exactly what plays he will call. He knows damned well they will work and we do too—because he's George Blanda."[21]

Now, in what appeared to be the twilight of his career, George Blanda had added a third reputation—miracle worker. His effort against Cleveland was the third game in a row he had saved the Raiders in the final seconds, and he wasn't done yet. The following week, November 15 against Denver, Lamonica left the field (either he got hurt again or coach John Madden realized the hot hand he had with Blanda). With four minutes left and the Raiders trailing 19–17, Blanda took over with Oakland on its own 20-yard line. When he hit Rod Sherman for 27 yards, then Warren Wells for 35 more to get deep inside Denver territory, the stage seemed set for another game-winning kick, but this time Blanda outdid even himself. He threw a 20-yard touchdown pass to Fred Biletnikoff and kicked the point after to win it for the Raiders, 24–19. The following week did not go down to the wire, but the difference was still a Blanda field goal, as Oakland beat San Diego, 20–17. "The guy almost embarrasses you," said Raider center Jim Otto. "He's out there, 43 years old, running the wind sprints, yelling all the time, coming in to pull it out for us."[22] By now, Blanda was having to screen his calls and was unable to keep up with the sacks of mail pouring in. "After five successive lightning bolts I began to think I was living in a goldfish bowl," he said.[23]

Playing less than a quarter against the Browns, Blanda completed seven of twelve passes for 102 yards and the game-tying touchdown; he had also kicked three field goals, including the game-winner, and accounted for seventeen of the twenty-three Raider points. In three quarters, Lamonica had completed only seven of twenty passes for 68 yards and a score. At this point, the Raiders must have been breathing a sigh of relief that a procedural move before the season worked out in their favor. During the preseason, the Raiders had released Blanda, meaning any other team in the league could have claimed him on waivers. Oakland had wanted to clear up roster space to look at some younger players, but figured nobody would have an interest in a forty-three-year-old kicker and backup quarterback. The Raiders were right and they quickly returned Blanda to the team, except he was mad enough at the time to consider retiring. "You've made it very clear that you see me as an ancient quarterback on his last legs," Blanda told Davis at the time, "and I'm not!"[24]

Had the Raiders figured wrong their season might have completely gone down the drain. As it was, Blanda had played a major role for five straight weeks, leading the Raiders to four wins and a tie, with three of the victories coming in the final seconds. The win over Denver on November 15 firmly established Oakland as the front-runner in the AFC West, ahead of the Chiefs and fading Broncos. Even though the Raiders split their last four games and finished with an 8-4-2 record, it was enough to give Oakland its fourth straight division championship by a game over Kansas City. Just for good measure, Blanda also kicked a game-winning extra point in the Raiders' week twelve win over the Jets, 14–13. And while he threw only twenty-five passes in the Raiders' last five games, the old man would get one more chance to shine in the AFC playoffs. By that time, *The Sporting News* had named him the AFC Player of the Year.

For the Browns, the last-second loss to Oakland was the second of three straight devastating defeats. The third came the following week when Cleveland lost its rematch in Cincinnati, 14–10, and the Bengals carried Paul Brown off the field. Brown passed directly under a banner in the stands that read, "Thank you, Art Modell," referring to the Cleveland owner who had fired Brown in 1963. A loss in Pittsburgh, then a brutal 6–2 defeat to Dallas in a quagmire in Cleveland Stadium, did in the Browns, who finished their first season in the AFC at 7-7 and a game behind the Bengals in the Central Division. It was just the second time since 1963 the Browns had failed to make the playoffs, and before the season even ended Blanton Collier announced his retirement. "I wanted to go out under my own power," he told reporters. "I didn't want them [the players] to feel they had to win games to me to save my job."[25]

It would be the Browns' first coaching change since Art Modell fired Paul Brown eight years earlier. "In my judgment," said Modell, "what happened to the Browns this season is in no way [Collier's] fault."[26] Nick Skorich guided the team to playoff appearances the next two seasons, but the Browns lost first-round games both times and the franchise would not win another playoff game until 1986. With the days of dominance under Paul Brown long gone, and the memories of 1964 growing dimmer, the Browns have yet to play in a Super Bowl.

WEEK THIRTEEN:
Green Bay Packers at Chicago Bears

The 1970 NFL season was nearing its end by the week of December 13, and by that point many teams were simply playing out the string. Not surprisingly, that included the Chicago Bears, a team that had finished 1-13 the previous season. The Bears played better in 1970, but the team went winless in October, and not even a victory over Green Bay would allow it to finish with a break-even record. The Packers could still end the year at .500, but for a franchise that had won five NFL championships in the 1960s, it was a tremendous comedown. Green Bay had started the season well, going 4-2, but a loss in San Francisco the first week of November led to four losses in five games and eliminated the Packers from playoff contention for the third straight year.

WHISTLING IN THE DARK

Vince Lombardi's departure from Green Bay in 1968—first to become the team's general manager, then to take over as coach in Washington the following season—seemed to take the life out of the franchise. In that 1968 season, even as Lombardi's shadow hovered over the team and his successor Phil Bengston, Packer players were determined to prove that their success was due to more than just coaching. "Yeah, we want to win for Phil," said defensive lineman Jim Weatherwax. "And we also want to win to show everybody that it wasn't just Lombardi these past few years, that it wasn't all him, that we can have a good season without him."[1]

Instead, the Packers fell to 6-7-1 and third place in the NFL Central, their first losing season since before Lombardi's arrival in 1959. Bengston had served nine years as a defensive assistant under Lombardi and knew both the players and the system well, but like many of those who follow coaching legends, he found the challenge almost impossible. "Phil is a softer man than I am," Lombardi had once said. "I don't say that critically. He is a fine coach, but it is not in him to be harsh and demanding and make the players hate him. You have to have someone on the staff who is a driver. If it isn't the head coach, then it has to be someone else."[2]

The veterans tried to provide that leadership by taking a more active and vocal role on the team. The core group consisted of Jerry Kramer, Ray Nitschke, and Willie Davis, men who went back to Lombardi's first championship team in 1961. "But we were all just whistling in the dark," Kramer said. "We meant well, but we'd forgotten how to motivate ourselves. We'd gotten lazy under Lombardi; he'd pushed us so hard we never had to push ourselves."[3] The harder the players tried, the more things seemed to go wrong, and by 1969 the Packers had to win their last two games just to finish with an 8-6 record.

As Lombardi made his exit from Green Bay, many of his great players seemed to be leaving right behind him. Davis, Kramer, Max McGee, Bob Skoronski, and Henry Jordan all soon retired, while Herb Adderley, Lee Roy Caffey, and running back Elijah Pitts were traded. In all, the team lost seven starters before the 1970 season—six of them former All-Pros. Those who did remain—such as future Hall of Famers Bart Starr and Ray Nitschke—were on the downside of their careers and not as productive. The thirty-seven-year-old Starr suffered with arm trouble all season in 1970 and would finish with only eight touchdowns compared to thirteen interceptions.

Turnover is nothing new in the NFL, but the Packers were not doing a good job of replacing their aging veterans. Donny Anderson and Jim Grabowski had never lived up to their promise as top draft picks in 1966. Anderson had his statistically best year in 1970, but he never rushed for more than 1,000 yards in a season and Green Bay traded him to the Cardinals in 1972. Grabowski scored only one touchdown all year before he too was traded, to the Bears, where he lasted only one more year. Green Bay drafted defensive lineman Rich Moore of Villanova University and Mike McCoy of University of Notre Dame with its number-one picks in 1969 and 1970. Moore would play only two years in the NFL, and while McCoy had a decent eleven-year career, it was certainly not what the Packers expected when they selected him right behind Terry Bradshaw as the number-two pick in the entire draft. It seemed the Packers might have missed Lombardi the general manager almost as much as Lombardi the coach.

Green Bay entered 1970 as something of a mystery team. Coming off a Super Bowl appearance, the Vikings were strong favorites to win the NFC Central, but it was generally believed that if the Packers could stay healthy and get strong performances from younger players they could contend for a wildcard playoff spot. Such assumptions were almost thrown out the window when the Packers opened the season with an embarrassing loss at home to the Lions, 40–0, the worst opening day defeat in team history. Detroit gouged the once-proud Packer defense for 266 yards rushing, including a 76-yard quarterback sneak by Greg Landry, while Starr threw an interception that was returned for a touchdown by Lem Barney, and was booed by the home crowd. If the Packers seemed confused during the game, Bengston was equally so afterward. "I just don't know," he kept saying to questions about what had happened. "This is the worst I ever experienced. I just don't know."[4] It marked the second home shutout for the Packers in as many years. In nine years under Lombardi, no Green Bay team had ever been shutout.

The Packers rebounded to win three in a row but lost to the Rams on "Bart Starr Day," when the quarterback was honored in a weekend celebration that included a visit from President Nixon. On November 15, Starr moved the Packers 80 yards in two minutes and scored the winning touchdown in a 20–19 thriller over the Bears in Green Bay. It was a victory that moved the Packers to 5-4 on the season and kept their slim playoff hopes alive, until losses to the Vikings and Cowboys ended the playoff talk.[5] The team came into the Chicago rematch with a 6-6 record. Even though the Packers had nothing to play for against the Bears, the week of the game Bengston moved workouts from the practice field to Lambeau Field and closed the stadium gates. "It wasn't secret," he insisted, but not very convincingly. "The turf is a lot better there." Were fans welcome to watch practice? "Well," he said coyly, "we didn't encourage them to come in."[6]

BEAR DOWN

Starting the 1970 season, George Halas had not coached the Chicago Bears for three years, but in every other respect it was very much *his* team. Halas had owned the Bears since the NFL began in 1920, and for fifty seasons as owner and forty-one as head coach he had shaped not only the team but the entire league. He had created an outfit in his own image—a tough, brawling, take-no-prisoners group that had justifiably earned the nickname, "The Monsters of the Midway." Halas had won six NFL titles in Chicago, the most recent in 1963 when the Bears beat the Giants, 14–10. "No game has meant as much to me as this one since we beat Washington, 73–0," said Halas, who was close to tears after beating New York. "I've waited a long time. I don't know what to say about it. It's too much."[7]

The Bears' 1963 championship win interrupted two straight Lombardi title teams in Green Bay and pushed the Bears-Packers rivalry to even greater heights. Not that the matchup needed any fuel with the cities separated by only 186 miles. The NFL's oldest rivalry started in 1921 and the teams had played at least twice a year since 1928. Even in the prehistoric era of NFL football, a Green Bay-Chicago game was not to be missed. "The Packers and Bears is the older definition of pro football," said author David Halberstam. "It dates to a time when the NFL wasn't slick or fancy, before the big salaries and the television cameras arrived."[8]

The arrival of Lombardi in 1959 to challenge Halas and the Bears turned an intense rivalry white hot. "Coach Halas, he'd burn your ears with language the week of the Green Bay game," said Rick Casares, a fullback who helped the Bears win the 1963 NFL title. "He'd say, 'We're gonna wipe that so-and-so smile off his face.'"[9] Like Casares, Johnny Morris played an important part in the '63 championship and understood the nature of the rivalry. "Halas pretty much made it clear that you beat Green Bay or else," he said. When the team stayed in Green Bay, "We'd be sleeping at two o'clock in the morning and here would come the Packer fans driving around and honking their horns."[10]

Lombardi beat Halas in thirteen of eighteen meetings before both men stepped aside after the 1967 season. Halas turned over the team to Jim Dooley, who in his first two years went 7-7 and then 1-13. His record against the Packers stood at only 1-4 after Green Bay's victory in week nine of the 1970 season. In that 20–19 come-from-behind win for Green Bay, several Packers suggested that Bears' star linebacker Dick Butkus had gotten a little too rough. Nothing illegal, the Packers said, but maybe some aggressive extracurriculars that Butkus could have avoided. Green Bay expected more of the same in the rematch. "I really don't think Dick is going to lay down and die, no matter what the record," said Green Bay center Ken Bowman. "So I figure I'd better go after him as aggressively as he comes after me."[11]

Butkus was one of the few star players on the Chicago roster, and in just five short years had become feared throughout the NFL for his ability and aggression. Butkus had made All-Pro or the Pro Bowl every season since his rookie year, and it was not just what he did, but how he did it. He raged, threatened, and intimidated opponents, not so much trying to beat them as destroy them. All the while, he kept hitting—sometimes legal and sometimes not.

"One time he bit me," said running back MacArthur Lane. "Another time he tried to break my ankle. Another time he tried to crack my leg. Nothing happened. Maybe my leg was too green."[12] Some coaches, like Lane's own coach Charley Winner, complained of Butkus' rough play, but no one could doubt his ability. When NFL coaches were asked before the season what player they would most want to have on their team, Butkus got more votes than anyone else.

The Bears' other bona-fide star was running back Gale Sayers, who like Butkus debuted in 1965 and immediately lit up the NFL. The highlight of his sensational rookie season came on December 12 in the mud of Wrigley Field. Sayers seemed to be the only one on either team not bothered by the playing conditions, as he tied an NFL record with six touchdowns—four rushing, one on an 80-yard pass reception, and yet another on an 85-yard punt return. Halas called it the single greatest performance he had ever seen in the NFL, and Sayers could have had a seventh score had he not slipped after losing defenders on another punt return. "You knock people down and they'll make five or six yards," said Sayers' teammate and running back Jon Arnett, "but very few have the instinct to cut across the grain, make things happen like Gale."[13]

Sayers led the NFL in rushing in 1966 and 1969, and seemed destined for a long career, but like Butkus he suffered from knee problems. Butkus could play through the pain, but Sayers's running style depended on his ability to run and cut through defenders at top speed, an ability he largely lost after a right knee injury ended his 1968 season. Sayers came back strong to lead the league in rushing in 1969, but in the 1970 preseason he got hurt again, this time tearing ligaments in his left knee. He tried to play once the regular season started, but could only manage 52 yards on twenty-three carries in two games. Once again, Sayers had to go under the knife, and although he tried to return in 1971 he would never be the same. As the *Chicago Daily News* aptly observed, "Gone are that instant acceleration from medium to top speed and the incomparable ability to change directions on a dime without hesitation or loss of speed."[14] The magic in the Bears' backfield was gone for good.

Sayers's season-ending injury climaxed a year of tragedy and turmoil in Chicago and the 1969 season ended with what some sportswriters described as "intrasquad rancor."[15] Bears' center Mike Pyle even admitted, "We're losers right now," midway through the season.[16] Quarterback Virgil Carter complained loud and long enough that Halas sent him packing to Buffalo for $100; others were similarly sold or traded away in a general housecleaning.[17] Then, as the Bears prepared for the 1970 training camp, popular running back Brian Piccolo passed away from cancer. Piccolo and Sayers had roomed together and formed an especially deep friendship, despite their racial differences. When Sayers received the George S. Halas award as the NFL's Most Courageous Player for returning from knee surgery, he told the audience, "You flatter me by giving me this award. But I accept it for Brian Piccolo. Brian is the man who should receive the award. I love Brian, and I'd like you to love him, too."[18]

Despite the loss of Piccolo, and the wreckage of the previous year, the Bears seemed a much better team in 1970. They opened the season with wins over the Giants and Eagles and had a respectable 3-4 record at the halfway point of the season. Much of the difference was due to the improved play at quarterback, especially Jack Concannon who had become the full-time starter. Before the season began, *Sports Illustrated* called the team's quarterbacking situation "sorry," but Concannon would go on to have a career year, throwing for sixteen touchdowns and more than 2,000 yards.[19] Backup Bobby Douglass was known more as a runner than a passer, but the second-year pro would throw four touchdowns in a win over Buffalo in November. Unfortunately, Douglass's season ended that same Sunday when he fractured his wrist. Dick Gordon was having a breakout year at wide receiver, and would eventually lead the NFL in catches (seventy-one) and touchdown receptions (thirteen) on his way to the Pro Bowl.

The Bears returned to earth with four straight losses in October, and as the season progressed it became apparent that without Sayers they had no ground game to speak of. By season's end, Ross Montgomery would lead the team with just 229 yards, as the Bears finished next-to-last in the NFL in rushing and scored just three touchdowns on the ground all year. Heading into the Green Bay game, Chicago had only four victories, and other than the win over the Giants it had beaten only the NFL's bottom feeders—Philadelphia, Buffalo, and Atlanta.

THE END OF TWO ERAS

The 104th meeting between the Bears and the Packers kicked off at Wrigley Field under relatively balmy conditions for mid-December in Chicago—thirty-two degrees and a brisk wind. Still unable to run, the Bears continued their season-long commitment to passing, and Concannon was off to his best game of the season. He started with a 15-yard scoring strike to Gordon, then followed up with a 42-yarder to rookie George Farmer. The two scores came in the first eight minutes of the game and gave Chicago a quick, 14–0 lead. Any chance of a Green Bay comeback ended when Bart Starr limped off the field after a first-quarter collision that left him groggy. "He was dizzy out there," Bengston said. "He tried to continue the game but couldn't."[20] Starr left after completing only two of five passes for 38 yards. After a Packer field goal, Concannon struck again, scrambling 15 yards for a second-quarter score that made it 21–3 Chicago at the half.

Concannon and Gordon essentially put the game away with a 25-yard scoring connection in the third quarter, and Concannon later threw a 6-yard pass to Ray Ogden for another score, giving him four touchdown passes on the day. With Starr sidelined, and backup Don Horn already out with a knee injury, Rick Norton and rookie Frank Patrick finished out the game for the Packers. "They had a rookie quarterback in there," Butkus said. "It was our job to keep him confused."[21]

Norton did manage a 29-yard fourth-quarter touchdown pass to John Hilton, but Green Bay could total only 82 yards passing as the Bears won, 35–17. For Chicago, it was the highest scoring output of the season, and it was done almost exclusively in the air. Concannon was the team's leading rusher with 31 yards, but he also finished twenty-one of thirty-four for 338 yards and four touchdowns. Gordon had seven catches, while Farmer caught nine for 142 yards. "I think the Packers were concerned about stopping Gordon," said Concannon. "Farmer had a real good day. That will give the other teams something to think about in the future."[22]

As the Bears walked off the field, they were saying goodbye to Wrigley Field, a stadium where they had won 221 of 332 games since 1921. Scheduling conflicts with the Cubs had caused constant headaches for Halas, one reason he had moved the September 27 game against the Eagles to Northwestern University's Dyche Stadium in suburban Evanston. Wrigley was also now officially too small since the NFL had passed a rule requiring all stadiums to have capacity for fifty thousand fans, so the Bears would move into new Solider Field in 1971. "I felt bad about moving," said linebacker Doug Buffone. "I never liked Soldier Field. It was too big. At Wrigley Field, there was only one thing to do—play football."[23]

The Bears finished the year with a 24–3 win in New Orleans, and their 6-8 record was a five-game improvement from the disaster of the season before. Coupled with the excitement of a new stadium, optimism ran high in 1971, but the team could not fulfill the promise. Sayers played only two games before retiring for good, while Concannon and Gordon both regressed from their outstanding 1970 seasons and were traded. After another 6-8 campaign in 1971, Dooley was fired and replaced by Abe Gibron, but the team would not return to the playoffs until 1977. Former tight end Mike Ditka took over in 1982 and led Chicago to its only Super Bowl title in 1985.

Change was also in the wind in Green Bay, especially after the Packers suffered another humiliating shutout loss to the Lions. "Let's go home," said a disgusted Donny Anderson after the Packers ended their season with a 20–0 defeat in Detroit.[24] Two days later, Bengston announced his retirement. The season record stood at 6-8, and his three years in Green Bay produced a record of 20-21-1. While some players complained of Bengston's coaching style, others realized the difficulty he faced in following Lombardi. "Phil did an excellent job," said safety Doug Hart. "The circumstances were just overwhelming. I don't think anyone else could have done a better job, either."[25]

Several men were discussed as possible replacements, including Joe Paterno of Penn State. The Packers did hire a college coach, naming Dan Devine from the University of Missouri as coach and general manager in January 1971. Devine lasted four seasons and got Green Bay back in the playoffs in 1972, but eventually he returned to college to coach at the University of Notre Dame. The Packers unsuccessfully tried to recapture the Lombardi magic by hiring Bart Starr and then Forrest Gregg as coaches, but their thirteen combined years brought only one playoff appearance. Not until the Mike Holmgren era in the 1990s did Green Bay win another Super Bowl, thirty years after Lombardi won the first one.

The Bears-Packers rivalry came into even sharper focus when the teams played for the 2010 NFC Championship, the first time they had met in the playoffs since 1941. Green Bay's 21–14 victory propelled them into the Super Bowl, where they beat the Steelers for their fourth Super Bowl championship. "We're proud to bring the Lombardi Trophy where it belongs: back in Green Bay," team president Mark Murphy told fans during a post–Super Bowl celebration at Lambeau Field. "There's a lot of history and tradition here. We gotta start winning some more to catch up with Lombardi!"[26]

The ghost of Vince Lombardi remains a powerful presence in Green Bay, something Phil Bengston and the 1970 Packers knew all too well.

★ 14 ★

WEEK FOURTEEN:
St. Louis Cardinals at Washington Redskins

A HISTORY OF FAILURE

When the St. Louis Cardinals dropped their opening game of the 1970 season to the Rams, 34–13 in Los Angeles, it certainly did not shock or surprise anyone in the NFL, least of all Cardinals' fans who had become accustomed to defeat. An original member of the NFL with roots going back to the first organizational meeting in 1920, the Cardinals were one of the oldest, but also one of the worst, teams in the history of the league. Even their brief flirtations with success were often clouded in controversy or tragedy.

The Cardinals began in Chicago and claimed an NFL championship in 1925 when they finished first in the league with an 11-2-1 record. But in those days, there were no championship games and teams were allowed to arrange their own schedules. As the season began to run out, teams began hastily scheduling games that would help them improve their record. This included both the Cardinals and the Pottsville Maroons of Pennsylvania, who played and beat a team of Notre Dame All-Stars to finish their season at 10-2. Even though the Maroons seemingly finished the season a half-game behind Chicago, Pottsville decisively beat the Cardinals on December 6. "As far as the Chicago Cardinals are concerned, Pottsville is the champion of the league," wrote the *Chicago Tribune*. "In the face of a driving attack by the Eastern eleven, the Cardinals curled up and were smeared in the snow on the gridiron at Comiskey Park yesterday, 21 to 7."[1] NFL Commissioner Joe Carr didn't see it that way, however, and awarded the NFL title to Chicago.[2]

Two decades of mediocrity followed until Chicago had its last shining moment in the NFL sun. The 1947 Cardinals, led by their "Dream Backfield" of Elmer Angsman, Charlie Trippi, and Marshall Goldberg, won the NFL Western Conference title, and then beat Philadelphia for the NFL Championship, 28–21. Against the Eagles, Angsman rushed ten times for 159 yards, including a 70-yard touchdown, and Trippi returned a punt 75 yards for another score. Even in victory, however, a pall hung over the Cardinals' celebration as owner Charles Bidwell had died earlier in the year. The Cardinals and Eagles met again in the championship game the following season, but playing in a blizzard in Philadelphia the Cardinals were shut out, 7–0. In terms of glory, that was about it for the Cardinals franchise, which sank to fifth place in 1950 and never finished higher than second for the next twenty years.

Bidwell's widow Violet took over the team, but control then passed to her new husband, millionaire Warner Wolfner. Wolfner spent the 1950s in a blood feud with George Halas and his cross-town Bears, often commenting about his rival, "I refuse to mention that man's name ever again!" Halas answered, "Wolfner? He's a real lovable specimen, isn't he?"[3] Halas could afford to be kind, seeing as how his Bears dominated the Cardinals in the standings and at the gate. On at least two occasions, Wolfner offered Halas a substantial amount of money to leave town and let the Cardinals have the city, but Halas turned him down every time.[4] Unable to pry Halas out of Chicago, and having lost around a million dollars since he took control of the team, Wolfner began looking for somewhere else to play. "It just got so that we weren't having any fun here anymore," he noted.[5]

In 1960 Wolfner moved the Cardinals to St. Louis, where they had the city to themselves, but their fortunes did not change for the better. Aside from a couple of nine-win seasons under Wally Lemm, the losing continued, and so did the bad luck. The Cardinals selected quarterback Joe Namath in the first-round of the 1965 draft, but he turned them down to play for the New York Jets of the AFL. Namath felt the Cardinals had "small-timed" him by rejecting his demand for a $200,000 contract at a time when the AFL-NFL bidding war was at its hottest. "When I met [Jets owner] Sonny Werblin," said Namath, "he said, 'I don't want to quibble over money. We want you. New York wants you. This is what I'm going to offer you and I want you to take it—$300,000 to play for the Jets.' This 300 went up a bit after we negotiated things."[6] The same year that Namath spurned them, the

Cardinals were featured on the cover of the November 1 issue of *Sports Illustrated* with the caption, "The Cardinals Take Wing." After the magazine appeared, the team lost six straight games and finished fifth in the NFL East with a record of 5-9.

A 'WINNER' IN ST. LOUIS

Coming off a 4-9-1 record in 1969, expectations were not high as the Cardinals entered the 1970 season. In its NFL preview issue, *Sports Illustrated* cuttingly observed, "[Philadelphia and] St. Louis will be a threat only to their coaches. Once again, the Cardinals are riven by cliques, dissension and unrest—or worse. With only a one-year contract, [head coach Charley] Winner cleaned house. Ten Cards left. Some were cut, others were traded."[7] One of Winner's main problems was trying to fill the quarterback position that Namath should have held. Charley Johnson and Jim Hart split time in 1969, but with Johnson's departure to the Oilers in the off-season, Hart would become the starter in 1970. "We all liked him," said Winner. "He had confidence in himself, and he could charge the other guys. There was no question he had the ability."[8] In the opening game loss to the Rams, Hart looked terrible, completing only twelve of forty-one passes. With the defense torched for three touchdown passes by Roman Gabriel, it seemed like another long season in St. Louis.

But suddenly, the team seemed to find itself and won four straight. In week two against Washington, MacArthur Lane bulled for 146 yards and two touchdowns on twenty-eight carries, as the Cardinals won, 27–17. Then Lane and Cid Edwards combined for 125 yards in a 20–7 win over Dallas. In an era that featured smallish running backs such as Kansas City's Mike Garrett and the Redskins' Larry Brown, Edwards was a 6-foot-3, 230-pound fullback who struck fear into defenders when he rumbled into the hole to block for the 6-foot-1, 225-pound Lane. "I played [that] whole damn game," said Cowboys linebacker Steve Kiner, "and they ran all over me. They would block down and here came [Cid] and it looked like a runaway train. [They] ran up and down the field."[9]

With Edwards clearing the way, Lane was on his way to a career season. Hurt and ineffective his first two years with the Cardinals, Lane was now finally healthy and extremely productive. He had 132 yards in a win over New Orleans and 125 more in a defeat of the Eagles. "I knew I had it all the time," Lane said about his success. "It was just a matter of getting the opportunity with the ball club. You can't perform on the bench. I never heard of anyone making all-pro while sitting down."[10] According to Winner, "Mac has things you can't teach. He has instinct, awareness of what's happening and tremendous reactions."[11]

Lane and Hart were also getting help from the defense, which did not give up more than twenty points in any game for the first six weeks of the season. Starting November 1 against Houston, the Cardinals defense would earn three shutouts in a row: 44–0 over the Oilers, 31–0 over the Patriots, and, finally, 38–0 over the Cowboys, tying an NFL record that dated to 1935.[12] The Cardinals held Houston to 160 total yards and forced Dallas into six turnovers. After the third shutout, *Dallas Morning News* sportswriter Bob St. John wrote, "Larry Wilson, the Cardinal free safety and defensive ring leader, said before the game that St. Louis was out to prove the earlier 20–7 victory over the Cowboys was no fluke. Well Larry, in a way, it WAS a fluke. The Cards only won that one by 13."[13] The win over the Cowboys put the Cardinals at 7-2 and in first place in the NFC East, one game ahead of the Giants and two in front of Dallas with just five games to play. "It's much too early" to talk about a division title, said Winner. "I've seen too many teams talk about championships, but do nothing about them."[14]

It seemed as if the Cardinals had finally found the right defensive pieces to put around Larry Wilson, whose reputation for toughness and determination would eventually land him in the Hall of Fame. A seventh-round pick of the Cardinals in 1960, Wilson terrorized offenses with his fearless safety blitzes and his all-around reckless play. On one occasion, he had all his teeth knocked out and kept playing; on another, he intercepted a pass while playing with a cast on each of his two broken hands. Packer guard Jerry Kramer, who often had to block Wilson's blitzes, called him "the finest football player in the NFL. He fire[s] up their whole team . . . his enthusiasm [is] infectious."[15] Wilson led the NFL with ten interceptions in 1966, and finished his career as an eight-time Pro Bowler and five-time All Pro. "I believe Larry Wilson is the greatest leader I've ever seen," said Rams' coach George Allen. "He's the only player I've ever seen fire up a team while holding for the extra point."[16]

With Wilson and the Cardinals' other future Hall of Famer, tight end Jackie Smith, having their usual outstanding seasons, St. Louis looked like a lock for the playoffs, if not the NFC East title. After beating the Eagles on November 29, the Cardinals were at 8-2-1, still a game and a half ahead of both the Giants and Cowboys with three games left. But reminiscent of 1965 and the *Sports Illustrated* cover story, the Cardinals suddenly went into a nosedive. The Lions held Lane to 32 yards rushing and intercepted Hart twice in a 16–3 Detroit victory. That was followed by a battle for first place with the resurgent New York Giants, who beat St. Louis handily, 34–17. Fran Tarkenton threw two touchdown passes and Lane once again had trouble finding running room, finishing with only 26 yards. Jim Hart could complete only thirteen of thirty passes, although he did throw a touchdown to Smith.

With one game left in the regular season, three of the five teams in the NFC East still had a chance at winning the division, or at least making the playoffs as a wild card. The Giants and Cowboys were tied for the division lead at 9-4, with the Cardinals just a half-game back at 8-4-1. The playoff scenarios for the final weekend had more mathematical complexity than a moon landing—St. Louis could win the division if New York and Dallas both lost, and even if that didn't happen it still had a chance of grabbing the wild-card berth because of two wins over the Cowboys. But any hopes for the post-season depended on a victory over the Redskins in Washington on December 20.

REPLACING A LEGEND

The Redskins came into the game with much less at stake, and were already assured of their fourteenth non-winning season in the last fifteen years. If not for the "Slingin' Sammy" Baugh era of the '30s and '40s that produced two NFL titles, the Redskins might actually rival the Cardinals for historical futility. Between 1956 and 1968, there were no titles, no playoff appearances, and not even a single winning season. "Back then," said Jerry Olsen, who ran the Redskins alumni association, "you could get all the season tickets you wanted."[17] It was also during this period that fans and sportswriters began referring to the team as the "Deadskins."

The man hired to bring the franchise back to life was none other than Green Bay legend Vince Lombardi. Lombardi admitted that the pressure of coaching forced his retirement in 1968, when he spent the season as the Packers general manager. A miserable season, as it turns out. The first day of training camp "I couldn't do anything but force myself to go down and watch," said Lombardi. "And, of course, I knew right then that I had made a horrible mistake by leaving coaching."[18] Lombardi wanted to get back into coaching, but realized he couldn't do it in Green Bay. Enter the Redskins, eager to see if the man who had never suffered a losing season in the NFL could work his magic in Washington. They named Lombardi executive vice president as well as coach and gave him full control of the team.

"Fellows, we will win," he told the team when it assembled for training camp in July 1969, "You believe that." And the Redskins believed. Quarterback Sonny Jurgensen had a fabulous year, leading Washington to a 7-5-2 record, its first winning season in fourteen years. Lombardi seemed to be the savior the team had so desperately needed, and he had the Redskins primed for even greater things in 1970. "I'd do anything for him," said fullback Ray McDonald. "He told us we had to love one another, to care for other players on the team if we were going to *be* a team. He's a genius, a genius."[19]

But even genius has its limits, its own mortality, and for Lombardi that came in the summer of 1970. Doctors diagnosed him with an extremely aggressive form of colon cancer in June, and by September he was gone. He died on September 3, 1970, mourned by the Packers, the Redskins, and almost everyone connected to professional football. Thousands lined the streets leading to his memorial service in St. Patrick's Cathedral in New York City, while inside former players and associates wept openly. Among the dozens of tributes and eulogies, Robert Lipsyte of the *New York Times* wrote, "[His players] bled for Lombardi because he offered them the opportunity to be the best. It all worked only because he came to his people offering them more than he asked."[20]

The man left to pick up the shattered pieces of the Redskins' season was assistant coach Bill Austin, whom Lombardi had officially named interim coach during training camp. Like Phil Bengston, a long-time assistant who took over for Lombardi in Green Bay, Austin had a monumentally difficult job. "I can't be Vince Lombardi but I can holler just as loud," said Austin, who was getting a second chance as a head coach after three years with the woeful Steelers.[21] Despite Austin's best intentions, Lombardi's illness and eventual death hung over the team all season. Lombardi stayed with the team as long as he could, attending practices and rookie scrimmages in late July, but by August it became apparent that Austin would be in charge when the regular season opened. "You win with people," Jurgensen said before the season began. "People win, not formations."[22] Now Washington was going to have to try and win without one of its best people.

The Redskins actually got off to a decent start, going 4-3 through their first seven games. Jurgensen and the offense were playing well, but it quickly became apparent that defense was going to be a problem. The Redskins gave up more than twenty-one points three times in those first seven games, and it was going to get much worse. A 19–10 loss on November 8 to Minnesota triggered a five-game losing streak in which the Redskins' defense was almost helpless. They gave up thirty-five points to the Giants, forty-five to Dallas, twenty-seven to the Giants again, then thirty-four more in the Cowboys rematch. The second game with Dallas was especially disturbing in that the Redskins were not only shut out, but they gave up an incredible 276 yards rushing; Dallas running back Duane Thomas had 102 yards by halftime. A Lombardi team had always prided itself on tough defense, but on the season, Washington would finish twenty-fourth out of twenty-six NFL teams in yards allowed and only four teams would give up more points. The Redskins pulled themselves together a bit on December 13, beating the Eagles, 24–6, and came into the regular season finale with a 5-8 record.

WIDE LEFT

The Cardinals did not play like a team whose season was hanging in the balance, at least in the first half, as Washington jumped out to a 21-10 lead. In a battle of All-Pro caliber tight ends, the Redskins' Jerry Smith outshone Jackie Smith, catching two touchdown passes from Jurgensen. Washington's Smith somehow always seemed to be in the shadow of the Cardinals' Smith, although they had remarkably similar careers. Jackie finished his career with 480 catches for 7,918 yards and forty touchdown receptions; Jerry had 421 catches for 5,496 yards and sixty touchdown receptions. Despite better numbers in several categories, Jerry Smith has not made the Hall of Fame. Jackie Smith was inducted in 1994.[23]

In addition to allowing Jerry Smith to run free through their secondary, the Cardinals were having continuing problems with their running game. Lane and Edwards had seemed unstoppable early in the season, but now the

Redskins defense was having little trouble stopping them. Lane would rush seventeen times for only 55 yards; his poor performances in the last three weeks of the season and against Washington would cost him a coveted 1,000-yard rushing season. He would finish with 977 yards, good enough to wind up third in the league in total yards rushing and to make the Pro Bowl. Cid Edwards added only 8 yards on four carries; throw in a couple of carries by Roy Shivers, and the Cardinals ground game managed only 69 yards on twenty-five tries, which averages only 2.8 yards per carry.

When Charlie Harraway skirted around the left end and into the end zone to open the fourth quarter, the Cardinals trailed 28–13 and seemed finished. Forced to pass, Jim Hart started to find some success. He quickly hit John Gilliam on a 57-yard catch-and-run score, his second touchdown pass of the day, and the Redskins' lead was cut to 28–20. It got even more interesting a few minutes later when the Chuck Latourette scooped up a Larry Brown fumble and ran 32 yards for another score. Suddenly, the Cards were within one, 28–27, and nearly half of the fourth quarter remained.

On the first play after the kickoff, Brown fumbled again and the Cardinals' Bob Rowe recovered deep in Redskins' territory. The much-criticized Washington defense held for three plays, so in came one of the better kickers in the league, Jim Bakken, who had already made two field goals, including a 45-yarder. This attempt would come from only 26 yards and if good, would give the Cardinals a 30–28 lead with less than four minutes to play. But with all the momentum, and a season riding on the outcome, Bakken somehow missed the chip shot wide left. St. Louis lost, 28–27—end of game, end of season, end of playoff hopes.

For a team that was cruising to a division title just a few weeks earlier, it was a devastating defeat, and one players later admitted was a "mammoth choke."[24] "You press to prevent it, then you're pressing too much," said offensive tackle Ernie McMillan "and that's it. Definitely, I think we were waiting for something like that to happen."[25] Dallas officially won the NFC East later that afternoon, while Detroit beat Green Bay to take the wild card. St. Louis ended the season with three straight losses and finished a game and a half out of the playoffs with a record of 8-5-1.

Winner put on a brave face after the game, saying, "No one thought we could be serious contenders before the season started. I'm happy with the development of this team. It's young and it's going to be strong."[26] But Winner was wrong on both counts, and he was more surprised than anyone when the Cardinals fired him less than a month later. "I felt it was totally unjustified," he said after receiving the news on January 6. "I thought I built a good team and a young one which will be a challenger for years to come. And now, I don't get a chance to reap the benefits."[27]

Neither did his successor, Bob Hollway, who went 4-9-1 the following season, in part because the team traded away the core of its youth, including Lane, Edwards, and John Gilliam, the team's best deep threat at receiver.[28] It was a tremendous comedown for a team that may have been the best in the NFL for a ten-week stretch in 1970. The Cardinals won eight of those games, including the three shutouts. "On film they looked like one of the best teams we had ever seen," said Cowboys defensive tackle Bob Lilly. "They were just killing people. I saw Jim Hart [after the season] and I asked him, 'What happened to you guys? You were as good as any team I ever saw for three or four games.' He told me, 'Attitude. We just couldn't handle success.'"[29]

The narrow victory helped take some of the sting out of a 6-8 season in Washington, but the team never fully recovered from Lombardi's illness and death. It was as if a black cloud settled over the Redskins in July and stayed there until December. "It was a nightmare," said Redskins' offensive lineman Ray Schoenke. "A season like this is an emotional drain on you. It's frustrating, depressing. The physical aspects are always tough, but the mental anxieties you go through are worse."[30]

It was believed that the victory might help Bill Austin keep his job, but Washington executives realized the only way to end the nightmare was to make a clean sweep of things. Considering all the points and yards they gave up in 1970, the Redskins needed a defensive-minded coach, and one just happened to be available when George Allen wore out his welcome again in Los Angeles. Washington was quick to scoop him up, hoping Allen could provide the same kind of rebuilding he brought to the Rams. Allen didn't believe in rebuilding, however, and thought his philosophy—tough defense, an "us against the world" mentality, and an emphasis on veteran players— would produce an immediate winner. He made nineteen trades before his first Redskins season ever started, giving up younger players and draft picks for older veterans, including several of his former Rams players. "An aging team is the least of my worries," Allen told reporters. "If you do things right, you don't have to build and rebuild to field a winner."[31]

At least not in the beginning. The Redskins went 9-4-1 Allen's first season and went to the playoffs. They made it all the way to the Super Bowl the next season before losing to the undefeated Dolphins. Allen led the team to five playoffs appearances and left football with the third-highest winning percentage in NFL history, but his "buy now, pay later" philosophy eventually caught up with him and made the Redskins a very old team.[32] He was fired after the 1977 season having coached seven seasons in Washington. "We knew that everything George did was for a purpose," said Redskins punter Mike Bragg. "Football was all he ever thought about, and when he said, 'Losing is like dying,' he really meant it. But when we won, nothing was too good for his players."[33]

WEEK FOURTEEN:
Houston Oilers at Dallas Cowboys

BACK FROM THE DEAD

That the Dallas Cowboys were even in the playoff race on the last weekend of the 1970 season was a miracle, considering that they had gone through a November that could kindly be called hellish. It began at the November 8 game against the Giants at Yankee Stadium—the Cowboys were at 5-2 and in their customary spot atop the division standings. Somehow, Dallas blew a 20–9 second-half lead, allowing a Ron Johnson 4-yard touchdown, followed by a late touchdown pass to Johnson by Fran Tarkenton. The Cowboys appeared to get in position to tie or win the game after Craig Morton hit Reggie Rucker with a pass to the Giants' 9-yard line, but Rucker was called for illegal motion on the play and Dallas lost, 23–20. "I knew something was wrong," said Rucker. "I heard the crowd yelling. I knew they weren't yelling for me."[1]

That was just the warm-up act for what followed on November 16, as Dallas hosted St. Louis in the first *Monday Night Football* game in franchise history. With an entire nation tuning in to watch, the Cardinals humiliated the Cowboys, 38–0, which seemed to end any hopes Dallas had of reaching the playoffs. The Cowboys dropped to third place in the NFC East with a 5-4 record and for all intents and purposes looked lifeless. "You remember the Cowboys, of course," wrote Bob St. John in the *Dallas Morning News*. "Those 40 outstanding individuals without a team, which is somewhat like a man without a country. When the Cowboys fall, few teams in the NFL fall harder."[2] It got so bad in the second half that fans at the Cotton Bowl looked toward the ABC broadcast booth and began chanting, "We Want Meredith!"

in reference to the Cowboys' former quarterback who was now working as a television analyst. "I ain't getting back out there,"[3] said Meredith, and few could blame him. It was the first time in the ten-year history of the franchise that the Cowboys had been shutout. "This is getting serious," noted Dallas general manager Tex Schramm.[4]

At this point, it seemed like things could hardly get worse, but three days after the loss, Lance Rentzel, one of the Cowboys' most popular players and a productive wide receiver, exposed himself to a young girl. Rentzel had had a similar incident when playing for the Vikings, who were able to keep it quiet, but this time the press got hold of the story. Rentzel was formally charged on November 30, and even though his teammates wanted him to keep playing, he agreed to go on the inactive list to get help. "I've made a mistake in my life before and now I've made a second one," he said as he broke down addressing the team. "Green Bay [on Thanksgiving] will be my last game."[5]

The two disheartening defeats, the loss of Rentzel, and memories of past playoff failures seemed to take the life out of the Cowboys' season, and even head coach Tom Landry. For all his qualities as a football coach, Landry was not a great motivator, and now, with the season teetering on the edge of complete disaster, the Cowboy players felt that he, the fans, and the media had given up on them. "Tom felt he had to put the season on the shelf," said cornerback Mel Renfro. "Because Tom was a statistics and numbers guy, and the statistics and numbers said, 'Hey, you guys. It's over.'"[6] Roger Staubach, at that point still a backup to Craig Morton at quarterback, added, "Coach Landry came into the locker room, and pretty much said he didn't think we could win."[7]

But in a players-only meeting after the St. Louis debacle, the team decided to ignore its coach and keep working. "We threw up our hands and said, 'To hell with the coaches,'" said linebacker Chuck Howley. "We said, 'The hell with this. Let's go play ball.' And then we started to win."[8] Howley kick-started the team's resurgence the following week by returning a fumble, which set up a touchdown in a 45–21 win over the Redskins, a game in which Duane Thomas ran for 104 yards and three touchdowns, and Morton threw two touchdown passes. Thomas would become increasingly valuable as the season continued.

Most of the credit for the turnaround belonged to the Dallas defense, which became the best in the NFL over the last five games of the season. After the Redskins scored a third quarter touchdown against Dallas on

November 22, the Cowboys went twenty-three quarters—the equivalent of nearly six full games—without giving up an offensive touchdown. They gave up only a field goal to Green Bay in week eleven, shutout Washington a week later, and permitted only a safety against the Browns. The 6–2 win in a rainy, muddy Cleveland Stadium on December 12 may have been the team's biggest of the season. "We lost in that Cleveland Stadium so many times when we were the better team," said Renfro. "Everybody was just muddy and dirty, and we rose to the occasion."[9]

While the defense soared, the offense was carried on the legs of Duane Thomas. Morton was playing hurt and his effectiveness was decreasing week by week. After going twelve of fifteen against the Redskins for 176 yards and two touchdowns on November 22, Morton hit only eight of twenty for 100 yards and one touchdown in the rematch on December 6. Obviously, the mud of Cleveland made it difficult to throw, and Morton went eight of seventeen for 72 yards against the Browns. Morton's problems were due in part to a variety of injuries, including a lacerated hand, infected elbow, and surgically rebuilt passing shoulder. "Because of Craig's injury, his confidence was shot," said Staubach. "The way we started to win was a ferocious defense. That last stretch our defense really got some momentum."[10]

As the Cowboys took the field for their regular season finale December 20 against the Oilers, the NFC East was bunched tightly together. The Giants and Cowboys were tied for first place at 9-4, although New York enjoyed a tie-breaker advantage. St. Louis was at 8-4-1 and still had a shot at the playoffs if either Dallas or New York (or both) lost. The Cowboys obviously knew they had to win, but even winning might not be enough. Depending on the outcome of the three games, Dallas could finish anywhere from first to third in the division. Such was not the case for the Houston Oilers, a team that had already clinched last place in the AFC Central and was now trying to win for only the fourth time that season.

"BACKSTABBING AND BUFFOONERY"

Ten years after the founding of the American Football League in 1960, most observers would have judged the Houston Oilers to be a success. They had won the first two AFL championships and came within double-overtime of winning a third. But the loss to the Dallas Texans in the 1962 AFL title game signaled bad times ahead—four straight losing seasons followed, fans began to abandon the team, and the Oilers began losing serious money. "I didn't mind losing money when we were competing with the NFL," said owner Bud Adams, who flirted with moving the team to Seattle. "We were fighting the other side, and it was fun. But now that we have merged, it's more businesslike and those losses don't appeal to me as a businessman."[11]

Adams's father was the chairman of oil giant Phillips 66, and staked with what he described as a "modest" claim, Adams spent decades expanding the empire in real estate, banking, and other various enterprises. One of his projects was the Houston Oilers, which became a charter member of the AFL in 1960. Unfortunately, Adams never had the football sense of the other two Texas oil barons who owned pro teams at the time—Lamar Hunt of the Dallas Texans and Clint Murchison Jr. of the Cowboys. Hunt and Murchison didn't know everything about football, but they were smart enough to hire good football people and let them run the organization.

While Adams publicly said that others were in charge of the Oilers, there was a feeling that he controlled far more than he admitted. The result, according to Houston sportswriter Ed Fowler, was a franchise run on "turmoil, intrigue, back-stabbing, and buffoonery."[12] Adams changed Oilers' employees like some executives change shirts; in its first six years of play the team had four general managers, five coaches, and played in three different stadiums. All the while, Murchison and Hunt kept their organizations stable, and Tom Landry and Hank Stram became two of the longest tenured coaches in the league.[13]

Two AFL titles should have made the Oilers the kings of Texas football, especially considering that at the same time the Cowboys were losing consistently as an expansion team. But as the Oilers began to slide following the 1963 season, the Cowboys began to get better, and by 1965 Dallas was the talk of Texas. Ratings showed that more people in Houston watched the Cowboys on television than watched the Oilers either in person or on the tube. As the Cowboys' success on the field began to catch and surpass the Oilers, the two teams became a focal point in the long-standing feud between the biggest cities in Texas. Even though they are only separated by 240 miles, "they are farther apart in style," wrote Bud Shrake of *Sports Illustrated* in 1969.[14]

"To folks in Dallas," noted *Time* magazine, "Houston is a loud, boorish, blue-collar place, overwhelmed by nouveau riche high rollers and overrun with Cadillacs and pickup trucks. To folks in Houston, Dallas is a dull, snobbish, white-collar town, dominated by banking and defense interests, and overrun with Rolls-Royces and Mercedes."[15]

THE NEELY CUP

In 1965 the feud got nasty when both teams coveted the same player, offensive tackle Ralph Neely from the University of Oklahoma. At that time, there were still separate NFL and AFL drafts, and Neely was selected by both the Oilers and Baltimore Colts. Wanting to stay in the south, Neely signed with Houston, but when the Colts traded his draft rights to Dallas, Neely signed a contract with the Cowboys and returned his $25,000 signing bonus to the Oilers.[16] Not one to take defeat lying down, Adams and the Oilers sued to enforce Neely's Houston contract. The Cowboys won the original trial, but the Oilers appealed and got the verdict overturned. In the decision, the Circuit Court chastised athletes like Neely who "one day agree to play football for a stated amount for one group, only to repudiate that agreement the following day or whenever a better offer comes along."[17]

That should have ended the matter and forced Neely to play in Houston, but the Cowboys desperately needed an offensive lineman, especially one of Neely's ability. Just as badly as the Cowboys wanted Neely, the Oilers wanted to play Dallas in a series of exhibition games in order to broaden their fan base in Texas. When Oilers general manager Don Klosterman suggested the series a few years earlier he was rejected by his Cowboys' counterpart Tex Schramm. "We've got a lot of fans in Houston," said Schramm. "You don't have any fans in Dallas."[18] But now, the Oilers had a bargaining chip and they worked out a deal—Neely for the exhibition games (and four draft picks).

The first two exhibition games were played in Houston and both were easy Cowboy victories, 30–17 in 1967 and 33–19 in 1968. But despite the losses, Oiler fans turned out in record numbers, and both games represented the largest crowds that had ever seen the team play. More than fifty-two thousand came to the Astrodome for the second game, and while Cowboys fans were well represented, the majority wanted to see the Oilers beat the hated wine-and-cheese crowd from Dallas. "A lot of emotion has been built up about this," said Klosterman. "The games we play with Dallas are always mean—well, let's say very brisk. The Cowboys get lots of publicity; they're supposed to be the best. It's like the Jets got tired of hearing about the Giants. We're tired of hearing about Dallas."[19]

By the time the third exhibition game was played in 1969, a trophy had been created called the Governor's Cup (which some sportswriters suggested should have been named the "Neely Cup"), and Governor Preston Smith was among another record crowd of 55,310 in the Astrodome. Tickets that would normally go for fewer than five dollars were openly scalped for thirty-five to sixty dollars. One Houston oilman offered one hundred dollars each for Houston television announcer Bill Enis's tickets. Enis didn't sell, but he "told his wife and kids they'd better enjoy this game."[20] Dallas won again, although by a much closer score of 14–11, and while they graciously accepted the Cup from Governor Smith, the Cowboys still refused to acknowledge that a rivalry even existed. "I don't mean to disparage Houston," said Schramm, who did just that, "but Kansas City would draw more people in Dallas than Houston would. I guess this could turn into a real rivalry with Houston sometime."[21] Sometime may have come during the 1970 preseason when the Oilers got their first-ever win over the Cowboys in the Governor's Cup.

Now, the on-again, off-again rivalry was coming to Dallas, and unlike the previous preseason games, this one would count. At least, it would count for the Cowboys; the Oilers had long since given up on 1970. After winning two of its first three games, Houston went eight weeks without another victory and came into Dallas after losing eight of its last ten. Part of the problem was at quarterback, where veteran Charley Johnson broke a collarbone in week five against Pittsburgh and missed the rest of the season. Back in training camp, coach Wally Lemm had said, "Getting Charley from St. Louis is the biggest single thing we've done since we've been here."[22] The Oilers traded for Johnson's stability and leadership, but he threw only seven touchdown passes before his injury. Houston's backup quarterback situation was a mess, and included Dallas castoff Jerry Rhome and rookie Bob Naponic.[23]

The bigger problem for Houston was defense, which despite the presence of future Hall of Famers Elvin Bethea and Ken Houston, allowed more points on the season (352) than every team in the league except for Boston (361). Linebacker George Webster, who had made all-AFL his first three seasons, was injured for most of the year and played only seven games. Webster would play six more years, but his injuries were so acute that after his retirement he applied to the NFL for benefits as permanently disabled. The Oilers also failed to get any defensive help in the 1970 draft, after going almost exclusively for offense. The one player of note was first-round pick Doug Wilkerson, who played only one season in Houston before getting traded to San Diego and becoming a three-time Pro Bowler at offensive guard with the Chargers.

Despite the possibility of their team winning the division or securing a playoff spot, Cowboys fans were less than enthusiastic about going to the Cotton Bowl on a foggy, drizzly December day. Only 50,504 showed up in a stadium that could seat nearly 76,000, which made it the smallest home crowd in five years. The weather was partly to blame, but there was also a sense that Cowboys fans had seen all this before. Winning in the regular season was not the issue; Dallas had won more than any other team in the NFL the past four seasons. The real test would come in the playoffs, if only the Cowboys could get there. "The hardest championship to win is the first," Landry admitted. "After that, a club knows that it is capable of winning and it gains a great deal in confidence."[24]

The teams traded field goals in the first quarter before the missing Dallas offense finally reappeared. Morton recently had four stitches removed from the cut on his throwing hand, but it apparently bothered no one but the Houston secondary. First, he connected with Rucker who, with Rentzel gone, was now an important part of the Dallas offense. It was a 52-yard touchdown in which Rucker did most of the work himself after taking a short slant pass over the middle. Then came the forgotten Cowboy, Bob Hayes—the same Hayes who had been benched earlier in the year and had complained long and loud about it. Back in Landry's good graces, and celebrating his twenty-eighth birthday, Hayes torched the Oilers for four consecutive scoring passes from Morton—from 38, 38, 15, and 59 yards. Hayes finished the day with six catches good for 187 yards and a club-record four touchdowns. "Hayes is a great example of how we turned this season around," said Landry. "He's been playing tremendous football and has been a major factor in our winning."[25]

Morton also had a record-breaking day, or at least a record-tying day, as his five touchdowns matched Don Meredith's performance in 1966.[26] Morton finished with thirteen of seventeen passing for 349 yards; easily his best day of the season and one of the best of his career. The five straight touchdowns gave Dallas a 38–3 lead, so the only remaining issue to be settled was whether the Oilers could break the touchdown-less streak of the Cowboys' defense. Dallas intercepted Houston's quarterbacks four times, knocked starter Rhome out of the game with a separated shoulder, and made life miserable for his replacement, rookie Naponic. The Oilers did score a touchdown, but it came when Johnny Peacock scooped up a Calvin Hill fumble and ran it in from 41 yards out; otherwise, Houston managed only 151 yards of offense and was completely overwhelmed, 52–10. In one final dig at the Oilers and their Governor's Cup win in Houston a few months earlier, center Dave Manders walked off the field shouting, "Remember the Astrodome!"[27]

Shortly after the game ended, the Cowboys got an early Christmas present when they learned that both St. Louis and the Giants had lost. With a possible playoff spot on the line, the Giants not only lost, they lost embarrassingly at home to the Rams, 31–3. Combined with the Cardinals' narrow 28–27 loss to Washington, it handed the NFC East title to the Cowboys, a team that was given up for dead in November. Despite a 1-3 record against the Giants and Cardinals, Dallas had won its last five games to finish at 10-4 and win a division title for the fifth straight year. The Cowboys would host Detroit in the first round of the NFC playoffs.

TEXAS'S TEAM?

The battered Oilers ended the year at 3-10-1 and immediately started thinking about the future. They replaced head coach Wally Lemm with Ed Hughes, who lasted only one season before giving way to the tragi-comic reign of Bill Peterson. Peterson had great success as a college coach, but that never translated to the NFL where the Oilers went 1-18 in his one-plus seasons of coaching. "The biggest joke I've ever been involved with in my life," said quarterback Dan Pastorini. "To this day I don't know how he ever got a coaching job here."[28] Houston sportswriter John McClain called Peterson "a master of the malaprop. He would tell the players to stand on their helmets with the sideline under their arms. How can you inspire players when you can't get the words out of your mouth correctly?"[29]

Things got significantly better in 1975 when the Oilers hired Bum Phillips, who immediately turned the team into winners and playoff contenders. It was also Phillips who guided the Oilers to perhaps their biggest win ever over Dallas, a 30–24 defeat of the Cowboys on Thanksgiving Day 1979 in Texas Stadium. By that point, Dallas was "America's Team," a name given to them by NFL Films because of the team's national popularity, but one that inspired hatred and jealousy from almost everyone else outside of Texas. After the Oilers had beaten the Cowboys for the first time ever in the regular season, Phillips said, "They may be America's Team, but we're Texas's team."[30]

The 1979 season was the last high point in the history of the Houston Oilers. That season, the team got all the way to the AFC Championship before losing to Pittsburgh, the second year in a row the Oilers had fallen one game short of the Super Bowl. The team made seven more playoff appearances through 1993, but never reached the Super Bowl, and in the 1992 playoffs Houston earned the dubious distinction of blowing the biggest lead in NFL playoff history, as Buffalo came back from a 35–3 second-half deficit to win in overtime, 41–38.

In 1987 Bud Adams agreed to a new ten-year lease at the Astrodome only after the Houston Sports Association made major concessions in terms of renovations and stadium upgrades, such as luxury boxes. The Astrodome was a palace when it opened in 1965, but over the years Adams had seen other teams build bigger, better, and more profitable stadiums. In 1994 he went to Houston city officials seeking a new domed stadium. When that failed, Adams found the city of Nashville was willing to build him a new $292 million facility, and he agreed to move the team to Tennessee, even if it meant breaking his lease a year early. "This is historic for all of us," NFL Commissioner Paul Tagliabue said when the Oilers' move to Nashville became official in 1996. "We are the first major sports franchise in Tennessee. And we are proud to be in Tennessee."[31] Those less proud included the city of Houston, Oiler fans, and even some NFL owners who worried about too many teams abandoning their cities. "Is this the last move for a while?" asked Wellington Mara, the owner of the Giants at that time. "I certainly hope so."[32]

The Oilers became the Tennessee Oilers, a regional name that came in handy their first season of 1997 because the new stadium was not ready and the team had to play its home games in Memphis. The franchise seemed to flourish when it finally reached Nashville and became the Titans, and in 1999 accomplished the one feat the old Oilers never could by reaching a Super Bowl. Even though the Titans lost to the Rams, 23–16, the franchise has been successful both on the field and in the community, regularly selling out its sixty-nine thousand seat stadium.

Ironically, the NFL not only put a new team in Houston in 2002, it put it in the same division as the Titans. Bud Adams and his former Oilers returned to Houston for the first time on December 29, 2002, to play the Houston Texans, and a record crowd of 70,694 came to boo Adams both before and the during the game. "It's a business and we had to win this game," Adams said after the Titans' 13–3 victory. "Outside of that, I love the Texans."[33]

But there are still hard feelings on both sides regarding the franchise that used to call Houston home. Adams wears an Oilers AFL Championship ring on his right hand, and a Titans AFC Championship ring on his left. When someone asked him what he would do if he ever won a Super Bowl ring, Adams said, "I'll put it on the middle finger and say to the mayor of Houston to take a look at it."[34] The people of Houston probably feel the same way.

★ 16 ★

THE PLAYOFFS

YOUNG GUNS

The NFC East logjam that Dallas broke through was not the only one to go down to the final weekend of the regular season. In week fourteen, San Francisco waxed its bay neighbor Oakland, 38–7 to finally clinch the NFC West by a game over Los Angeles; despite losing, the Raiders still won the AFC West by a game over Kansas City. Cincinnati's 45–7 rout of the Patriots made the team AFC Central champions, albeit with a mediocre 8-6 record. "I'm a very happy man right now," said Paul Brown after the game. "It's a dream come true."[1] Minnesota and Baltimore finished with the best records in their respective conferences and would host playoff games at least in the first round. Even with an uneven performance from quarterback Gary Cuozzo, the Vikings looked even more imposing than in their Super Bowl season, winning the NFC Central at 12–2 and allowing a league-low 143 points. On the season, NFC teams had a record of 27-12-1 against teams from the AFC.[2]

Those teams that finished out of the playoffs could console themselves with some impressive individual performances. Dick Gordon of the Bears almost pulled off a receiving hat trick, catching seventy-one passes for 1,026 yards and thirteen touchdowns; another 75 yards and he would have passed San Francisco's Gene Washington and swept all three season receiving categories. On the ground, a relatively unknown Larry Brown of the Redskins topped the NFL in rushing with 1,125 yards. Brown had not done much his rookie season and he always seemed to be late coming off the ball. When Washington coaches suggested a hearing test, results showed that Brown

163

was almost completely deaf in one ear. Outfitted with a special hearing aid in his helmet, Brown made the first of four consecutive Pro Bowls in 1970. "You don't tackle Brown," said St. Louis defensive tackle Bob Rowe. "You just hit him and hope help comes along."[3]

For some teams, there was no consolation. The Saints endured yet another losing season, finishing at 2-11-1, and after four years in the NFL their overall record was 14-40-2. Charlie Waller lost his job in San Diego, as did John Rauch in Buffalo after a 3-10-1 season. Harvey Johnson replaced Rauch and the team promptly sank to 1-13 the following year. But perhaps no team suffered more than the Boston Patriots. Boston finished with a 2-12 record, scored the fewest points in the league (149), gave up the most points (361), and, perhaps to cover up the embarrassment, changed its name to the New England Patriots in the off-season.

The NFL's wildcard format, in which the non-division-winning team with the best overall record would make the playoffs, brought some fresh faces to the postseason. The most surprising was the Miami Dolphins, a team just four years removed from expansion that had never had so much as a winning season. But when Don Shula left the Colts to coach in Miami, he brought with him discipline, a winning track record, and most of all, toughness. "It really dawned on me that I'd better be concentrating every second," said running back Larry Csonka, "because the time you least expect it, you're going to get Shula's foot in your rear."[4] Quarterback Bob Griese also praised his coach saying, "Shula is a big factor for us. Maybe it's just that he's a winner and we know it. It gives us confidence."[5]

Only in his fourth season, Griese was among Miami's many young players who were just coming into their own. Backs Mercury Morris (second season), Jim Kiick (third), and Csonka (third) gave Shula the running game he needed for his ball control offense. Csonka was the power gear in Miami's attack, preferring to run over defenders rather than to run around them. Against the Bills on October 18, Csonka avoided a tackle by bowling over safety Pete Richardson with a forearm, a move that earned him a penalty for roughing. "I've never had a ball carrier called for unnecessary roughness on a tackler before," marveled Shula. "It shows you what a competitor he is."[6] Csonka finished fifth in the NFL in rushing with 874 yards, and as a team the Dolphins ranked third in the league behind only Dallas and Detroit.

Even though Miami had to give the Colts a first-round selection in order to hire Shula, the team stockpiled more young talent in the NFL draft. Future starters drafted in 1970 included tight end Jim Mandich (second round), defensive back Tim Foley (third), defensive back Curtis Johnson (fourth), and linebacker Mike Kolen (twelfth). Perhaps the steal of the draft was safety Jake Scott, who lasted until the seventh round, but played nine years in the league and won MVP honors in Super Bowl VII. Two veterans helped provide the young Dolphins with experience and leadership: linebacker Nick Buoniconti, who was in his second season in Miami after seven years with the Patriots, and Paul Warfield, who came over in a trade with Cleveland and gave Griese a deep threat at wide receiver. Both players would eventually make the Hall of Fame.

As befitting a young team, Miami played inconsistently, starting with the season opener, which it lost to the dreadful Patriots. The Dolphins then won four in a row, lost three straight, and finished with six consecutive wins to close the season and earn their first-ever playoff spot as a wildcard team. Proof of the team's resiliency came in its rematch with the Colts, the team that had routed Miami, 35–0, on November 1 in Baltimore. Three weeks later, the Colts found the young Dolphins had very much grown up, as Miami won easily, 34–17. "The two biggest difficulties for expansion teams are a lack of consistency and a lack of depth," said Dolphins owner Joe Robbie. "It's the first year we've had either."[7]

On the final weekend of the regular season, the Dolphins could secure a playoff spot with a win over Buffalo, but would have to do it without injured starters Warfield and defensive lineman Manny Fernandez. Jim Kiick rushed for three short touchdowns, and the defense forced four turnovers as Miami built a 31–0 halftime lead. The Dolphins would have had a shutout if not for a late, meaningless touchdown, but still won handily, 45–7. "I could look across the field and see the Bills aching to get it over with and clear out," said Griese, who threw a touchdown pass, but sat down with the rest of the starters midway through the second half. "That's about the way it has been with us before this year."[8] When someone asked Robbie before the season if he would give Shula time to produce a winner, he remarked, "Sure. He's got all summer."[9] The new coach had missed the mark by only six months.

Over in the NFC, the wildcard spot went to the Detroit Lions, a team that seemed on the brink of collapse in November. With its record at 5-4 and all hopes of winning the division gone, Detroit closed out the season with five straight victories, four of them coming over teams leading their division at the time. A 20–0 victory over Green Bay in the season finale clinched the wildcard spot and marked the second shutout on the season over the Packers, a team the Lions outscored 60–0 in two meetings. "They're fantastic," Green Bay's Donny Anderson said after the game. "They're the best we've played in the last four-five weeks," a span that included both Dallas and Minnesota.[10]"Now we've got an opportunity to possibly go to the Super Bowl," said Joe Schmidt. "This is our greatest progress in four years."[11]

PLAYOFF SATURDAY: DECEMBER 26

The first game of the playoff weekend looked like a mismatch on paper. Cincinnati, which had barely won more games that it lost and would be playing in its first-ever postseason game, would go on the road against Baltimore, a team with a ton of playoff experience that was highly motivated to avenge its loss in Super Bowl III. The Bengals were also somewhat handicapped at quarterback, where Virgil Carter was playing with a broken rib, busted lip, and gashed tongue. Unable to eat solid food for a week, Carter dropped ten pounds, and said his specially designed rib protector would restrain him, but not bother his passing.

Realizing it would be a monumental upset to beat the Colts in Baltimore, the Bengals accepted the underdog role and just seemed happy to be in the playoffs. "When you realize the Rams and Kansas City didn't get a chance to play," said Cincinnati coach Paul Brown, "we were flattered to get into this game."[12] Bengals' defensive end Royce Berry was a bit less humble. "We're going to be ready," he warned. "You can almost feel it building up inside you, just like before the Boston game last week."[13] Berry admitted that getting pressure on Unitas was going to be a key for Cincinnati's young defense.

With Carter somewhat disabled, the Bengals relied heavily on the run, which got nowhere against Baltimore's defense. For the game, Cincinnati managed only 63 yards on twenty-two carries; Paul Robinson was the leading ground-gainer with just 25 yards. After a short time, it became obvious that Cincinnati had nowhere to run and nowhere to pass. "We knew from watching films that their running game had to work against us if they were going to succeed," said Baltimore linebacker Ray May. "If their running game doesn't go, then their passing doesn't either."[14] Carter hit only eight of twenty-one passes for 93 yards and an interception, as the Bengals crossed midfield only once and finished the day with a grand total of 139 yards of offense.

Baltimore also wanted to run, and proved much more effective than the Bengals. Norm Bulaich, the rookie runner who had replaced an injured Tom Matte in the opening game of the season, bowled his way for 116 yards on twenty-five carries. The success of the Colts' running game opened things up for Johnny Unitas through the air, and although Unitas did not have a statistically great afternoon, hitting just six of seventeen passes, he threw touchdowns of 45 yards to Roy Jefferson and 53 yards to Eddie Hinton. Jim O'Brien kicked a field goal and that was it for the scoring. The Colts weren't necessarily impressive, but they got the win everyone expected, 17–0. "We got in a little deep," admitted Brown after the game. "The Colts are big and mature, and when it gets down to the end of the season for the money, it takes the same kind of people to play them. We've only been in existence that long."[15]

The playoff opener between Baltimore and Cincinnati may have seemed like a somewhat listless affair, but it was a piece of football art compared to what followed later that afternoon in Dallas. The Cowboys and Lions, two evenly matched teams with strong defenses and powerful running games, may have set offensive football back an entire generation in their meeting at the Cotton Bowl. It started normally enough, with Mike Clark of the Cowboys kicking a first-quarter field goal for a 3–0 lead, but that was it for the offenses the rest of the day. "When we got those three points," said Cowboys running back Walt Garrison, "I told [linebacker] Dave Edwards, 'There's three for you. Now all you got to do is shut them out and we win.'"[16]

The Lions went almost exclusively with Landry at quarterback and he could do nothing against the Cowboys' defense, hitting seven of twenty passes for 92 yards, while their ground game managed just 76 yards on twenty-seven carries. Detroit's deepest penetration came early in the second period when it reached the Dallas 29, but Altie Taylor fumbled the ball over to the Cowboys. The Dallas offense seemed even feebler than the Lions, mainly because Craig Morton was having a terrible day, completing four of eighteen passes for an incredible 38 yards. Giving up on the pass in the fourth quarter, Dallas called fifteen straight running plays, mostly with Duane Thomas, to drive inside the Lions' 5-yard line. Dallas coach Tom Landry gambled on fourth and goal from the 1, and even though the Lions held, the resulting field position set up the game's final score. The Cowboys' Jethro Pugh and George Andrie combined to sack Landry for a safety and a 5–0 lead with 4:45 to play. "I'd have to say that Dallas is the best defensive team we've faced this year," said Detroit linebacker Mike Lucci.[17] Added tackle Rocky Freitas, "They didn't give up on a single play."[18]

Still, a touchdown one way or another would win the game, and Detroit seemed poised to get it late in the fourth quarter. Munson replaced Greg Landry and led the Lions on a desperate drive, converting a fourth and 10 that put the ball on the Cowboys' 29 with less than a minute to play. But once again the Dallas defense made the big play, this time Mel Renfro intercepted a tipped pass to preserve the game and the shutout, 5–0, in what remains as the lowest-scoring game in NFL playoff history. "I have," said Renfro, "been waiting for that one all season."[19] "You saw the zero," said Dallas' Tom Landry after the game. "That about sums it up. This is the best defense we have ever played."[20]

The best defense, maybe, but there were still lots of questions about the Dallas offense. "It's games like this that made baseball lower the mound," quipped sports columnist Dick Young.[21] Thomas did run for 135 yards on thirty carries against one of the best rushing defenses in the league, but watching Morton try to throw the ball did not inspire much confidence that the Cowboys could beat their second-round playoff opponent, especially if it turned out to be the powerful Vikings. For the moment, Dallas had survived, and that in itself was a major accomplishment after four straight years of crushing playoff defeats. "This was the biggest win we ever had," said Landry. "I think the problem we had with winning big games is behind us now."[22]

PLAYOFF SUNDAY: DECEMBER 27

As the Cowboys gathered around their televisions to watch the second NFC playoff game the following day, they fully expected to meet the Minnesota Vikings for the NFC Championship. While San Francisco had a strong team, led by league MVP John Brodie at quarterback, the Vikings had lost only two games all season, gave up the fewest points in the NFL, and ranked behind only the 49ers in points scored. What's more, Minnesota would be at home in the frozen confines of Metropolitan Stadium, where the team believed it enjoyed a psychological advantage in cold weather. While there was no snow and the field was relatively dry, the temperature at game time would be ten degrees above zero, with a wind chill of six below. "There were hard patches—ice—around midfield along the sideline and inside the 10-yard line at both ends," said Brodie after the game. "I guess, secretly, we were a little scared of it. But we found out it didn't bite."[23]

If anything, the Vikings' offense seemed frozen shut. Cuozzo hit only nine of twenty-seven passes and threw two interceptions, as Minnesota turned over the ball four times. The only Vikings' points of the first half came when Paul Krause returned a fumble for a touchdown, but Brodie immediately responded with a 24-yard score to a wide-open Dick Witcher. That and a Bruce Gossett field goal gave San Francisco the lead at halftime, 10–7.

The Vikings never did solve the 49ers' defense, which had started to come into its own toward the end of the season. Dazzling cornerback Bruce Taylor would lead the league in punt return yardage and win NFC Rookie of the Year honors. He was joined in the defensive backfield by Jimmy Johnson, who would go on to intercept forty-seven passes in a sixteen-year career that landed him in the Hall of Fame. Another rookie, defensive end Cedrick Hardman, teamed with Tommy Hart and Earl Edwards to give San Francisco a formidable pass rush.

The most interesting figure up front was twelve-year veteran defensive tackle Charlie Krueger, a tough Texan who still used the two-bar facemask more common to quarterbacks. Krueger looked like an old, beat up pickup truck, in part because he was always willing to play in pain. In a November game against the Oilers, pieces of his left femur and tibia broke off, but he never came out and finished the rest of the season. "If they said I could play, I played," he later said. "I played because it was my job. Pro football's a hard place to make a living."[24] He also made life hard for opposing offenses. "No one is able to gain running at Charlie Krueger," said Tom Landry.[25]

Krueger and the 49ers' defense kept Minnesota bottled up most of the second half, and late in the game forced a punt deep in Vikings' territory that Taylor returned to the 14-yard line. A run by Ken Willard to the 1 set up a Brodie quarterback sneak that put San Francisco ahead, 17–7, with less than three minutes to play. Cuozzo finally threw a touchdown pass to Gene Washington, but it came with just one second on the clock, and the defending NFL champions and playoff favorites were eliminated, 17–14. It was the first loss for the Vikings at home in seventeen games, dating back to December 1968. "We are just too basic a football team to win with that many mistakes," said Minnesota coach Bud Grant.[26] The 49ers also used their underdog role as a motivator. "It was like everybody knew the Vikings were going to the Super Bowl and it was just a matter of whom they were going to play," said Johnson.[27] Now it was the 49ers advancing to play the Dallas Cowboys for the first-ever NFC Championship, with the game to be played in San Francisco. "There's not a guy in the house that's cold right now," Brodie said of his team after the game.[28]

As Oakland took to the field for its home playoff game against Miami, it learned of the 49ers' upset over Minnesota. It was news the Raiders later admitted motivated them to avoid a similar fate in their game, which was also against a team playing in its first playoff game in franchise history. Adding to the Dolphins' confidence was the fact that they had beaten the Raiders, 20–13, back on October 3 in Miami. "Don Shula said they were sky high, and they probably were," said Raiders running back Marv Hubbard, who rushed for 58 yards on the day. "But it doesn't matter how high you get before a game or how high you are after a game. When it gets to be one o'clock that's when it counts and that's when we get emotional."[29]

The Oakland Coliseum is typically damp because it lies below sea level, but steady rains had turned the field into a muddy "cow pasture," according to Miami's Garo Yepremian.[30] Yepremian, the NFL's most accurate kicker in 1970, missed two field goal attempts from just twenty-four yards out during the game, while Oakland's George Blanda misfired from the twenty-three. "The officials put in a new dry ball on every play," said Bob Griese, "but it was always wet by the time I got it."[31] Griese hit only thirteen of twenty-seven passes, but his 16-yarder to Paul Warfield in the second quarter gave Miami a 7–0 lead.

The lead further fanned the Dolphins' emotional flames, but they were quickly snuffed out by the big-play Raiders, a team accustomed to playoff pressure, having played in a Super Bowl just three seasons before. Daryle Lamonica quickly hit Fred Biletnikoff with a 22-yard scoring pass, and then in the third quarter, Willie Brown intercepted Griese and ran it back for a 50-yard touchdown.[32] "I had no idea I could go all the way," Brown said. "I just dropped back in my zone and saw the ball coming directly at me. I figured I'd hug the sidelines and try to scoot it in."[33] When Griese slipped throwing the ball, "Willie had nothing to do but run it in," said Shula.[34]

Clinging to a 14–7 lead in the fourth quarter, Oakland finally finished the Dolphins with an 82-yard strike from Lamonica to Rod Sherman. "My job was to take my man deep as quickly as possible to open up the zone," said Sherman of the play that clinched the game. "I was surprised to see the ball coming my way, but it was so perfectly thrown it was easy to take since I had my man beaten."[35] Griese added a late touchdown to Willie Richardson, but Oakland held on, 21–14.

Lamonica had a solid game, hitting eight of sixteen passes and the two touchdowns, but in some ways the Raiders played as sloppy as the field conditions. They fumbled four times leading to two Miami recoveries, one of which the Dolphins converted into an easy touchdown, and a defensive holding penalty kept alive a Miami drive that led to another score. "We've got to cut our turnovers down to nothing if we're going to beat Baltimore next Sunday," said guard Gene Upshaw. "The Colts don't make mistakes and, if we do, we'll be out of it."[36]

Still, the Raiders had accomplished their main objective of the weekend—survive and advance. They would have to play in Baltimore for the AFC Championship, but that was nothing new for an experienced team. They had turned back the emotion of the young Dolphins and now, another step closer to the Super Bowl, were able to feel a little emotion themselves. "There were eight teams and now there are four," said Hubbard. "The lower the number gets the more emotional we get."[37]

CHAMPIONSHIP SUNDAY: OAKLAND AT BALTIMORE

"This will be like the American Football League versus the National Football League," said Oakland coach John Madden of the AFC Championship matching the Raiders and Colts.[38] Baltimore would be at home and its 12-2-1 record was the best of the four teams left in the NFL playoffs. Oakland would bring a much more pedestrian 9-4-2 record into the game, but the Raiders were not about to accept the role of underdog.

Befitting a team run by Al Davis, the Raiders expressed a confidence that bordered on arrogance. "When Unitas looks across the line of scrimmage Sunday," said cornerback Willie Brown, "he's going to see the best defense in football, no matter what anyone says. For a long time we weren't playing as a unit. Now we are."[39] So confident was Oakland that it planned to ship all its gear directly from Baltimore to Miami, the site of the Super Bowl. "[Defensive back] George Atkinson told me, 'Yeah, we're going to go right from here to Miami,'" said Colts defensive tackle Bubba Smith. "I said, 'What? You guys going to the game? You got tickets? Because we're going to beat the hell out of you.'"[40] Davis was just as combative. "So those are the Colts," he said as the teams took the field. "I hate the Colts. Just getting this far isn't enough. We've got to beat them."[41]

Two days before kickoff, emergency crews had to clear five inches of snow from Memorial Stadium, leaving only bare field and swirling dust. The Colts had long ago become accustomed to their "Dirt Bowl," as coach Don McCafferty called it, simply painting the end zones and logos at midfield.[42] The stadium was technically multi-purpose, and the Colts shared the facility with the Orioles, who just a few months earlier had won the World Series. The Orioles had torn up the field after the long season, and even though the Colts tried to re-sod, it never really took. Colts' players looked at it as just another home-field advantage.[43]

The game was billed as a quarterback duel between Unitas and Lamonica, but the Oakland quarterback left in the second quarter after a hit from Bubba Smith and sat out the rest of the game with a groin injury. In came the forty-three-year-old Blanda to battle the thirty-seven-year-old Unitas, which made the matchup seem more appropriate for an Old-Timers' game than the AFC Championship. The only touchdown of the first half came after Atkinson, perhaps thinking of his upcoming trip to Miami, muffed a punt. A Unitas pass to Hinton set up a short Bulaich touchdown, and Baltimore led at halftime, 10–3.

In the second half, Blanda began to find himself and conjure up images of his miraculous November. He led the Raiders on a nine-play, 80-yard drive, which he finished with a 38-yard touchdown pass to Biletnikoff. Suddenly, the game was tied at ten, and the Colts were wondering if Blanda was going to add another chapter to his storybook season. "We were just waiting for the Cinderella finish," said tight end John Mackey. "The Cinderella man was in there and his tricks were working."[44]

Blanda would finish the day seventeen of thirty-two for 271 yards, and he threw a second touchdown pass to Warren Wells in the fourth quarter, but there would be no miracles this day. Unitas had a much poorer statistical day, connecting on only eleven of thirty passes, but he hit the one that counted—a 68-yard touchdown pass to Ray Perkins in the fourth quarter with Baltimore clinging to a 20–17 lead. "It was bump-and-run," said Perkins, "and [defensive back Nemiah] Wilson expected me to make a sharp outside cut for the first down. Instead, I kept going."[45] Unitas dropped the third and 11 pass right in Perkins' hands for the touchdown that gave the Colts a 27–17 lead and put away the game. "It was this week's special play," said McCafferty, who admitted that it was an uneasy win.[46] "The only breath I took was with 29 seconds left."[47]

The unusually emotional Colts carried their rookie coach off the field in celebrating their return to the Super Bowl. It was not just a chance to win a championship; it was a chance at redemption. In essence, they were returning to the scene of the crime with an opportunity to rewrite the ending. "Intensity," center Bill Curry said of the difference between the Colt teams of 1968 and 1970. "Maybe even a tangible sense of unity. I could feel it in the locker room, on the sidelines, even in the hotel room last night."[48] Linebacker Mike Curtis said, "Our '68 team executed far better than this one. But we might have learned something from the trip to Miami that year. Maybe we won't relax as much as we did then."[49]

CHAMPIONSHIP SUNDAY: DALLAS AT SAN FRANCISCO

While the Colts sought to erase the memories of a single Super Bowl afternoon, the Cowboys took the field in San Francisco for the NFC Championship trying to overcome four years of playoff failures. There was a growing belief, especially after their uninspired win over the Lions, that next year still had not arrived for "Next Year's Champions."

"Week in and week out, the Dallas Cowboys may be the best team in professional football," wrote Tex Maule in *Sports Illustrated*. "But in the big-money games, the Dallas Cowboys are the best team at coming up with fascinating ways to lose. Or, as many fans contend, they choke."[50] Another writer noted that the Cowboys "have discovered more ways to fold than a piece of origami."[51]

San Francisco brought its own ghosts into the game, never having won a playoff game in its history until the week before. This was all new to the 49ers—the big-game atmosphere and the pressure of playing for the Super Bowl. Dallas had a clear edge in experience, but not necessarily confidence. "We're going all the way," said 49ers running back Ken Willard the week of the game. "Dallas is a fine team, but we will go to the Super Bowl."[52] His coach, Dick Nolan, was more reserved, but admitted that the 49ers wouldn't "embarrass ourselves. This is what we've been shooting for all year."[53]

Nolan had played with Landry on the Giants, and then coached under him for six seasons before leaving to become the 49ers head coach in 1968. He brought to San Francisco many of Landry's strategies, and led by Brodie, the 49ers finished first in the league in scoring, passing offense, and total offense. But San Francisco had finished a modest fourteenth in defense, while Dallas had become the best defensive unit in the league. "Defense controls the playoffs," said Landry, "and we've played the best defense we ever have."[54]

One factor working in San Francisco's favor was a home-field advantage at Kezar Stadium, where the 49ers had played since 1946 in the days of the old All-America Football Conference. Much like some of the wine of nearby Napa Valley, Kezar was an acquired taste; locals either loved it or hated it, and sometimes both. Situated just blocks from the bay, the stadium was tiny, cramped, and fertile ground for stray sea gulls. "About four o'clock, here'd come the sea gulls," said Art Donovan, the Hall of Fame defensive tackle who played for the Colts in the 1950s. "They'd start shitting on you like they were aiming. The final indignity was that the sea gulls seemed to be trained only to bombard the visiting team. I found out later the 49ers always took the sunny side of the field, and the sea gulls always felt more comfortable shitting in the shade. I'll never forget the look of dread visiting teams wore going in to play San Francisco."[55]

Because Kezar also hosted high school and college games, the field was often a muddy mess, and the grounds crew would cover it with black cinders. Donovan and other visiting players called it "a disgrace," but the 49ers loved it, and they won six and tied one in their seven home games in 1970.[56] "I always loved playing at Kezar, with the mud and the seagulls and the intimate setting," said Gene Washington. "We had a real home-field advantage there."[57] That home-field advantage would be tested for the final time against Dallas; with the 49ers moving into Candlestick Park the following season, the NFC Championship game would be Kezar's last NFL game. "It is a wreck, a shambles and an embarrassment," wrote Wells Twombly. "Yet, there is warmth to the joint that pretty nearly defies description. It is a beautifully eccentric way of life."[58]

Kezar went out with somewhat atypical San Francisco weather—sunny and forty-six degrees with almost no wind. Both teams played tentatively in the first half, which ended 3–3. "Neither team played very well in the first half," admitted Landry. "We went into the half pretty down. The players were mumbling because they thought they played terrible."[59] But the low score was an indication that the Dallas defense was getting the upper hand on San Francisco's powerful offense. The Cowboys' defenders would make the two biggest plays of the second half. First, linebacker Lee Roy Jordan intercepted a pass deep in 49ers territory, a pass Brodie was simply trying to throw away. "I'm sure if John had seen me in the zone he wouldn't have thrown," said Jordan. "He had to hurry to throw and it was short and low and I caught it right off the ground."[60]

"I was trying to dump the ball," said Brodie. "Their guy made a helluva play."[61] On the very next play, Duane Thomas ran 13 yards for a touchdown that gave Dallas a 10–3 lead. Thomas continued his stellar rookie season, finishing the day with 143 yards on twenty-seven carries. With Morton's continuing problems at quarterback, Thomas and the running game carried the Dallas offense almost entirely by themselves, accounting for 229 of the Cowboys' 319 yards of total offense.

The second big play came after the Thomas touchdown. Brodie went for broke, sending a long pass to Washington, but he was intercepted by Mel Renfro, who returned the ball to the Dallas 38. The Cowboys got a big break on a pass interference call on Mel Phillips against Bob Hayes, which put the ball on the 5-yard line. From there, Morton finished the drive with a touchdown pass to Walt Garrison—one of only seven passes Morton completed on the day in twenty-two attempts as the Dallas passing game managed only 90 yards.

The 49ers finally scored a touchdown late in the third quarter on a pass from Brodie to Witcher. It was the first touchdown allowed by the Dallas defense in twenty-three quarters, and it cut the lead to 17–10. But San Francisco never threatened again, and when Dallas broke up a fourth-down pass to Ken Willard with two minutes to play the 49ers' season came to an end. "The farther you go the farther you want to go," said a disappointed Nolan. "We really worked well as a group. But we just didn't have enough experience to get over the hill. We'll be back again. We have a young team."[62]

For the Cowboys, it was the biggest win in the ten-year history of the franchise, and a victory that, at least temporarily, quieted the critics who said the team could not win the big one. "You can't imagine how we feel about beating the 49ers," said Landry. "This was by far our greatest win. You can't imagine how much we've suffered the last four years."[63] Said Morton of his poor passing performance, "As long as we win it doesn't make any difference if I'm one of 100 or 15 of 16. A lot of guys were jittery out there."[64]

There figured to be quite a bit of frayed nerves for Super Bowl V in Miami against the Colts. The previous two seasons, the Cowboys had played in Miami in the Playoff Bowl, the now-defunct game matching the losers from first-round playoff games. "Everybody called it the Nothing Bowl and the Losers' Bowl," said Hayes. "I guess it was. I used to enjoy that game, though, because it was kind of like a vacation. But this one will be better."[65]

★ 17 ★

SUPER BOWL V

"If the Super Bowl is the ultimate, they wouldn't play it again next year."[1]
—**Duane Thomas, Dallas running back at Super Bowl V press day**

MAN-FOR-MAN STANDOFF

The Super Bowl had experienced some growing pains in its four-year history. The first game in 1967 between the Chiefs and Packers had failed to sell out, the first two games had been NFL blowouts, and Super Bowl IV had been plagued by gambling rumors and terrible weather in New Orleans. But despite all that, the game had become one of the preeminent events in American sports, and in five short years had grown from curiosity to bona fide spectacle.

"The event lacks tradition," sportscaster Howard Cosell wrote at the time, "yet it ranks with a heavyweight championship fight and the World Series as one of the three super events in American sport."[2] Super Bowl V sold out several weeks in advance, and the game seemed prepared to take yet another step in becoming the dominant event in American sports culture. "We could have sold 100,000 tickets for this game if we had the room," noted NFL public relations director Don Weiss.[3] The tickets sold at face value for fifteen dollars, but scalpers were demanding, and getting, much more.

Yet, as the Colts and Cowboys prepared for the game in Miami, there were some disturbing signs, most notably the lack of the old NFL-AFL rivalry. Realignment had put the Colts in the AFC, and they did not carry the banner of an upstart league that the Jets had in Super Bowl III or the Chiefs had in Super Bowl IV. "Sorta takes a little zing out of the game for old AFL fans, noted sports columnist Dick Young."[4] The Colts especially sensed it and came to Miami feeling unloved and unappreciated. "We came into a new league this season and nobody wanted to see us win the championship," said the center Bill Curry. "And they still don't."[5] Unitas was just as blunt, saying, "My only allegiance is to Baltimore."[6] The two teams had played just the season before, with the Cowboys beating the Colts in Dallas, 27–10. Sportswriter Leonard Koppett didn't even want to call the game the Super Bowl anymore. "The game between Baltimore and Dallas in Miami," he wrote, "[is] the NFL championship game, and nothing else."[7]

Without an NFL-AFL rivalry, the matchup suffered from lack of a compelling storyline. Super Bowl I was defined by novelty, Super Bowl II by Lombardi's impending retirement, Super Bowl III by Namath's brash prediction, and Super Bowl IV by the end of the AFL. On the surface, Super Bowl V had nothing to commend itself, especially since the two teams were significantly lacking in star power, aside from Unitas. The *New York Times* noted, "The matchup inspires less curiosity than any of the four prior Super Bowls."[8]

There was also a nagging sense that these were not so much championship-caliber teams as they were the best of a mediocre lot. Baltimore sportswriter Sam Lacy observed, "In no fewer than half of their games during the regular season the Colts were disturbingly unimpressive. The team was flat, the fans were disgruntled, and the town itself was in no mood for football."[9] The Cowboys were similarly viewed with skepticism, especially in light of their 5-4 start and the pitiful November loss to the Cardinals. "They became winners only when faced with the prospect of humiliation," wrote Marty Ralbovsky. "That they did succeed indicated a great deal of pluckiness, but there remained something suspect about this team."[10]

The Colts had the additional burden of returning to Miami, where just two seasons before they had suffered a Super Bowl upset at the hands of the Jets. Baltimore had somewhat atoned for that by beating New York twice during the regular season, but the stigma had not completely gone away. "That was the biggest game of my life," said Colts quarterback Earl Morrall, who threw three interceptions against the Jets. "I've tried to shrug it off, but

I just can't. I keep thinking about it and I still get flashbacks. Now that I'm back in the Super Bowl, I'll be returning to the scene of the crime. I guess there is no way I can escape it."[11] Morrall's wife Jane said, "I think the Lord put this extra burden on Earl to test him to see if he was strong enough to handle the disappointment as well as the success. And I believe that he has more than proved himself."[12]

Unitas also came in for some criticism after his spotty play in the AFC Championship. "The quarterbacks who got here didn't burn up any worlds," wrote Dave Eisenberg in *The Sporting News*. "Johnny Unitas was more like an elderly gent engaging in a Married Men vs. the Single Men game when Baltimore beat Oakland."[13] Meanwhile, Dallas quarterback Craig Morton had lost so much confidence that during the season he began seeing a hypnotist. Morton said that the sessions may have helped his several injuries, but also admitted, "It is supposed to work on the subconscious and that's unmeasurable [*sic*]."[14] Morton also suffered the indignity of having his plays called from the sideline by Tom Landry, a rarity in an age when most quarterbacks ran their own huddle. Landry said he made the move to take pressure off Morton, and shuttled his tight ends to bring in the plays. "No quarterback likes to have plays called from the sideline," said Dallas running back Dan Reeves, "but Craig was man enough—mature enough—to accept the help. If we hadn't been successful, I'm sure he would have rebelled. But it worked."[15]

That Landry took the play-calling away from Morton said as much about the coach as it did about the quarterback. The general view of Landry was that while brilliant, he was too controlling and too detached to motivate his team in a big game. The *Dallas Times-Herald* ran a cartoon consisting of eleven panels depicting Landry putting on his "game face." The joke was that all eleven panels were exactly the same, and in the last panel Landry says, "Want to see me do it again?"[16] At a Tuesday press conference during Super Bowl week, Detroit sportswriter Joe Falls observed, "I am fascinated because he almost smiles twice. He doesn't quite make it, but I can see he is trying. I kind of hope he wins on Sunday."[17]

Colts coach Don McCafferty was seen as Landry's antithesis—kindly, smiling, outgoing—but that was not universally considered a good thing. *Time* magazine wrote, "The Colts are a plodding and unspectacular team, which reflects, in part, the unobtrusive personality of their first-year head coach."[18] *Time's* preview of the game focused on what Super Bowl V represented to many football fans: a game not to determine a deserving champion but rather a desperate fight to avoid further humiliation. "Both teams will be [more] concerned with banishing their reputations as losers," the article observed. "Come Sunday, the Pride Bowl will decide which team will suffer some more through a long, hard winter."[19]

Time did not venture to pick a winner, but the combination of Landry's persona, Morton's problems, and the Cowboys' repeated failures in the big game made the Colts a slight favorite among the nation's media. Falls may have secretly wanted Landry to win, but in print he picked Baltimore, 33–13, reasoning, "Johnny Unitas is going to get it rolling early and he's going to take the Cowboys apart."[20] Sam Lacy of the *Baltimore Afro-American* also picked the Colts to win big, writing, "The Colts will whip the Dallas Cowboys Sunday in the Super Bowl. Baltimore will win in a rout at Miami."[21] *The Sporting News* called the game a man-for-man standoff, which was more in line with official odds makers, who either listed the game as dead-even or gave Dallas a slim one-point advantage. The prospect of a tight game should have thrilled NFL executives, considering the closest of the previous four Super Bowls had been the Jets' nine-point win over the Colts. "But [that] silver lining could not diminish the prospect of these two less-than-spectacular teams plowing through the trenches in a dull, unexciting game," countered Ralbovsky. "The bland leading the bland."[22]

TURF BATTLE

At the time of Super Bowl V, the event was just starting to come into its own as an American sports spectacular. The NFL had put two weeks between the Super Bowl and the conference championship games in order to build interest and publicity, and the nation's sports media descended on sunny Miami in droves. [23] But it was not the 24/7 sports media that predominates today, and many of the sportswriters went down to Miami for the week mainly to soak up some sunshine. "The conditions suddenly grow abominable on Miami Beach," wrote Falls in his Super Bowl diary. "The temperature drops from 82 to 81 and the sun doesn't come out until 9:30 in the morning, which leaves only 7 ½ hours for sunbathing."[24] Lowell Reidenbaugh wrote, "A cruise to Nassau, a trip to the golf course or an interview with [boxer] Floyd

Patterson, who was to fight a local bellhop in yet another comeback attempt, held over-riding allure for many scribes."[25]

NBC handled the television broadcast of the game, and for the fifth straight year a record audience tuned in. According to Nielsen Media, forty-six million viewers watched the game in twenty-three million homes, good for a solid 39.9 rating. The game also attracted a share of 75, which means that 75% of all television sets turned on that Sunday afternoon were tuned to the game.[26]

Even so, the people of Miami would not be able to see the game without a ticket. NFL blackout policies at the time prohibited showing the game live within a seventy-five-mile radius. A local lawyer named Ellis Rubin sued to have the blackout lifted, but three days before the game a circuit court refused to issue an injunction, saying it had no authority in the matter. The blackout policy was a continuing thorn in the side of the NFL, especially because teams and fans often found a way around it. For the 49ers-Vikings playoff game, hotels in the Twin Cities used equipment to pick up a signal from an Iowa television station broadcasting the game, and the piracy undoubtedly contributed to nineteen hundred unsold tickets. Some five thousand fans in Baltimore skipped the Colts-Bengals playoff game because they could pick up the game broadcast on a Washington, D.C. station. "We are going to take a hard look at our broadcast patterns," said Jim Kensil of the NFL. "We may not permit as much signal penetration as in the past."[27]

The frustration of south Floridians in not being able to watch the game on television was symptomatic of the general level of local excitement. The Greater Miami Chamber of Commerce estimated that the game would bring forty thousand to fifty thousand people to the area, and it figured that each visitor would spend on average around one hundred dollars per day. "The Super Bowl visitors are the biggest spenders of all," said Chamber executive vice president Lester Freeman, who scoffed at estimates by the Florida Commerce Department that visitors would spend only twenty-five dollars per day. "That's very low," he added. "Why, they'll spill $25 per day."[28] The most conservative estimates suggested the cash inflow to Miami would be in the $35 million range.[29]

Restaurants and hotels figured to pick up most of that money, and they began preparing months ahead of time. "The Super Bowl is the biggest football game of the year to the fan and the sports concessionaire," said Gerry

Ward, director of marketing for Restaurant Associates Industries. "We used more than 1,000 employees. Most were from Miami, but we also flew in some of our top people from New York, Detroit and Chicago."[30] By the time the game ended, Ward figured the Orange Bowl crowd had eaten sixty-five thousand hot dogs and twenty thousand bags of peanuts, and drank one hundred and forty thousand sodas. That represented a 25 percent increase over the last time Miami hosted the Super Bowl two years earlier.

Orange Bowl Stadium itself had been upgraded for the event, with an additional 4,500 seats added for the game. The new seats had already helped the stadium set an attendance record of 80,699 when Nebraska and LSU played in the Orange Bowl on New Year's night. Super Bowl V would also introduce two other innovations that have since become league standards: it would be the first Super Bowl played on artificial surface, and the NFL would put nets behind the goal posts to keep kicks from bouncing into the stands. The switch to artificial turf would prove more significant.

In 1970 artificial surface was considered the wave of the future, and seven of the league's twenty-six teams were already using it in their home stadiums. By 1985, that number had grown to sixteen of twenty-eight teams. The original artificial surface, called AstroTurf, was developed by Monsanto for the Astrodome in 1966. The Astrodome originally had real grass and skylights, but baseball outfielders found that the translucent lights made it virtually impossible to follow fly balls. Painting over the lights killed the grass, so the solution was the world's first artificial playing surface.

At first, the new surface was hailed as a breakthrough. It was easier to maintain, made playing conditions more uniform, and eliminated the problems associated with playing in mud. The surface at the Orange Bowl was called Poly-Turf, and it consisted of a carpet of finely woven green fibers laid over padding and asphalt. The Poly-Turf was installed by American Biltrite, whose executives crowed, "The Orange Bowl is our showcase. We'll put in a new field every year if we have to."[31] According to *The Sporting News*, "The new Orange Bowl playing surface, installed last summer, has drawn few complaints, from home or visiting teams."[32] NFL Commissioner Pete Rozelle predicted, "In five to 10 years, we'll have artificial turf on all of our fields."[33]

But almost everyone underestimated the hot Miami sun, which cooked the artificial field like an electric skillet, and field temperatures sometimes reached 120 degrees. Kermit Alexander of the Rams called the artificial turf an "oven," so when he played on it he wrapped his feet in tinfoil. Then there were the injuries. Medical experts across the country weighed in—Dr. Joseph Torg, an orthopedic surgeon and football team doctor in Philadelphia, recommended a moratorium on the turf, while orthopedist Dr. William Smith talked about a 50–60 percent increase in injuries. "Every time we play on it we seem to get somebody hurt," said Lions coach Joe Schmidt.[34] A Congressional subcommittee began investigating and the NFL Players Association withdrew its endorsement of Poly-Turf.[35]

Miami quickly fell out of love with its new surface. The Florida sun baked the Poly-Turf, causing it to lose traction and turn blue in places. When workers painted the field for special games, such as Super Bowl V, it took months to get the paint off. Exasperated, the city of Miami, which owned the Orange Bowl, stopped payments on the turf the following season. By 1977, the city gave up and put natural grass (Prescription Athletic Turf) back in the Orange Bowl, where it remained until the stadium was demolished in 2008.

The bloom eventually came off the rose for Poly-Turf and its synthetic cousins such as AstroTurf and Tartan Turf. By 2013, almost every team in the NFL had moved back to natural grass or switched to a new product called FieldTurf, which reportedly is much safer, softer, and easier to maintain. But in some cases, the more things change the more they stay the same. A study by the NFL's Injury and Safety Panel found that between 2002 and 2008, knee injuries were 88 percent higher on FieldTurf compared to natural grass. "We challenge the manufacturers to use this data to improve these surfaces," said Dr. Elliott Hershman, chair of the panel.[36]

Cowboys' quarterback Craig Morton blamed his infected elbow on an AstroTurf rug burn, and Dolphins' safety Jake Scott complained, "It's easier to get new players than it is to tear out artificial turf and maintain a regular field. I've never had a sprained ankle in my life, but this year I've already had two on that awful rug."[37]

THE GAME

Both teams came into the game relatively healthy. Walt Garrison was still healing from a variety of injuries, including a chipped collarbone, and although not at 100 percent he would play the entire game. Morton recovered from his laryngitis during the off-week, but his shoulder still caused him difficulty while throwing. The Colts reported no significant injuries on either side of the ball.

Perhaps having learned its lesson from the previous year, the NFL kept the pregame ceremonies simple and low-key, at least by Super Bowl standards. The year before in New Orleans, a pregame hot air balloon launch almost ended in disaster when the balloon had trouble getting off the ground and crashed into the stands. Luckily no one was hurt, but the league didn't take any chances this time around. The only sour note of the festivities was hit on the national anthem when the four Air Force jets sent for a flyover arrived two minutes after the song ended. Otherwise, the NFL could not have asked for better conditions, and the game kicked off under perfect, sunny skies at 1:50 p.m. (EST). The weather would be the only perfect thing about the game that followed.

From the very outset, defense dominated Super Bowl V. The Cowboys took the kickoff, ran three plays, and kicked to the Colts, who also ran three plays and punted it back. After another Dallas three-and-out, it looked like the game would turn into the plodding affair so many had predicted, but at that point predictability went right out the window. Unitas was intercepted by linebacker Chuck Howley, who had clear sailing to a touchdown, but somehow allowed Unitas to make the tackle. The Colts' defense forced another punt, but this time the kick was fumbled by Ron Gardin inside the 10-yard line. "There was nowhere to hide," Gardin said after the game. "All I could think of was what my mother would think. She doesn't know that much about football, but she would know I had done something stupid."[38]

With a first and goal, Dallas still couldn't move—Morton overthrew a wide open Reggie Rucker in the end zone—and Mike Clark was forced to kick a short field goal for a 3–0 lead. The Colts responded with yet another three-and-out, and this time the Cowboys finally made some headway. Morton would have another miserable day passing, although he connected on a long pass to Hayes, who caught the ball while sandwiched in between Charlie Stukes and Jerry Logan. The 41-yard gain was helped by a roughing the passer penalty, and suddenly the Cowboys had the ball on the Colts' 6-yard line as the first quarter ended. Unfortunately, visions of past playoff failures began to surface as the Cowboys moved closer to the end zone. To avoid a sack, Morton tried to throw away the ball, but was penalized for intentional grounding. The 15-yard penalty killed the drive, which Clark rescued with another field goal for a 6–0 lead.[39]

Up to this point, the Colts had done nothing offensively, having run seven plays for a grand total of 12 yards and an interception. Unitas immediately threw two more incompletions, which set up the most controversial play of Super Bowl V. On third down, Unitas overthrew Eddie Hinton, who managed to get a hand on the ball and deflect it. At this point, the ball was either touched or not touched by Mel Renfro, before settling into the arms of John Mackey, who took it the rest of the way for a 75-yard touchdown. At the time, NFL rules stated that a ball could not be batted or deflected from one offensive player to another without a defensive player touching it in between, and the Cowboys argued violently that Renfro never touched the ball. But the officiating crew, led by veteran referee Norm Schachter, disagreed and the score stood. Replays from several different angles suggest that the ball's flight and rotation changed slightly in between Hinton and Mackey. "I had no sensation of touching the ball," said Renfro. "I never said I didn't touch it. I may have."[40] The ball also may have touched safety Charlie Waters, who just missed knocking it away from Mackey.

In came Jim O'Brien to attempt the usually automatic extra point. NFL kickers had missed only 21 of 722 extra points during the regular season, which translates to a 97 percent success rate, but O'Brien had accounted for two of those misses and he again failed to connect. Mark Washington cleanly blocked O'Brien's kick, leaving the score tied, 6–6. "When I kick a football I like to take a divot, and on artificial turf you can't get one," said the Colts' straight-ahead kicker. "Your foot kind of gets jammed up. It doesn't feel right as you kick."[41]

The game seemed destined to stay tied for some time, as the next three possessions ended in three-and-outs. Just when the Colts were ready to make it four, a scrambling Unitas fumbled after a hit from Lee Roy Jordan, and Jethro Pugh recovered on the Baltimore 28. From there, Dallas had its most successful offensive series of the day, with Morton throwing to Dan Reeves and then Duane Thomas for a 7-yard touchdown. Clark's extra point gave Dallas a 13–6 lead with 7:53 left in the second quarter.

Aside from the fluke touchdown pass to Mackey, it had been a forgettable day for Unitas, and it would soon get worse. On the Colts' next possession, Unitas threw deep for Hinton, but was intercepted by Renfro. On the play, George Andrie had slammed into Unitas, sending him to the sidelines for the rest of the day with badly bruised ribs. There would be no Unitas magic in the Super Bowl—take away the touchdown to Mackey, and he finished just two of eight passing for 13 yards, with two interceptions and a fumble. "It felt bad, but I thought I could play," said Unitas, who also admitted that he had come into the game suffering from headaches since the playoff game with Cincinnati. "Thank God we've got six months to rest."[42]

After another Dallas punt, into the game for Unitas came Earl Morrall, who immediately sensed the rare opportunity he had been given for Super Bowl redemption. Morrall's first pass was a 26-yard completion to Hinton, and he followed that up with a 21-yarder to Roy Jefferson. All of a sudden, the Colts were inside the Dallas 5-yard line with less than a minute to play in the first half. But three straight runs by Norm Bulaich got nothing, bringing up fourth-and-goal from the 2 with twenty seconds left. Perhaps thinking of O'Brien's kicking difficulties, McCafferty rolled the dice and came up snake eyes. On fourth down, Morrall overthrew Tom Mitchell in the end zone and the half ended with Dallas leading, 13–6.

"If their players had a bad day, the coaches made it unanimous," wrote Bob Oates. "Even if completed, the pass [to Mitchell] would have been a bad call, an unnecessary gamble. It was set up by three other bad calls—three line bucks into the heart of the Doomsday Defense."[43] Said McCafferty, "If we had lost, it would have been the worst call I made this year. But someone had to make the decision."[44]

Just thirty minutes from exorcising their championship demons, the Cowboys got another huge break on the second half kickoff. Jim Duncan fumbled the return—the Colts' fifth turnover of the day—and Dallas recovered at the 31. The Cowboys swiftly moved to the 2, and seemed poised to put away the game, but as Thomas was preparing to cross the goal line, he fumbled. Replays clearly showed Dallas center Dave Manders recovering the ball and handing it back to an official, but Colts defensive end Billy Ray Smith began yelling, "Our ball, our ball," and line judge Jack Fette awarded the ball to the Colts.

"I know Manders recovered it," said Dallas lineman John Niland. "I was right there on the ground next to him. There was no way it should have been Baltimore's ball."[45] Said Bubba Smith, "We ought to give a game ball to Billy

Ray. He conned that official right out of the Super Bowl."[46] A touchdown at that point would have made it 20–6, an almost insurmountable lead considering how the Dallas defense was playing. "That was the turning point," said Landry. "If we'd scored there the ball would have to bounce around three or four times for them to get that many points."[47]

The rest of the third quarter passed uneventfully. Morrall led Baltimore on a good drive that ended when O'Brien missed another kick, this one from 52 yards. A 45-yard Morrall completion to Tom Nowatzke got the Colts down to the Dallas 12-yard line as the quarter ended. Once again, the Cowboys' defense made a saving play in the shadow of its own goal line—on the first play of the fourth quarter Howley made his second interception of the day, stealing the ball from Bulaich in the end zone.

Baltimore quickly got the ball back and returned to the Dallas 30, setting up the strangest play of a strange Super Bowl. Morrall lateraled to Sam Havrilak, who was supposed to throw back to Morrall on a flea-flicker. But when Pugh intervened, Havrilak decided to throw to Mackey. Hinton stepped in front of Mackey, caught the pass, and seemed headed for the end zone, but he was stripped from behind by Cornell Green at the 10-yard line and the ball started bouncing toward the goal line. "I could see the end zone in front of me when someone knocked the ball out of my hands from behind," said Hinton. "I tried to get to it, but someone else tackled me and I couldn't reach it."[48] Several Colts and Cowboys took turns trying to recover the loose ball, which eventually bounced out of the back of the end zone for a touchback and the Colts' seventh turnover of the afternoon.

At this point, the Cowboys had the ball and the lead with eight minutes to play, and considering their offensive futility for most of the game, simply trying to run down the clock might have been a wise decision. But Landry and Morton decided to throw, and a third down pass to Walt Garrison sailed high, bouncing off his hands into the arms of Rick Volk. Volk returned the pass all the way to the Dallas 3-yard line, and this time there was no heroic stop. It took two tries, but Nowatzke bulled in and the game was tied at 13.

The teams traded punts, after which Dallas got the ball back at the Baltimore 48 with 1:52 to play. A first down or two would put the Cowboys in field goal position and give them a chance to erase fifty-eight minutes of Super Bowl sloppiness, not to mention years of frustration, with a dramatic win. Instead, Dallas went backward: Thomas lost a yard, and then Morton lost nine more on a sack, which, combined with a holding call, pushed the ball back to the Dallas 28. Morton attempted a relatively safe pass to Reeves, but the high throw bounced off his hands and into the arms of linebacker Mike Curtis, who returned to the 27. It was the Cowboys' final—and fatal—mistake of the afternoon. "You might be inclined to pack it in and hope for sudden death overtime at this point," sportswriter Jim Murray said of the play, "but Morton went to the ricochet pass. I didn't see the hand that pushed it toward Mike Curtis, but I know it was there."[49]

Now the Colts had the ball in field goal range and they were content to let O'Brien try to win it. Bulaich ran into the line twice for three yards, as the clock ran down to nine seconds. Jim O'Brien, the rookie kicker who had already missed one field goal and had an extra point blocked, would now attempt to make the first game-winning kick in Super Bowl history. "The day before the game we were practicing and he was having trouble kicking on the turf," said Colts public relations director Ernie Accorsi. "He said, 'I hope they're not counting on me tomorrow.' Well, who else are we going to count on?"[50]

Yet, O'Brien did not appear nervous. "I asked him if he wanted a full time out to compose himself," said teammate Dan Sullivan. "He said, 'Get up to the line of scrimmage and get this —— thing over with.'"[51] O'Brien recalled "the Cowboys didn't help matters by calling a timeout to increase the pressure. They hollered at me, 'You're not going to miss this, are you kid?' But I was accustomed to such things because in practice Billy Ray Smith does the same sort of things to help improve my concentration. He screamed louder than the Cowboys did."[52]

Late in the year, the Colts had acquired veteran snapper Tom Goode for just such an occasion. In his only appearance of the season and the last of his career, Goode's snap was perfect and so was the 32-yard kick that broke the tie with five seconds to play. "When I looked up there it was a little to the right," said O'Brien. "It was the most beautiful picture I ever saw. I had this dream about a week ago. It was about a long field goal winning the game. The only thing was the dream didn't identify the kicker, so it could have been me or Mike Clark." But O'Brien's mother assured him that he couldn't lose. "She's big on astrology and she figured it all out. I was born on February 2,

1947. This is the Age of Aquarius, isn't it? I'm an Aquarius."[53] The Cowboys still had one final play, but from his own 40 Morton threw yet another interception, this time to Logan, and Baltimore had won, 16–13.

THE POST-MORTON

In the immediate aftermath of Super Bowl V, Morton was considered the chief contributor to the Cowboys' failures. He finished the day twelve of twenty-six for 127 yards, with one touchdown and three interceptions, and completed only one pass to a wide receiver the entire game. There are some who suggest that any kind of competent quarterbacking would have tipped the game in Dallas's favor. "Against Baltimore, all we had to do was have a halfway good passing game," said backup quarterback Roger Staubach, who did not play in the game.[54] "If I ran the Cowboys I would call Boston while the Colts are still celebrating and better anyone's offer for [Stanford quarterback Jim] Plunkett," wrote Larry Felser. "It's impossible to overcome Dallas' death wish and the absence of a quarterback, too."[55]

The Dallas defense played well, as did Howley, who was named the game's Most Valuable Player for his two interceptions.[56] But Howley and the other Cowboys were inconsolable after losing "the Big One" yet again. Immediately after O'Brien's kick, defensive tackle Bob Lilly threw his helmet 30 yards in disgust.[57] "To lose like we did," he said, "was the lowest point of my career. The Ice Bowl, the Cleveland games, they were bad. But the Baltimore game was the worst I ever felt."[58]

"What can you say?" said Landry after the game. "It was all there and we lost it."[59] Had the Cowboys played a great game and lost, the feeling might have been different. But there was no escaping the fact that on the game's biggest stage they had slipped on the banana peel one more time. "We tried to give them the game every way possible," said Nowatzke, "but they just wouldn't take it."[60]

Thus, the unwanted title of "Next Year's Champions" would stick with the Cowboys for at least one more season. If anything, Super Bowl V only further convinced sportswriters that either Dallas simply did not have what it took to win a championship game or that the fates were not going to allow it. "Dallas has found the black cat once again," wrote Murray, "the dark lining in the silver cloud. The pot at the end of the rainbow doesn't have gold in it."[61] Cowboys' beat writer Bob St. John observed, "So the Big String Puller, who frowned on the Cowboys twice in title games with Green Bay, did it again at the end of this one, the biggest one. Now the Cowboys, who had their hands on everything, feel as if they have nothing."[62]

For their part, the Colts were feeling more relief than jubilation. Yes, they had won the Super Bowl, but their play had hardly been of championship caliber. The Colts managed just 69 yards on the ground in thirty-one carries and turned the ball over seven times. "Hell," said veteran receiver Jimmy Orr, who retired after the game, "we've been that bad all year and winning."[63] Morrall finished seven of fifteen for 147 yards and somewhat atoned for his Super Bowl III defeat. "You'd like to dream Walter Mitty dreams," he said. "You'd like to be Frank Merriwell and come off the bench and throw the winning touchdown pass. But really, I wasn't dreaming about it. I wasn't thinking about two years ago. I studied all week and tried to be ready. That was all."[64]

The public reaction to Super Bowl V was one of disgust, as if one had been promised a steak dinner and ended up instead with cold hot dogs. And the media immediately dismissed the game as an affront to professional sports, suggesting that somehow the Colts and Cowboys had cheated the American public. To this day, Super Bowl V is still considered one of the worst championship games in NFL history, if not in all of sport. "It was supposed to be a great spectacle," wrote Wells Twombly. "Instead, the result was pure slapstick humor."[65] Tex Maule wrote in *Sports Illustrated* that after the combined eleven turnovers between the two teams, "Perhaps the game should be called the Blunder Bowl from now on. To think that television was worried that situation comedy was dead."[66] And in his syndicated column, Red Smith observed, "Space does not permit a catalogue of the crimes and misdemeanors, the mortal and venial sins, the errors of commission and omission that made up this exercise in foolishness."[67]

Much of the blame was directed at realignment and the parity within the merged NFL. "It is not easy to explain why such an important event should be so poorly played, but the seeds were laid long ago," wrote Oates. "The Colts won the championship of the NFL's inferior American Conference without much offense. Unitas made a few big plays, and with the defense he had, that was enough."[68] Some suggested that the Super Bowl itself was to blame. "Perhaps the [game] is just too immense," wrote Twombly. "So much depends on the outcome. So many people are watching at once. At least in the World Series if a team looks dreadful, there is always tomorrow. The Super Bowl is too concentrated. It is downright eerie."[69]

Perhaps the best explanation of what happened came from the Colts. "The Cowboys were known as 'next year's champions'—they couldn't win the big one," said Accorsi. "And we were trying to overcome the scars of Super Bowl III. It was a game played in total desperation, which is why I think it was so frantic."[70]

"I think we were pressing too hard," said Curtis. "They weren't relaxed and I wasn't relaxed going in to the game. The guys put a lot of pressure on themselves to push harder, for both sides, and I think that's why it was a carnival."[71]

"Super Bowl V evokes for me a sense of not carrying our share of the load," said Colts center Bill Curry. "It was not the redemption we desperately sought for what went on before. It was the most mixed sense of achievement in my career."[72] Even as he was walking off the field, Bubba Smith acknowledged that he was depressed. "I knew I was supposed to be feeling good," he admitted, "but I wasn't feeling that way, because I was supposed to look at my other ring from Super Bowl III."[73]

The Colts could still console themselves with the winner's share, which at that time was $15,000 per player. (The Cowboys would get $7,500 per man). Today, the winners get around $83,000 and the losers $42,000, although when adjusted for inflation, the $15,000 is actually a better payday.

It is one of the few things people would say was better about Super Bowl V.

★ 18 ★

THE AFTERMATH

OF COLTS AND COWBOYS

Super Bowl V represented a turning point for both the Cowboys and Colts. For Baltimore, it was the last glimpse of glory for an aging team and town. The following season the team made the playoffs again, but was shut out by the up-and-coming Dolphins, 21–0, in the AFC Championship. When the Colts started 1-4 in 1972, McCafferty was fired and the team ultimately failed to make the playoffs.[1] Unitas departed after that season and finished his long career with a forgettable season in San Diego, while Earl Morrall left and won two more Super Bowl rings backing up Bob Griese in Miami. When Griese got hurt in 1972, Morrall played a significant role in the Dolphins' undefeated season.

Super Bowl hero Jim O'Brien kicked for another three years in the league, but like most straight-ahead kickers, his days in the NFL were numbered. It also didn't help that O'Brien's eye was seriously damaged when he was hit by a beer bottle in a bar in 1975. "I tried a couple of times; had a couple of tryouts and didn't make it," said O'Brien, who in 2010 was a project manager for a real estate company in Los Angeles. "But I can't blame that on [the incident] specifically. It was just one of those things—wrong place wrong time."[2]

The same might be said by Colts fans of Robert Irsay, the man who acquired the franchise in 1972. Much has been written about Irsay's stormy ownership period in which he routinely hired and fired coaches, made promises he never intended to keep, and ultimately moved the Colts from Baltimore to Indianapolis in 1984. "He lied and he cheated, and he was rude and he was crude and he was Bob Irsay," said Bert Jones, who quarterbacked the Colts in the 1970s. "He doesn't have any morals. It's a sad state for the NFL to be associated with him."[3]

It was Irsay who wanted a better stadium in Baltimore and when he didn't get it, moved the Colts to Indianapolis in the middle of the night on March 28, 1984. The previous day, the Maryland Legislature passed a law allowing the city to take over the franchise by eminent domain, and Irsay was concerned that the team would be seized at daybreak. "They not only threw down the gauntlet, but they put a gun to his head, cocked it and asked, 'Want to see if it's loaded?'" Michael Chernoff, the team's general counsel, said after the move. "They forced him to make a decision that day."[4]

The Colts became something of a league laughingstock under Irsay in Indianapolis, making the playoffs only once between 1984 and 1994, but the team began to improve when Irsay handed over control to his son Jim.[5] The Colts began to draft wisely, including the selection of quarterback Peyton Manning in 1998, and during the 2000s they became an NFL power. Starting in 2002, the team made the playoffs nine straight years and won a Super Bowl in 2007.

By then Baltimore had a new team, the Ravens, which started play in 1997, but the fans never forgot their Colts. The Baltimore Colts Marching Band, now known as Baltimore's Marching Ravens, continued to play even after the Colts left town. They were a reminder of the bond between town and team, and a wound that never completely healed. "I remember being sort of dumbfounded," said filmmaker Barry Levinson about the Colts move. Levinson paid tribute to the band in his film, *The Band That Wouldn't Die*. "I was at the very first Colts game in 1953—my dad had gotten tickets—and I was there every year until I went off to college. It's one of those devastating things that you think is inconceivable."[6]

While the 1970 Baltimore Colts basked in the glow of a Super Bowl championship, the Cowboys were left to suffer another season as "Next Year's Champions." Yet, the team had taken a significant step in reaching its first Super Bowl, and the players expressed confidence that they would recover from their humiliating defeat. "I'm not taking any shit about this game," said linebacker Lee Roy Jordan after Super Bowl V. "We'll be back. We've got good personnel, we're playing the defense; all we need is a little better passing game."[7]

That came in the form of Roger Staubach, who took over for Craig Morton full-time after the Cowboys stumbled to a 4-3 start in 1971.[8] Staubach was completely unlike the fun-loving Morton and his predecessor, Don Meredith. A Heisman Trophy winner at the Naval Academy in 1963, he had served a tour of duty in Vietnam before attempting a professional career with the Cowboys. "Roger Staubach was a different kind of person than your normal homo sapiens," said teammate and running back Walt Garrison. "He'd take his [Navy] leave and come to training camp and work out. We'd see him sweating his ass off through two-a-days and we'd say, 'What in the hell is he doin' here? He can't even play for three, four more years.'"[9]

Staubach provided the Cowboys with the passing game and leadership that had been missing in previous years, and along with another dominating defense, he took the Cowboys to Super Bowl VI to face the Dolphins. This time, Dallas played a near-perfect game, routing Miami, 24–3 and chasing away the demons of defeat that had followed it for six years. "Free at last!" was how Bob St. John opened his account of the game in the *Dallas Morning News*.[10] "It was certainly a great thrill," said Jordan, "but for us, it was more the lifting of a heavy burden that we had been carrying since 1966. The victory itself wasn't that big; it was almost anti-climactic. It was more important to get the 'bridesmaid-but-never-a-bride' tag removed."[11]

Staubach ushered in an era in which the Cowboys became "America's Team" and he became "Captain Comeback," a quarterback known for his clean-cut living and his ability to rescue the team from desperate situations.[12] With Staubach and Tom Landry at the helm, the team won consistently, and became glamorous and exciting in doing so. Dallas captured another Super Bowl after the 1977 season and made the playoffs seventeen times in the eighteen seasons between 1966 and 1983. The team's success dipped in the 1980s, and a 1989 takeover by businessman Jerry Jones turned ugly when he fired Landry and replaced him with college coach Jimmy Johnson. But after a 1-15 season in 1989, the Cowboys returned to NFL dominance winning three Super Bowls in four years starting in 1992. To date, they have five Super Bowl championships.

The Cowboys have not won a Super Bowl since January 1996, but they are probably the most recognizable and successful team in the NFL. A 2010 study called the Nielsen Sports Media Exposure Index indicated that the

Cowboys were the runaway most popular team in the NFL based on television and Internet exposure. In a Harris Interactive poll conducted at the same time, fans ranked the Cowboys as the league's most popular team for a fourth straight year. The Steelers have more Super Bowls, and teams like the Packers and Bears have longer histories, but in many ways, the Dallas Cowboys are the face of the modern NFL.

FLYING HIGH

The shadow of the late Vince Lombardi still hung over the NFL in the early 1970s, especially in terms of offense. Lombardi's conservative philosophy based on running predominated in the NFL, in which teams ran first and usually passed only out of necessity. Tom Landry was often credited as a genius with his multiple offense, but in Super Bowl VI the Cowboys set a record with 252 yards rushing, while passing for only 100.[13] By 1972, the trend became a stampede, as ten NFL backs rushed for more than 1,000 yards in a fourteen-game season, headlined by O. J. Simpson's 1,251 yards for the Bills. (The next season, Simpson would become the first back to break the 2,000-yard mark, rushing for 2,003.) The 1972 Miami Dolphins had two backs surpass 1,000 yards: Larry Csonka with 1,117 and Mercury Morris with exactly 1,000. When the Dolphins completed their perfect season with a 14–7 win over Washington in Super Bowl VII, Bob Griese threw only eleven passes the entire game, good for 88 yards.

The Jets, Colts, and Dolphins all won Super Bowls scoring less than seventeen points, and there was genuine concern among league owners that the game had become too focused on running, defense, and kicking. As more teams began using soccer-style kickers, kicking accuracy went up and teams began settling for field goals rather than touchdowns. The league responded in 1974 by moving the goal posts from the goal line to the back of the end zone, and also instituting a fifteen-minute "sudden death" overtime period to resolve tie games. Both rules seemed to help—in 1974 there was only one tie game (ironically in the very first overtime game between the Steelers and Broncos) and field goal attempts fell from 860 in 1973 to 518.

Scoring, however, was still somewhat lacking. In 1974, when the new rules went into effect, seven teams scored more than three hundred points for the season. But the previous year, eight teams had done it and even in the ground-oriented season of 1970, nine teams broke three hundred points. In 1977 NFL teams averaged just 17.7 points per game, the lowest scoring output since 1942.[14] So, in 1978 the NFL changed the rules again, this time to encourage more passing. Offensive linemen were allowed to extend their arms and open their hands when pass blocking. More important, defensive backs were now limited to contact with a receiver only within five yards of the line of scrimmage, where before they could harass them anywhere on the field. "So many great, physical cornerbacks now had limitations," said Michael Silver of Yahoo! Sports. "It was like Christmas for wide receivers."[15]

The rules had an immediate effect. From 1970 to 1977, not one quarterback threw for more than thirty touchdown passes in a season. Between 1978 and 2009, it happened thirty-nine times. By 1979, the league-wide completion average reached an all-time high of 54.1 percent, and the following season pass plays outnumbered running plays for the first time in a decade. As the game opened up, so did the minds of NFL coaches, who sought to take advantage of the new rules. By the 1980s, the league was finally ready to accept the West Coast offense.

The West Coast offense was actually being used years earlier—Sid Gillman ran an early version of it in the 1960s, and Bill Walsh refined many of those concepts when he worked under Paul Brown as an assistant coach with the Bengals. "The West Coast offense was born in Cincinnati," said former Bengals' tight end Bob Trumpy. "Walsh didn't care if a play made only two yards because it made the defense defend the entire field."[16]

The West Coast offense has many variations, "but its core philosophy is that a team can keep possession and move the ball down the field with a multidimensional passing game," wrote former Brigham Young coach Lavell Edwards, who used the offense to win a national college championship in 1984. "Spread the field out, present the defense with different looks, make more receivers available than can be covered, and get the ball to the open receiver."[17]

Walsh used the West Coast offense to win three Super Bowls in San Francisco during the 1980s, and variations of the attack remain in the league today. It represented a major shift in offensive thinking—that the ball, and the game, could be controlled with passing rather than running—and that philosophy dominates the modern NFL. Consider some of the passing records that have been set just in the past decade:

- Aaron Rodgers's 122.5 passer rating in 2011
- Tom Brady's fifty touchdown passes in 2007
- Drew Brees's 468 completions and 71.6 completion percentage, both set in 2011
- Brees's record of throwing a touchdown pass in 54 straight games set in 2012
- Passer rating of 83.8 for the NFL as a whole in 2012

In 1970 Don Shula had the reputation as a ball-control coach who emphasized the ground game. Shula's conservative philosophy turned around the Dolphins, who went on to win back-to-back Super Bowls in '72 and '73 behind the running of Csonka, Morris, and Jim Kiick. By 1984, Shula had the Dolphins back in the Super Bowl with a new breed of quarterback—gunslinger Dan Marino—who in that season threw forty-eight touchdown passes and became the first NFL quarterback to pass for more than 5,000 yards (5,084). Miami went 14-2, scored a team record 513 points, and its passing yardage surpassed its ground yardage by an almost 3-to-1 margin. After a 35–17 win over the Redskins in October, in which Marino threw five touchdowns, no interceptions, and had a near-perfect passer rating, Paul Zimmerman of *Sports Illustrated* wrote, "There was something arrogant, even irreverent, about the way Marino bombed Washington. The Skins had prepared for a nasty kind of game, a slugfest, trench warfare, but Marino opened up the skies. Marino's rainbows had taken the Skins off the ground and into the airways, and the game was over."[18]

Just a few years later, Zimmerman asked, "Is the running game doomed? Not likely. Football is cyclical," and indeed, rushing has rebounded substantially.[19] But the modern NFL game remains in the air, thanks in great part to the lessons learned in 1970.

THE MOD SQUAD

Just as the NFL of the 1970s was beginning to rethink Lombardi's conservative approach to the game, it was also moving away from his style of coaching.

Coaches like Lombardi, Shula, and Van Brocklin represented the ultimate authoritarian figures; men who demanded respect and inspired fear in their players. When these coaches told players to do something, they did it, or risked losing their jobs. "Lombardi tells guys when to quit here," said Bud Lea, who covered the Packers in the 1960s for the *Milwaukee Sentinel.* "Nobody makes decisions but him. Everyone had feared the guy, and he wanted it to stay that way."[20]

Lombardi's style worked because the players he coached had not known any other way. It was the generation that had fought, and survived, World War II, and to many of them, professional football was simply an extension of combat. Art Donovan said his first pro training camp with the Colts in 1950 was so brutal, he and teammate Sisto Averno both wanted to quit. "But in those days, I guess authority meant something," recalled Donovan. "When [assistant coach Wayne] Milner threatened to kick our asses unless we dragged them down into that death hole, we both sheepishly complied."[21]

But the generation of players that came along in the late 1960s was a different, and sometimes radical, breed. Many of them had come directly to the NFL from college campuses that were in racial and generational conflict. Just four months before the 1970 season had kicked off, four students at Kent State University in Ohio were killed in an anti-war demonstration on campus. The Vietnam War, along with the Civil Rights, Hippie, and Free Love movements, profoundly affected the young NFL players of 1970. Instead of embracing authority, they often questioned it, or even openly rebelled.

"Football was so violent that thinking wasn't encouraged in that atmosphere," said former Cowboys receiver Pete Gent. "You really couldn't think beyond what you were doing that day. You'd say to yourself, 'How can I survive doing this?'"[22] Gent played five seasons in Dallas and became a magnet for other young, disaffected Cowboys' players, some of whom were heavily involved with drugs.[23] Like Gent, Dave Meggyesy turned his NFL experiences into a best-selling book. *Sports Illustrated* called Meggyesy, who played seven seasons with St. Louis, "an anti-football guru" for his outspoken criticism of the dehumanizing aspects of pro football, which he chronicled in his book, *Out of Their League.*[24]

Perhaps no player more symbolized the new breed of NFL player more than Tim Rossovich, a linebacker for the Eagles who in 1970 was just two years removed from his college days at USC. Born near San Francisco, Rossovich seemed to embody the anti-establishment youth of 1960s California. He often slept on the floor with his head facing magnetic north in order to reenergize himself.[25] "Tim Rossovich eats light bulbs," wrote *Sports Illustrated*. "He wears tie-dyed shirts and shower-of-hail suits, Dracula capes and frontier buckskins and stands on his head in hotel lobbies."[26] Rossovich added, "I live my life to enjoy myself. I can't explain things I do much beyond that."[27]

Old-school coaches, described by one psychiatrist in 1969 as "the remaining stronghold of the archaic family structure," found it easier to get rid of these difficult players rather than try to deal with them.[28] The season after he nearly carried the Cowboys to a championship in Super Bowl V, Duane Thomas demanded the team tear up his contract and give him a new one. When Dallas refused, Thomas became isolated, moody, and unwilling to listen to coach Tom Landry, whom he famously called a "plastic man."[29] Landry dealt with the problem by trading Thomas (and another problem child, linebacker Steve Kiner) to the Patriots in the summer of 1971, but Thomas's stay in New England lasted only a couple of days. He didn't listen to the Patriots' coaches, either, and New England petitioned the league to have the trade rescinded. So Thomas returned to Dallas, still unhappy, and he vowed not to speak to the media for the rest of the season.[30]

Tom Landry never did figure out how to handle the enigmatic Thomas, who came back and led the Cowboys to a Super Bowl title, although his presence created deep divisions among the team. "The worst anguish Tom ever went through was with Duane Thomas," said Mike Ditka, a Dallas tight end that championship season. "I've never seen a man suffer in trying to do what he thought was best for the football team, for the individual and for everyone concerned. It was very agonizing and tough for Tom, but he did it."[31]

Landry finally solved the problem for good in 1972 by trading Thomas to the Chargers, but he was not the only coach caught in changing cultural tides. Hardly anyone in the NFL could figure out what to do with John Matuszak, the number-one overall draft pick of the Oilers in 1973. Shortly after he was drafted, Matuszak noted, "If you really like to play the game and go about it with unabashed enthusiasm, then you can play better. By unabashed enthusiasm I mean going crazy."[32] It was a comment that should have tipped off Houston, and the rest of the league, as to what it was getting. Matuszak unquestionably had the talent to star in the NFL, but ended up playing for four teams in an eight-year career that *Sports Illustrated* described as a "legacy . . . of a brawling, incorrigible miscreant who occasionally played hard but always partied harder."[33] Matuszak wore out his welcome in Houston, Kansas City, and Washington, before finally finding a home with the Raiders, who seemed to become something of a halfway home for NFL troublemakers.[34] Matuszak helped the Raiders to a win in Super Bowl XV, but died of heart failure in 1989 at the age of thirty-eight.

Certainly, there have always been drinkers, carousers, and free spirits in the NFL, but up through the 1970s such players were typically handled like Thomas and Matuszak. Even Hall of Fame quarterback (and Hall of Fame drinker) Bobby Layne played on four different teams. But as the power of the players began to grow in the 1970s, and their salaries began to escalate dramatically, the relationship between coach and player began to change. As players became more outspoken, more demanding, and more valuable, it was up to coaches to adjust to them, not vice versa. When the Falcons drafted Deion Sanders with their top pick in 1989, he announced, "They don't pay nobody to be humble. I'm a businessman now, and the product is me. Prime Time. I'm the first defensive back to make a million dollars a year. Set a record for a bonus. Cash up front."[35] The coach for Sanders' rookie season was sixty-year-old veteran Marion Campbell, but Campbell lasted only that one year before the team brought in Jerry Glanville, a man with his own set of eccentricities (he left free tickets for Elvis at various NFL venues), and a younger coach who might better understand how to deal with the team's top commodity. Glanville and Sanders lasted four years together in Atlanta; the coach departed after two straight losing seasons, and Sanders left for more free agent money.

POWER TO THE PLAYERS

Millionaire players are a reality in the modern NFL, and their development can be traced back to the seemingly inconsequential players' strike of 1970. Though brief, that strike laid the groundwork for future action, particularly as the game became more successful and players began to demand a bigger piece of the NFL pie. Things came to a head in September 1982, when the NFL

Players Association announced the first regular-season strike in the game's history. It was a strike over money—the players originally wanted 55 percent of the league's gross revenues, but later asked for $1.6 billion in television money—and it brought the NFL to a standstill. "There will be no practices, workouts, or training," said NFLPA leader Gene Upshaw, the former Raiders guard. "No games will be played until management abandons its unlawful course. We are prepared to withhold our services, however long it takes."[36]

After fifty-seven days, the two sides finally settled, but hard feelings remained, and the labor peace lasted only five years.[37] When the NFL players struck again in 1987, the owners were prepared and used replacement players for the three games the regulars missed. Some starters crossed the picket line, but most teams filled in their rosters with marginal talent. "It's like the high school coach hanging a sign outside the gym, saying, 'All those who want to try out for football report at 5 p.m.,'" said Redskins general manager Bobby Beathard.[38]

But it was a clear sign that the players' power was growing. As part of the collective bargaining agreement that came out of the strikes, the players acquired free agency, which allowed them to sign with other teams when their contracts expired. The obvious effect was to increase players' average salaries: from $23,000 in 1970, to $198,000 in 1986, and to $1.8 million today.[39] In return, the owners got a salary cap in 1994 with the idea that it would help keep their expenses relatively low. Unfortunately, the salary cap and collective bargaining agreement ended after the 2010 season, which resulted in yet another work stoppage in 2011.

The 2011 lockout ended after four and a half months and resulted in substantial gains for the players. That represents a dramatic change from 1970, when owners controlled every aspect of the game, including the players, whom they viewed as mere chattel. A case in point is Joe Kapp, who quarterbacked the Vikings to the Super Bowl in 1969 but had difficulty signing a new contract the following season. When the Vikings stalled the negotiations, then issued an ultimatum to Kapp in the summer of 1970, he exploded. "Damn it," he said, "I don't answer ultimatums. I'm not some kind of slave."[40] Kapp did not re-sign with Minnesota, and the Vikings did not return to the Super Bowl until they traded for veteran quarterback Fran Tarkenton.[41]

Flash forward to 2010, when the same Vikings were trying to convince quarterback Brett Favre to hold off retirement and play another season. Team officials, including coach Brad Childress, made several trips to Favre's Mississippi home. "I played a long time, I went to four Pro Bowls and I never had a coach fly down to Mississippi to talk to me in the offseason and see how I was doing," said former quarterback Rich Gannon, the NFL MVP in 2002. "[But] I think in this situation it's warranted."[42] According to NFL sources, the Vikings were expected to increase Favre's contract to $16.5 million from $13 million, which did not include a potential $3.5 million in performance incentives. Favre's agent Bus Cook observed, "If they want to reward him, nobody's going to walk away from that. But it's not a factor in his decision."[43] "You've got to remember," said former NFL receiver Gary Collins, "that some of the guys today are making more than [Art] Modell paid for the [Browns] franchise."[44]

THE YEAR-ROUND LEAGUE

The players have certainly benefited financially in the new NFL, but they have also lost some things. As the league, and the money, got bigger, so did the pressure and the commitment level. Before the explosion in salaries, NFL players routinely got off-season jobs as an economic necessity. Art Donovan and Lou Groza were salesmen; Donovan sold liquor and Groza insurance. Paul Warfield co-owned a tire dealership. "All of our guys worked," said former Browns guard John Wooten, who was also math teacher. "Nobody just sat around and 'worked out.'"[45]

Now, there is no off-season. The Super Bowl is played in February, and teams start conditioning programs in March, followed by quarterback schools, organized team activities, minicamps, and then training camp. "They started doing the off-season weight program," said former Browns linebacker Dick Ambrose. "Then all of a sudden the coaches were coming and wanting the guys to watch film with them in the off-season. And then we'd almost have little mini-organized workouts, all in the off-season. So, at some point, I'd say the early to mid-'80s, it started to become a year-round job with about a month, month-and-a-half off in between, depending on when your season ended."[46]

Coaches like Tom Landry, who worked in insurance, real estate, and oil, also had to give up their off-season jobs and commit full-time. Some went beyond full-time. Former Eagles coach Dick Vermeil routinely worked twenty-hour days and slept in his office, before abruptly quitting after the 1982 season due to what he called "burnout"; a term unknown at the time, but one that became common in the 2000s. Before Vermeil arrived in Philadelphia in 1976, "It was great," said lineman Stan Walters. "Practice at one, get off the field by two-thirty. I was off to play golf, the whole bit. Coach Vermeil made it a year-round, 40 hour-a-week job."[47] When John Gruden coached in Tampa Bay, he arose at 3:15 every morning and headed to work. "At 3:45 a.m., he's going to work and, hell, I'm just coming in," joked former defensive tackle Warren Sapp. "Why would you not want to kill for a man like that? When you're sleeping, he's working. When you're working, he's working. And when you're off? He's still working."[48]

The commitment level, especially in regard to off-season workouts, began to show in bigger and better conditioned players. In 1970 few NFL teams were into serious weight training, and the league's bigger players were usually born that way. The Cowboys' Bob Lilly developed his strength from hauling hay as a youngster, and at 6-foot-5, 260 pounds, he was about average for the Cowboys' defensive line at the time. Bob Vogel was 6-foot-5, 250 pounds, and the biggest member of the 1970 Colts offensive line, which averaged about 6-foot-3 and 240 pounds. When the Saints won the Super Bowl in 2009, the *smallest* member of their offensive line was center Jonathan Goodwin at 6-foot-3, 318 pounds; every other member of the New Orleans line was at least 6-foot-4 and 315 pounds. It's not just offensive lineman who got bigger; in 2007 the Raiders selected quarterback JaMarcus Russell with the first pick in the NFL draft. At the time, the LSU quarterback stood 6-foot-6 and weighed 250 pounds.[49] Writer Michael Rosenberg asked players of the early 1970s, "Do you understand that if you could enter today's NFL with the body you had in your prime, today's mammoth linemen would snap you in two, dip you in ketchup, and eat you?"[50] No wonder that even in 1970, Green Bay's 6-foot-4, 245 pound defensive end Lionel Aldridge noted, "I'm not big enough anymore. The game's outgrown me."[51]

Unfortunately, some of today's athletes got bigger by using banned substances such as steroids and performance-enhancing drugs, the use of which is certainly nothing new. Shot putter Dave Maggard said that if they had more sophisticated steroid testing at the 1968 Olympics, "You would have had an awful lot of people dropping out of events because of instant muscle pulls."[52]

The Olympic Games, Major League Baseball, the Tour de France, and professional wrestling have all suffered through highly publicized steroid scandals in recent years, and while the NFL has so far escaped major embarrassment it has not remained untainted. The most famous case involved defensive lineman Lyle Alzado, who after his career ended admitted to using steroids and lying about it. "All along I was taking steroids, and I saw that they made me play better and better," he said. "I kept on because I knew I had to keep getting more size."[53] Alzado blamed steroid use for the brain cancer that ultimately killed him in 1992.

The NFL adopted a strict steroid policy in 1987, and the league has beefed it up since then to include more testing, as well as game suspensions for violators. But as the money and pressure continue to grow in the NFL, the temptation will always remain. In 2010 the league suspended Houston Texans linebacker Brian Cushing for four games and stripped him of his Defensive Rookie of the Year award for testing positive for a banned substance.

GOODBYE ROCKPILE

A year after the success of *Monday Night Football* in 1970, Carl Lindemann of rival NBC somewhat jealously announced, "The novelty is rapidly wearing thin."[54] Lindemann and other detractors could not have been more wrong, as *MNF* became the single most important development of the 1970 season. Its popularity confirmed the NFL as the sport of the future, and suggested there was no limit on America's football appetite.

The NFL reacted aggressively, eventually expanding its season from fourteen to sixteen games in 1978. In 2012 there was talk of an eighteen-game season, although safety concerns have kept the discussions from becoming too serious. The playoff format went from eight teams in 1970 to ten in 1978, then to twelve in 1990. The league itself kept growing, too, adding Seattle and Tampa Bay in 1976, and then expanding again in 1995 (Carolina Panthers and Jacksonville Jaguars), 1999 (the "new" Cleveland Browns), and 2002 (Houston Texans). When the Texans joined in 2002, the NFL realigned for the first time since 1970 in order to find a place for its thirty-two teams and expanded from three divisions in each conference to four.

More teams mean more attendance, which has grown steadily for the NFL since 1970. NFL games attracted 9,533,333 fans in 1970, and by 2000 that number had grown to 16,387,289, a 72 percent increase. Starting in 2003, the NFL broke its own live attendance record for six straight years, which peaked in 2008 at an average of 68,034. Even during the recession in 2009, the league has the best average attendance of any sport in the world. That season, 17,282,225 seats were sold for 256 NFL games, or an average of 67,509 per game.[55]

Even in an age when it has become easier and cheaper to watch the game at home, NFL attendance has not unduly suffered. In 1973 the league revised its television blackout policy, allowing home teams to show their games locally if the game was sold out seventy-two hours in advance. That season, the NFL set yet another attendance record, suggesting that fans still valued the live game experience. The challenge for the league in the 2010s is in the living room— namely, the big screen, high definition televisions, surround sound systems, and channels that allow viewing of multiple games at the same time. All that new technology, combined with higher ticket prices, makes it much easier for a NFL fan to watch at home, and television ratings have exploded in recent years. "We aren't just going to invest on new technologies that serve people at home," says Brian Rolapp, the NFL's vice president for digital media. "We will continue to invest to make the stadium experience better."[56]

Part of that means building better stadiums. In 1970 the Buffalo Bills played their home games in creaky War Memorial Stadium; an old tub that was affectionately known by locals as the "Rockpile." Today, the Rockpile is gone, and twenty-three of the twenty-six stadiums that NFL teams used in 1970 are either demolished or no longer used. The three places still stand-ing—Lambeau Field in Green Bay, the Oakland Coliseum, and Qualcomm Stadium in San Diego—have undergone major renovation. In 2009 the Cowboys opened a $1.2 billion, 100,000-seat stadium in Arlington, Texas, equipped with a 60-yard-long high definition video board suspended ninety feet above the field. The following season, the Jets and Giants began play in a similar $1.6 billion facility. By 2012, almost all NFL stadiums had added HD screens and wireless Internet access.

The Internet and digital television have exponentially increased the NFL's visibility and popularity. In 1970 the NFL television experience was typically limited to three games per Sunday and another on Monday. CBS or NBC would take turns televising a doubleheader on Sunday, leaving the other network with a single game, while ABC had the *Monday Night Football* showcase. In 2012 the NFL fan could watch thirteen weekend games through the NFL's "Sunday Ticket" package, as well as a Sunday night game, a Monday night game, and a Thursday night game on NFL Network.[57]

That information has made the fan much more knowledgeable, involved, and passionate. Fantasy football, which allows fans to create teams and compete against each other based on the statistical performance of NFL players, began to gain popularity in the 1990s and today is a $2 billion industry involving between twenty and thirty million people. Fantasy leagues also reflect the growing problem of gambling on the NFL. Betting on the NFL was an issue in 1970 just like it is today, but the scale was drastically smaller. Thanks to the Internet and online gambling sites, an estimated $4 billion is bet illegally on the NFL, with nearly $100 million bet on the Super Bowl alone.[58] The NFL continues to maintain a vigorous anti-gambling stance, but policing gets harder to do with each passing year. "The NFL's policy on this issue has been consistent for decades," said Brian McCarthy, the NFL's director of communications. "Sports gambling threatens the integrity of our games and all the values they represent, especially to young people. The NFL has been an active proponent of federal and state efforts to combat sports gambling."[59]

Even those that do not bet can use the Internet to feed their NFL passion. The NFL fans of 1970 could only rely on newspapers, magazines, radio, and television, and such content was limited and often outdated. The NFL fans of 2013 not only have seemingly unlimited, instant access to content through message boards, fan forums, and blogs, they can also create, distribute, and share their own information. Hundreds of fans have created websites dedicated to coverage of their favorite teams, and in some cases these sites rival the traditional coverage offered by newspapers and magazines. In 2011, for example, the blogs Dawgs by Nature, Browns Gab, and Dawg Pound Daily, all created and run by fans of the Cleveland Browns, had thousands of subscribers. "I think blogs are the wave of the future because they give a voice to the ordinary fan that has an intelligent opinion, but in the past didn't have the medium to voice it," said Marc James, who created a sports commentary blog that eventually had a staff of forty people and published about 120,000 posts per week. "People want to hear less of what the so-called experts have to say and more of what the sports geek down the street thinks."[60]

Such fans are pouring millions into NFL coffers. When you add up the money the NFL makes from its media properties, especially television, and other sources such as merchandising and live attendance, the league annually takes in more than $8 billion in revenue. A study by the NFL Players Association shows the average rate of return on an NFL team is about $100 million a year, considering profit and franchise appreciation. Those numbers are just as staggering today as they would have been in 1970. Carroll Rosenbloom owned the Colts in that Super Bowl season, but two years later decided he would rather own the Los Angeles Rams. To do that, Rosenbloom pulled off a complicated deal in which Robert Irsay bought the Rams, then switched franchises with Rosenbloom. In 1972 getting control of the Baltimore Colts cost Irsay $19 million. Today, the Indianapolis Colts are worth an estimated one billion dollars.

ROZELLE'S UTOPIA

The 1970 season represented an important shift in the organizational thinking of the NFL. Throughout its fifty-year history, the NFL had faced external challenges from leagues like the AFL, or situational crises, such as the financial instability caused by the Great Depression and World War II. But as the newly merged league now enjoyed both peace and prosperity, it shifted its focus from survival to expansion, and it did so thanks primarily to the efforts of Commissioner Pete Rozelle. When he became commissioner in 1960, Rozelle sought to move the league away from its "every man for himself" approach and embrace an attitude of "one for all, and all for one." Some called this philosophy parity, and Rozelle made it an institutional goal in all areas of the NFL during his twenty-nine years as commissioner.

Economically, Rozelle wanted the clubs to stop competing against each other and work together for the benefit of all, and primarily this meant sharing television revenue. In the 1950s each team had cut its own television deal. "It was a growth that was kind of segmented," said long-time Dallas general manager Tex Schramm. "The Chicago Bears and Chicago Cardinals had their own networks. George Preston Marshall and the Washington Redskins had their southern network. And [the Rams] tried to have the west coast network."[61] When CBS threatened to air only the games of big city teams like the Giants and Bears, Rozelle stepped in and convinced owners that they needed to share television revenues equally. Congress approved, and in 1962 the first league-wide television contract began with CBS paying the fourteen NFL franchises a fee of $4.65 million, which did not include rights to the championship game.

The NFL has fully embraced what Rozelle started in the 1960s. Today, revenue sharing is the economic basis for the league's operation, and it helps ensure that teams in small cities, like Green Bay, receive roughly the same revenues as teams in bigger cities. The NFL makes in the neighborhood of around $8 billion annually from television deals, merchandising, national sponsorships, and ticket sales, and nearly 60 percent of that money is pooled and redistributed equally among teams. "This league was based on people being partners and being together and helping out," Pittsburgh Steelers owner Dan Rooney said. "It's one of the strong points of our league. It's a matter of fairness."[62]

Rozelle also wanted that kind of fairness on the field, believing that the league was healthier with tighter division races and more competitive teams. Cynics like sportswriter Jerry Green suggested that Rozelle's version of parity included "all 26 teams finishing at 7-7. This is the Utopian concept," which, while an obvious exaggeration, was not that far from the truth.[63] Coincidence or not, the 1970 season played out like Rozelle wrote the script, with four of the six divisional races going down to the final weekend. The closest thing to a dominant team, the Minnesota Vikings, went 12-2, but they also got bounced from the playoffs in the first round. "There is now a wide-ranging balance of power in the NFL," wrote Bob Oates at the time. "From here on, the Super Bowl can be considered up for grabs."[64]

The NFL fully believed that, too, even after a decade of dominance by Lombardi's Packers. "There's not more than two touchdowns' difference between the playing talent of any of the 26 pro football teams," noted Chiefs defensive lineman Aaron Brown during the 1970 season. "Most games are so close, one break can be the deciding factor."[65] Added Raiders quarterback Daryle Lamonica, "There won't be any more 12-1-1 or 13-1 teams."[66]

Parity took a little longer to flower. In the rest of the '70s, the Dolphins won two Super Bowls and the Steelers won four, but both teams were able to keep their rosters intact for a long period of time, something that is much more difficult in the recent era of free agency and escalating salaries. "Free agency and salary caps encourage players to abandon championship juggernauts and play for larger salaries on lesser teams," said sportswriter Frank Deford. "[It] also destroys would-be dynasties."[67] Kevin Demoff, the executive vice president of football operations for the St. Louis Rams, countered that statement, saying, "Parity is not designed to make every team equal. Parity is designed to give every team a chance if they operate right. The goal is for everybody to begin the year feeling like they have a chance, and for the most part, everyone does."[68]

The Rams were a perfect example of that, rising from a 4-12 record in 1998 to 13-3 and a Super Bowl championship the following season. When the Green Bay Packers went to the Super Bowl after the 2010 season, they were the tenth different NFC team in ten years to get there. Since the current thirty-two-team, eight-division setup began in 2002, fifty-two of ninety-six playoff berths went to teams that missed the postseason the year before. In ten of the twelve years prior to 2009, a team that was 9-7 or worse the year before went to the Super Bowl. "We have a very unique situation in our league," said Demoff, "because our system works."[69]

AROUND THE WORLD

Like any growing corporation, the NFL began to look for ways to expand its empire. Internal expansion was one such avenue, and the NFL grew from twenty teams in 1970 to thirty-two by 2002, but the success of the post-merger NFL convinced league executives that the game could also succeed overseas. Starting in 1986, the NFL staged a series of eight exhibition games before sellout crowds at Wembley Stadium in London, England. The games, which became known as the American Bowl, were considered successful, even though as former NFL player John Offerdahl observed, "Because it was an exhibition, after one or two series all the good players were off and the Brits were saying, 'Hey, this stinks!'"[70] In 2007 the Giants and Dolphins came to Wembley for the first regular season NFL game outside the U.S. "The [NFL] owners approved two regular season games per year [abroad] and this has been a tremendous success even before the game's been played," said NFL Commissioner Roger Goodell. "I would anticipate that we will be back here on a regular basis."[71]

The success of the American Bowl prompted more expansion in Europe, and in 1990 the NFL created the World League of American Football, a developmental league with teams in such cities as Barcelona, Frankfurt, and London. The league went through several incarnations before the NFL pulled the plug in 2007. The growth of high definition television, the Internet, and other media technologies convinced NFL owners that it was easier, and cheaper, to expand their product digitally rather than by operating permanent franchises overseas.

"We will continue to build our international fan base by taking advantage of technology and customized digital media that make the NFL more accessible on a global scale than ever before and through the regular-season game experience," said Mark Waller, senior vice president of NFL International. "The time is right to re-focus the NFL's strategy on initiatives with global impact, including worldwide media coverage of our sport and the staging of live regular-season NFL games."[72]

Waller is part of an NFL International division that has offices in five countries on three continents. The league has growing fan bases in Japan, where the NFL has staged fourteen exhibition games, and China, where more than seven million people watch games on television. One of the strongest markets is in Mexico, where the NFL claims the largest number of fans (16.5 million) outside the U.S. The six games played in Mexico between 1994 and 2005 drew an average of more than 100,000 fans, and the 1994 exhibition between the Cowboys and Oilers at Estadio Azteca in Mexico City set the record for the largest crowd ever to watch a single NFL game, with 112,376 fans attending. "The world, as we know it, is getting smaller," said Darin Perry of Marketing Arm, an international consulting agency. "The boundaries of all kinds are disappearing. And as that happens, whether you're a corporate brand or a sports league, there's a push to reach new growth opportunities."[73]

FINAL OBSERVATIONS

Comparing the NFL in 1970 to the NFL in 2013 is like comparing a 1970 Volkswagen Beetle to a 2013 Lamborghini Murciélago. Even considering the

strides the league made under Pete Rozelle, the NFL in 1970 still had something of a pastoral feel to it. Stadiums like Kezar in San Francisco, Municipal
in Kansas City, and Franklin Field in Philadelphia were all located in city
neighborhoods, where it was still possible to walk up on game day and buy
a ticket for five dollars, and then maybe talk to players going home from the
game. There seemed to be a strong connection between players and fans, in
part because those playing the game didn't make much more in salary compared to those watching.

But in the last forty years or so, the NFL has transitioned from a league
that emphasized competition into a multi-billion dollar conglomerate that
emphasizes profit. The teams moved out of the neighborhoods and into glass
and steel palaces in the suburbs, such as the Cowboys' move from the Cotton
Bowl to Texas Stadium in 1971. "The whole place is weird," tight end Billy
Truax said that season. "You're down there on the field, and you know they're
up there. It's like the lions and the Christians all over."[74] In 2009 Dallas moved
again, this time to the $1.2 billion Cowboys Stadium in Arlington. "We are
facing different economic realities than we have in prior years," NFL
spokesman Greg Aiello said in 2010. "For the most part, these new realities
reflect a significant increase in costs, including the cost of building, maintaining and operating stadiums."[75]

Ticket prices kept going up to pay for those stadiums and rising player
salaries. The ticket that cost five dollars in 1970 averages seventy-eight dollars today, and that does not include the potential cost of a personal seat
license that many teams require simply to have the chance to buy tickets.[76]
For the San Diego Chargers home opener in 2010, a family of four had to pay
$288 for tickets, $40 for hot dogs and drinks, and $25 for parking. The face
value of a Super Bowl V ticket was $15; by Super Bowl XLV, tickets were
$600 face value, and the average price paid was more than $4,600.

Compounding the problem is an economy suffering from a recession.
The NFL has seen overall attendance and average attendance fall every year
since 2008 to their lowest levels since 2002. Television blackouts also
increased dramatically. "We know some of our fans are struggling. We don't
need to see the statistics," said Eric Grubman, executive vice president of
NFL Ventures and Business Operations. "That works its way into the equa-
tion."[77] Admitted Baltimore Ravens president Dick Cass, "It's been difficult.

Everything has been flat. If businesses continue to struggle, it could become a concern."[78] Of even greater concern was the end of the NFL's collective bargaining agreement, which expired in March 2011. The players decertified their union, which allowed them to file anti-trust lawsuits against the owners. Although a settlement was eventually reached, for much of 2011 the possibility of no football seemed very real.

Lockouts. Blackouts. Salary caps. Life in the NFL of 2013 is more complicated than ever. It is also bigger and richer than the NFL of 1970 could have ever imagined. But the dreams of forty-three years ago have their place just the same. They were dreams of a game and a time that remain fixed in memory, and serve as a reminder that bigger is not always better.

APPENDIX I

1970 NFL FINAL STANDINGS

1970 NFL FINAL STANDINGS

Team	W	L	T	Win %	Points Scored	Points Allowed
AFC East						
Baltimore Colts	11	2	1	.846	321	234
Miami Dolphins*	10	4	0	.714	297	228
New York Jets	4	10	0	.286	255	286
Buffalo Bills	3	10	1	.231	204	337
Boston Patriots	2	12	0	.143	149	361
AFC Central						
Cincinnati Bengals	8	6	0	.571	312	255
Cleveland Browns	7	7	0	.500	286	265
Pittsburgh Steelers	5	9	0	.357	210	272
Houston Oilers	3	10	1	.231	217	352
AFC West						
Oakland Raiders	8	4	2	.667	300	293
Kansas City Chiefs	7	5	2	.583	272	244
San Diego Chargers	5	6	3	.455	282	278
Denver Broncos	5	8	1	.385	253	264
NFC East						
Dallas Cowboys	10	4	0	.714	299	221
New York Giants	9	5	0	.643	301	270
St. Louis Cardinals	8	5	1	.615	325	228
Washington Redskins	6	8	0	.429	297	314
Philadelphia Eagles	3	10	1	.231	241	332

Team	W	L	T	Win %	Points Scored	Points Allowed
NFC Central						
Minnesota Vikings	12	2	0	.857	335	143
Detroit Lions*	10	4	0	.714	347	202
Chicago Bears	6	8	0	.429	256	261
Green Bay Packers	6	8	0	.429	196	293
NFC West						
San Francisco 49ers	10	3	1	.769	352	267
Los Angeles Rams	9	4	1	.692	325	202
Atlanta Falcons	4	8	2	.333	206	261
New Orleans Saints	2	11	1	.154	172	347

*Qualified for playoffs as wild card team

1970 NFL PLAYOFF RESULTS

Winner	Loser	Score	Site
First Round			
Baltimore	Cincinnati	17–0	Baltimore
Dallas	Detroit	5–0	Dallas
San Francisco	Minnesota	17–14	Minnesota
Oakland	Miami	21–14	Oakland
Conference Championships			
Baltimore	Oakland	27–17	Baltimore
Dallas	San Francisco	17–10	San Francisco
Super Bowl V			
Baltimore	Dallas	16–13	Miami

APPENDIX II

STATISTICAL LEADERS

The following is a list of statistical leaders for the 1970 season and how they compare to 2012 and all-time leaders. The trend toward more offense is evident in that almost all individual and team offensive records have been set since 2000.

It is important to remember that the 2012 season was sixteen games, compared to fourteen in 1970, but in terms of averages, total offense yardage has gone up 19 percent since 1970, while passing offense has increased about 36 percent. The only decline is in rushing average, where there was a 4 percent drop. At the same time, touchdowns per game and scoring have not significantly increased. This could be attributed to better, more sophisticated defenses or to more accurate field goal kickers. In 1970 field goal kickers hit only 478 of 805 attempts, for a success rate of 59.4 percent. In 2012 the numbers rose to 852 of 1,016, or 83.9 percent. The rate of success from 40 yards and beyond is even more astounding—74 percent in 2012 compared to 37 percent in 1970.

Passing numbers also show the influence of the West Coast offense and horizontal passing game. NFL teams in 1970 believed in a vertical, down-the-field passing attack, and Bob Hayes's yards-per-catch average of 26.1 that season is still one of the highest in NFL history. That same season, seven other receivers had averages over 20 yards per catch. In 2012 no receiver did.

INDIVIDUAL STATISTICS

	1970 Leader		2012 Leader		All-Time Leader		
Passing							
Touchdown passes	John Brodie	24.0	Drew Brees	43.0	Tom Brady	50.0	(2007)
Completion percentage	Sonny Jurgensen	59.9	Peyton Manning	68.6	Drew Brees	5,476.0	(2011)
Yards passing	John Brodie	2,941.0	Drew Brees	5,177.0	Drew Brees	468.0	(2011)
Rating	John Brodie	93.8	Aaron Rodgers	108.0	Aaron Rodgers	122.5	(2011)
Rushing							
Rushing attempts	Ron Johnson	263.0	Arian Foster	351.0	Larry Johnson	416.0	(2006)
Rushing yards	Larry Brown	1,125.0	Adrian Peterson	2,097.0	Eric Dickerson	2,105.0	(1984)
Rushing touchdowns	MacArthur Lane	11.0	Arian Foster	15.0	LaDainian Tomlinson	28.0	(2006)
Yards per carry	Duane Thomas	5.3	Robert Griffin III	6.8	Michael Vick	8.4	(2006)
Receiving							
Total receptions	Dick Gordon	71.0	Calvin Johnson	122.0	Marvin Harrison	143.0	(2002)
Yards receiving	Gene Washington	1,100.0	Calvin Johnson	1,964.0	Calvin Johnson	1,964.0	(2012)
Touchdown receptions	Dick Gordon	13.0	James Jones	14.0	Randy Moss	23.0	(2007)
Yards per catch	Bob Hayes	26.1	Vincent Jackson	19.2	Jimmy Orr	27.6	(1958)

	1970 Leader		2012 Leader		All-Time Leader		

Scoring/Kicking

	1970 Leader		2012 Leader		All-Time Leader		
Points	Fred Cox	125.0	Stephen Gostkowski	153.0	LaDainian Tomlinson	186.0	(2006)
Field goals	Fred Cox and Jan Stenerud (tied)	30.0	Blair Walsh	35.0	David Akers	44.0	(2011)
Field goal percentage	Garo Yepremian	75.9	Kai Forbath	94.4	Six players tied:	100.0	
					Gary Anderson		(1998)
					Shayne Graham		(2010)
					Mike Vanderjagt		(2003)
					Jeff Wilkins		(2000)
					Tony Zendejas		(1991)
					Garrett Hartley		(2008)
Punting average	Dave Lewis	46.2	Brandon Fields	50.2	Sammy Baugh	51.4	(1940)
Kickoff return average	Jim Duncan	35.4	Percy Harvin	35.9	Travis Williams	41.1	(1967)
Punt return average	Ed Podolak	13.5	Leodis McKelvin	18.7	Jack Christiansen	21.5	(1952)

Defense

	1970 Leader		2012 Leader		All-Time Leader		
Interceptions	Johnny Robinson	10.0	Tim Jennings	9.0	Night Train Lane	14.0	(1952)
Fumbles recovered	Alan Page	7.0	Patrick Peterson	5.0	David Carr	12.0	(2002)
Sacks	*		J. J. Watt	20.5	Michael Strahan	22.5	(2001)

*Sacks not kept as an official NFL statistic until 1982.

TEAM STATISTICS

	1970 Leader		2012 Leader	
Total offensive yards	Oakland	4,829.0	New England	6,846.0
Total yards per game	Oakland	344.9	New England	427.9
Passing yards	San Francisco	2,923.0	New Orleans	4,997.0
Passing yards per game	San Francisco	208.8	New Orleans	312.3
Rushing yards	Dallas	2,300.0	Washington	2,709.0
Rushing yards per game	Dallas	164.3	Washington	169.3
Points scored	San Francisco	352.0	New England	557.0
Offensive points per game	San Francisco	25.1	New England	34.8
Fewest points allowed	Minnesota	143.0	Seattle	245.0
Defensive points per game	Minnesota	10.2	Seattle	15.3

OVERALL TEAM STATISTICS

	1970 Leader	2012 Leader
Total offensive yards per game	281.8	347.2
Rushing yards per game	120.4	115.9
Passing yards per game	161.4	231.3
Yards per pass	5.5	6.2
Offensive touchdowns per game	2.0	2.3
Points per game	19.3	22.8

All statistics from: Pro-Football-Reference.com

APPENDIX III

1970 PRO BOWL

On January 24, 1971, the NFC beat the AFC, 27–6, at the Pro Bowl in Los Angeles, California. Mel Renfro returned two punts for touchdowns and was named offensive MVP; defensive MVP was Fred Carr of Green Bay. It was the first time NFL and former AFL players met in an All-Star game.

"It's a matter of pride and I think we're all aware that we represent the league this year," said Giants' quarterback Fran Tarkenton.[1] From the losing side, Denver's Rich Jackson observed, "I don't think this is a true test of the strengths of both conferences."[2]

Rosters for the game are listed below (* indicates players eventually elected to the Hall of Fame).

Quarterbacks:

John Brodie (San Francisco)
*Bob Griese (Miami)
Daryle Lamonica (Oakland)
*Fran Tarkenton (New York Giants)

Running Backs:

Larry Brown (Washington)
*Larry Csonka (Miami)
Hewritt Dixon (Oakland)
Mel Farr (Detroit)
Ron Johnson (New York Giants)
*Leroy Kelly (Cleveland)
MacArthur Lane (St. Louis)
*Floyd Little (Denver)
Dave Osborn (Minnesota)

Wide Receivers:

*Fred Biletnikoff (Oakland)
Marlin Briscoe (Buffalo)
Carroll Dale (Green Bay)
Gary Garrison (San Diego)
Dick Gordon (Chicago)
Paul Warfield (Miami)
Gene A. Washington (San Francisco)
Gene Washington (Minnesota)
Warren Wells (Oakland)

Tight Ends:

Raymond Chester (Oakland)
*Charlie Sanders (Detroit)
*Jackie Smith (St. Louis)
Bob Trumpy (Cincinnati)

Offensive Linemen:

*Bob Brown (Los Angeles)
Ed Budde (Kansas City)
Charlie Cowan (Los Angeles)
Ed Flanagan (Detroit)
Gale Gillingham (Green Bay)
Len Hauss (Washington)
*Gene Hickerson (Cleveland)
Winston Hill (New York Jets)
*Tom Mack (Los Angeles)
Ernie McMillan (St. Louis)
Jon Morris (Boston)
John Niland (Dallas)
*Jim Otto (Oakland)
Len Rohde (San Francisco)
Harry Schuh (Oakland)
Walt Sweeney (San Diego)
Jim Tyrer (Kansas City)

Defensive Linemen:

*Junious "Buck" Buchanan
    (Kansas City)
*Carl Eller (Minnesota)
John Elliott (New York Jets)
*Joe Greene (Pittsburgh)
Claude Humphrey (Atlanta)
Rich Jackson (Denver)
*David "Deacon" Jones
    (Los Angeles)
Gary Larsen (Minnesota)
*Bob Lilly (Dallas)
Jerry Mays (Kansas City)
*Merlin Olsen (Los Angeles)
*Alan Page (Minnesota)
Bubba Smith (Baltimore)

Linebackers:

*Bobby Bell (Kansas City)
*Dick Butkus (Chicago)
Fred Carr (Green Bay)
Mike Curtis (Baltimore)
Jim Houston (Cleveland)
*Willie Lanier (Kansas City)
Paul Naumoff (Detroit)
Tommy Nobis (Atlanta)
Andy Russell (Pittsburgh)
Larry Stallings (St. Louis)
Dave Wilcox (San Francisco)

Defensive Backs:

*Willie Brown (Oakland)
*Ken Houston (Houston)
*Jimmy Johnson (San Francisco)
Karl Kassulke (Minnesota)
Jerry Logan (Baltimore)
Jim Marsalis (Kansas City)
Zeke Moore (Houston)
Lemar Parrish (Cincinnati)
*Mel Renfro (Dallas)
Johnny Robinson (Kansas City)
*Roger Wehrli (St. Louis)
*Larry Wilson (St. Louis)
*Willie Wood (Green Bay)

Place Kickers:

Fred Cox (Minnesota)
*Jan Stenerud (Kansas City)

Punters:

Bobby Joe Green (Chicago)
Jerrel Wilson (Kansas City)

Kick Returner:

Cecil Turner (Chicago)

APPENDIX IV

1970 MAJOR AWARD WINNERS

Most Valuable Player, Associated Press:
John Brodie, Quarterback, San Francisco

Most Valuable Player, Newspaper Enterprise Association:
John Brodie, Quarterback, San Francisco

NFC Player of the Year, *The Sporting News*:
John Brodie, Quarterback, San Francisco

AFC Player of the Year, *The Sporting News*:
George Blanda, Quarterback/Kicker, Oakland

Player of the Year, NFL Bert Bell Award:
George Blanda, Quarterback/Kicker, Oakland

Offensive Rookie of the Year, Associated Press:
Dennis Shaw, Quarterback, Buffalo

Defensive Rookie of the Year, Associated Press:
Bruce Taylor, Defensive Back, San Francisco

APPENDIX V

THE MEN OF 1970: WHERE ARE THEY NOW?

Herb Adderley retired in 1973 after a twelve-year NFL career that landed him in the Hall of Fame. Along with forty-eight interceptions, he won six NFL championships—five with Green Bay and another one with Dallas. After his retirement, Adderley briefly did some coaching and also broadcast games for the Eagles and Temple University. He has become a strong advocate for the rights of retired NFL players, and in 2007 sued the NFL Players Association on behalf of two thousand former players who claimed that the union broke licensing agreements by using their images in media such as video games. The NFLPA eventually settled and paid the players $26 million. "I'm just grateful and happy that this thing is finally over and my hope is to bring everyone together," Adderley said.[1]

George Allen never coached again in the NFL after his surprise firing by the Rams in 1978. He served as a television commentator for a few years but could not get coaching out of his blood. Allen coached two teams in the USFL, and in 1990 at the age of seventy-two took over the program at Long Beach State University. Allen said the one season at Long Beach was the most rewarding of his career, as he took a team that finished 4-8 the season before and led it to a 6-5 record. "He was just so excited about the winning season he had at Long Beach State," said Jack Pardee, one of his former players. "Coach Allen always thrived on building something out of very little."[2] But Allen complained of poor health after his team showered him with ice water after a season-ending victory, and he died on New Year's Eve 1990.

Lance Alworth retired after two seasons with the Cowboys, but played a big part in their 1971 championship season, catching a touchdown pass in Super Bowl VI. Although his statistics pale in comparison to some of today's receivers, Alworth was elected to the Hall of Fame in 1978 and named to the NFL's seventy-fifth anniversary team. He has also had a successful post-football career, creating a nationwide chain of self-storage facilities. "A player comes along once in a lifetime who alone is worth the price of admission," said AFL receiver Charley Hennigan. "Lance Alworth was that player."[3]

George Blanda finally retired after the 1975 season, just missing the Raiders' Super Bowl title of the following year. While some of his records have been broken, his longevity mark of twenty-six pro seasons remains intact, as do his heroics from the 1970 season. "I went through the most exciting year any football player ever enjoyed," said Blanda of that year, "and I don't mean only as a field-goal kicker tiptoeing out there to try for three and then running for the sidelines. I mean as a complete football player, doing the *whole* job week after week."[4] Much like his football career, Blanda stayed out of the limelight in retirement. He passed away in 2010 at the age of eighty-three.

Terry Bradshaw had a rocky first few seasons in Pittsburgh, drawing the ire of both Steeler fans and coach Chuck Noll. At one point during the first Super Bowl season of 1974, Bradshaw was benched in favor of "Jefferson Street" Joe Gilliam. "I wasn't used to booing," Bradshaw said. "The first time I heard it, my knees shook. I came close to being a No. 1 flop, but I learned a lot."[5] Bradshaw eventually got his job back, and then went on to win four Super Bowls in six years. He retired after the 1983 season and was inducted into the Hall of Fame in 1989. Bradshaw has done some country and western singing and acting, but he is primarily known for his work as an NFL studio analyst with the Fox television network.

John Brodie finished his seventeen-year NFL career (all with San Francisco) in 1973, and then became an NFL and college football commentator for several years. As a testament to his athletic ability, Brodie joined the Senior PGA Tour and in 1991 won the Security Pacific Senior Classic. He had that one win and twelve other top-ten finishes in a seventeen-year pro golf career. A

massive stroke in October 2000 left him with a lengthy and difficult reha-
bilitation, but he continues to make public appearances. The 49ers retired
Brodie's number 12 jersey but briefly brought it out of retirement in 2006
for quarterback Trent Dilfer, who said he wanted to publicize Brodie's case
for the Hall of Fame.

Bill Brown never got much publicity during his thirteen years in Minnesota,
but his character both on and off the field has made him one of the most
beloved players in Vikings' history. Brown made four Pro Bowls and played
in three Super Bowls, ending his career as a member of the Vikings' kickoff
team in 1974. He still lives in the Twin Cities and attends several games every
season, along with charity work and personal appearances. Brown was
scheduled to be inducted into the team's Ring of Honor in 2003, but he was
bumped until the following year when Cris Carter was inducted ahead of
him. "Bill was very, very gracious," said Bud Grant, who coached Brown.
"He's the nicest guy you'd ever want to know."[6] "He was a real football player.
A tough guy," said long-time Minnesota sportswriter Jim Klobuchar. "If you
have to go into a dark alley, this is the guy you want at your side because
you'll come out. On the other hand, he's a real human being. A warm, car-
ing person."[7]

Paul Brown retired from coaching after leading the Bengals to the playoffs
in 1975, but stayed on as the team's president and saw the Bengals reach two
Super Bowls in the 1980s. His feud with Art Modell was one of many he had
in the NFL because of his rigid, autocratic style. Protégé and former assistant
Bill Walsh said, "[He] worked against my candidacy" to be a head coach anywhere in the league. "And then when I left him, he called whoever he thought
was necessary to keep me out of the NFL."[8] Brown passed away in 1991 and
today the Bengals are run by his son Mike.

Norm Bulaich, the rookie who filled in so well for Tom Matte in 1970, lasted
only three seasons in Baltimore. He was slow to recover from an injury in
1971, and the Colts traded him to the Eagles. After two years in Philadelphia,
he played five more seasons in Miami, and then retired after the 1979 season. For more than a decade, Bulaich has lived outside Ft. Worth, Texas, and

worked for one of the largest solid-waste management companies in the country. But he still has vivid memories of his Super Bowl–winning season with the Colts. "Baltimore was different in that they were a family," Bulaich said. "I came there as a 22-year-old rookie and lined up in the huddle with legends. I'm in awe of that. And I was able to start my rookie year, so it was an extra bonus just to be in that arena with them and go to the Super Bowl and win it."[9]

Dick Butkus came to personify the position of linebacker, and especially a linebacker who loved violence. "I never liked the NFL players I butted helmets with," he once said. "I didn't want to be their friend. I couldn't be friends with someone who, at any moment on the field, could bring an end to my utopia—playing football."[10] Knee injuries finally forced Butkus to retire after the 1973 season, and he was elected to the Hall of fame in 1979. Butkus gravitated toward broadcasting and acting, appearing in several movies and television shows, as well as doing radio work on Bears' games for several years. He has also been actively involved in charity work, and the Butkus Award annually honors the nation's best high school, college, and NFL linebackers for their work on the field and in their communities.

Howard Cosell stayed with *Monday Night Football* through 1983 and also worked in a variety of roles for ABC, including boxing, baseball, and the Olympics. Throughout the 1970s he was considered the most powerful voice in sportscasting, and although his influence began to wane in the 1980s, he still remains one of the most iconic figures in sports television history. "Whether you liked him or not, you couldn't help but notice him," said sportscaster Bob Costas. "He could only be, whether you loved him or hated him, Howard Cosell."[11] Cosell retired in 1992 and died three years later.

Larry Csonka went on to win two Super Bowls with Miami and also earned game MVP honors in Super Bowl VIII. His Hall of Fame career included five Pro Bowl and three All-Pro selections. After his retirement in 1979, Csonka has appeared in several outdoor-related television shows and projects. While taping for a television show in 2005 in Alaska, his boat was caught in a severe storm; Csonka and his crew had to ride through the storm for ten hours before the U.S. Coast Guard rescue team could reach them. Despite the incident, Csonka still lives in Alaska and continues to produce outdoors programming. "Coach [Don] Shula used to demand complete attention," Csonka said of his playing days. "He would get in my face and say, 'I don't know where you are, but I know you are not here. Would you please tell me where you are?' He was right. Where I was was in a stream in Alaska."[12]

Gary Cuozzo found himself expendable in Minnesota when the Vikings reacquired Fran Tarkenton in 1972. Cuozzo played that season in St. Louis, then retired to practice orthodontics in his native New Jersey. When his oldest son, Gary Jr., was murdered as part of a drug deal in 1990, Cuozzo began lecturing teenagers on the dangers of drugs and became national chairman of the Fellowship of Christian Athletes from 1995 to 1998. Another son, Patrick, followed in Cuozzo's footsteps and became an orthodontist in New Jersey.

Bill Curry's NFL career lasted until 1974, at which point he worked in both television and coaching. Curry served as a commentator for college football on ESPN but also was the head football coach at Georgia Tech, the University of Alabama, and the University of Kentucky. In 2010 he took over as head coach at Georgia State University, a school just starting its football program. "To be with a group of young people, most of whom have been told they're not good enough, and show them how to succeed and have a meaningful life," he said, "I haven't felt like this in a long time."[13] Curry retired from Georgia State after the 2012 season.

James "Mike" Curtis has a Super Bowl ring from 1970, but perhaps the singular image fans have of him took place the following year. When a drunken fan ran out on the field at Baltimore's Memorial Stadium and tried to make off with the football, Curtis leveled him with a vicious hit. The four-time Pro Bowler remains just as competitive in commercial real estate, where he has worked since his NFL retirement in 1978. "It sounds corny but I want to provide a service and that means I have to learn the business better than anyone else," he said in 2009. "And that's how I compete. All the people who loaf around end up croaking."[14]

Al Davis eventually put the Raiders on top, winning three Super Bowls between 1977 and 1984, but his reputation suffered major damage. It began in 1982, when Davis successfully challenged the NFL in court for the right to move the team to Los Angeles. By the time the Raiders returned to Oakland in 1995, their dominance had ended, and starting in 2003 the franchise endured ten straight non-winning seasons. Davis reacted with petulance and impatience, firing four head coaches during that span and in some cases, refusing to pay money he owed them. By 2011, there was a great sense that the game had passed by Davis, and in a national poll he was voted the most disliked sports figure in the country.[15] Sportswriter Rick Reilly wrote that Davis had become "exactly like those Members Only jackets he wore—fashionable once, dreadfully dated forever after."[16] Davis was elected to the Hall of Fame in 1992 and he died in 2011 at age eighty-two.

Tom Dempsey had his shining moment in 1970, but it was also his last season in New Orleans. With more teams going to soccer-style kickers, Dempsey and his fellow straight-on kickers were becoming outdated, and even his record was somewhat tainted when, in 1977, the NFL passed the "Dempsey Rule," which outlawed all odd-shaped kicking shoes and surfaces. Dempsey bounced around with four more teams before finishing his NFL career in 1979, still looking to recapture the magic of November 8, 1970—when he was the greatest kicker who ever lived. "I don't think about it a lot," said Dempsey, who settled in New Orleans in retirement and had to rebuild his home after Hurricane Katrina. "I'm very proud of what I accomplished. It helped me get where I was going. A lot of times people forget where they came from and who helped them get there."[17]

Roman Gabriel stayed with the Rams until he tore up a knee during the 1972 season and figured his career was over. But he was traded to the Eagles and had three more productive seasons, including 1973 when he led the league in touchdown passes and passing yards and was named NFL Comeback Player of the Year. Gabriel retired after the 1977 season and did some acting, broadcasting, and coaching. He also created a company that produces hats, shirts, and other golf-related attire, and has raised millions for charity in his native North Carolina. "There's been more good things that have happened to me, far above the bad things," he said. "Naturally, when you play as a player in the NFL, the ultimate goal is you wish you can get to the Super Bowl and win. I'm glad I didn't get there and not win. I can't imagine getting there and not winning it and never getting the chance to get back. But sure, I miss that fact that I wasn't on a Super Bowl team that won."[18]

Mike Garrett went on to get a law degree after retiring from the NFL in 1973, and for several years was involved in a variety of business projects in the southern California area. In 1993 Garrett became the athletic director at University of Southern California, the school where he had won the Heisman Trophy in 1965. Under Garrett's direction, the Trojans became a football powerhouse, but in 2010 the NCAA imposed major sanctions on USC related to alleged recruiting violations and payment of players. Garrett was forced out as athletic director in July 2010, but he remained unrepentant. "As I read the decision by the NCAA, I read between the lines and there was nothing but a lot of envy," he told a USC booster club meeting. "They wish they all were Trojans."[19]

Harry "Bud" Grant retired as Vikings' coach in 1983, and then came back for one ill-fated season in 1985 before leaving for good as the eighth-winningest coach in NFL history. He produced eleven division championships and took Minnesota to four Super Bowls, although he shares with Marv Levy the record for having lost all four. Grant was elected to the Hall of Fame in 1994 and continues to work with the Vikings as a consultant. In addition to hunting and fishing, he has also become an outspoken advocate for environmental reform and wildlife preservation.

Bob Griese had a much longer career as a television football analyst than he did as an NFL quarterback. After his fourteen-year pro career ended with two Super Bowl wins and induction into the Hall of Fame, Griese embarked on a twenty-nine-year career as an analyst for pro and college games. He had a variety of broadcast partners over the years, but perhaps is most well-known for the twelve seasons he spent doing college games with Keith Jackson. "Bob is a great analyst and an even better man," Jackson said. "We had the ability to play off each other which isn't always the case with announcer teams. It worked for us."[20] Griese retired from broadcasting in 2011, saying, "I've had a wonderful career and now it's time to experience new things."[21]

Jim Hart enjoyed a nineteen-year career in the NFL; not bad for a free agent who went undrafted out of college. He still holds Cardinals' franchise records for passing yards, touchdowns, and completions. After eighteen years in St. Louis, Hart spent one season in Washington and then retired in 1985. He served several years as athletic director of his alma mater, Southern Illinois University, and now lives in retirement in Florida, where he does not see much football. "I enjoy watching the Monday Night games," he said in 2008, "but I would rather play golf on Sundays."[22]

Bob Hayes was elected to the Hall of Fame in 2009; an honor many in the NFL believed was long overdue. What may have kept Hayes out of the Hall so long was a dark post-football career that saw him serve ten months in prison for selling drugs to an undercover police officer. Although Hayes pleaded guilty, he adamantly denied guilt until his death from kidney failure in 2002. In his autobiography, Hayes admitted the 1979 conviction destroyed his life, and he struggled with addiction his remaining years. "That was it," said former teammate Pete Gent. "That was one of those where once you're out of the game, life kills you."[23]

Chuck Howley is still the only player from a losing team named as Super Bowl MVP. He intercepted another pass in Super Bowl VI and shares (with Rod Martin of Oakland and Larry Brown of Dallas) the record for career Super Bowl interceptions with three. A knee injury in 1972 effectively ended Howley's fifteen-year NFL career. In retirement, he spent several years in the dry-cleaning business, and more recently has raised quarter horses at his ranch in east Texas. "There is a whole different world outside of sports," he once said, "but a lot of things that help you succeed in football also help you succeed in life."[24]

David "Deacon" Jones finished his career in 1975 and was named as either All-Pro or a Pro Bowl selection thirteen times. He was named to the Hall of Fame in 1980, his first year of eligibility. Jones worked for a variety of companies after his retirement, but since 1997 he has mainly focused on the Deacon Jones Foundation, an organization designed to help young, disadvantaged kids in inner-city neighborhoods. "Coming from a poor, inner-city neighborhood myself, I have an intimate knowledge of all of the problems people face there," he said. "When kids from the ghetto enter college and the workplace, they don't know a thing about what they hear. And they are never told exactly what their commitment to their own neighborhoods must be."[25]

Lee Roy Jordan played fourteen seasons for the Cowboys, earning a spot in the team's Ring of Honor, the Texas Sports Hall of Fame, and the College Football Hall of Fame. He played for two of the iconic coaches of his era—Paul "Bear" Bryant at the University of Alabama and Tom Landry with the Cowboys. "Playing under both men I learned there are two different ways, two approaches to winning," Jordan said.[26] Landry called Jordan a leader and "an extremely tough competitor. Not everybody liked him, but they respected him."[27] Jordan entered the business world after his retirement in 1976 and today owns Lee Roy Jordan Lumber Company in Dallas.

Joe Kapp did not play in the NFL again after the 1970 season, and he still carries hard feelings about the way he had been treated by both the Patriots and Vikings. Kapp eventually sued the league, claiming that the standard player contract was restraint of trade, and his legal victory ultimately helped pave the way for NFL free agency. Kapp returned to coach his alma mater, the University of California, Berkeley, and was on the sidelines in 1982 when the Bears stunned Stanford on a last-second kick return, now known simply as "The Play." Even at seventy-three, his reputation for toughness still remains. In 2011 Kapp got into a cane-swinging public fight with a former rival player at a Canadian Football League reunion. "These guys, despite their age, what is bred in their bones is a warrior's streak," said Ron James, who emceed the event.[28]

Alex Karras seemed larger than life, both on and off the field. Many argue that the three-time All Pro belongs in the Hall of Fame, and may be kept out because of his one-year suspension in 1963 for gambling on NFL games. After his thirteen-year career with the Lions ended in 1971, Karras became a successful actor and his credits include memorable roles in the movies *Blazing Saddles* and *Victor Victoria*, as well as the television series *Webster*. He also spent three seasons in the *Monday Night Football* booth where he once noted that Raiders defensive lineman Otis Sistrunk was from the "University of Mars." When he died in 2012 at the age of seventy-seven, the official cause was listed as kidney failure, although Karras also suffered from dementia. He was one of the many former NFL players to sue the league over head-related injuries. "This physical beating he took as a football player has impacted his life," said Karras's wife, Susan Clark, shortly before he died. "He is interested in making the game of football safer and hoping that other families of retired players will have a healthier and happier retirement."[29]

Karl Kassulke's NFL career was cut tragically short in 1973 by a motorcycle accident he suffered while riding to training camp. The accident nearly killed Kassulke and left him permanently paralyzed. "Bud [Grant] broke down and started to cry," recalled defensive tackle Bob Lurtsema of the moment the Vikings' head coach gave the news to the team. "Tears were coming down my cheeks. You could hear a pin drop. . . . That says more for any individual of being the total package for a coach to respect him that much."[30] After the accident, Kassulke worked with Wings Outreach, a Christian ministry for the disabled. He died of a heart attack in 2008, at age sixty-seven.

Leroy Kelly had a difficult season in 1970, rushing for just 656 yards and six touchdowns. He never again rushed for more than 1,000 yards in his NFL career, which ended after the 1973 season. Kelly played briefly in the World Football League, and then settled down to a life of card shows and personal appearances. He was elected to the Hall of Fame in 1994, one of his moments in the sun after spending his career in the shadow of Jim Brown. "I'm just glad he quit when he did," Kelly said of Brown. "If he had played a few more years—and he certainly could have done that—I might never have had the chance I had. All I ever wanted to do was to be Leroy Kelly and do the best job I possibly could."[31]

Steve Kiner defined the hard-partying, rebellious young NFL player of the early 1970s, and his lifestyle helped cause his exit from Dallas after only one season. After playing for the Patriots and then the Oilers, Kiner retired in 1978 and embarked on a personal transformation. He got married, raised three daughters, and earned two master's degrees. He currently manages emergency psychiatric services for Emory Healthcare at Emory University in Atlanta, Georgia. "They gave the crazy guy the keys to the asylum," he joked.[32]

Daryle Lamonica still holds the Oakland record for most touchdown passes in a single season with thirty-four in 1969. In fact, he's also second on that list with thirty touchdowns in 1967. The "Mad Bomber" retired after the 1974 season with five Pro Bowl and two All-Pro selections in his twelve-year career. He now lives a relatively quiet retirement in the Fresno, California, area, close to the high school football field named in his honor. "That's one of the highest honors I've ever had," he said.[33]

Tom Landry won 270 games in his NFL coaching career, all with the Cowboys, which ranks him third all-time (behind Don Shula and George Halas). His twenty career playoff wins and twenty-nine years coaching the same team are both NFL records. After Landry was fired by Jerry Jones in 1989, the city of Dallas celebrated "Hats Off to Tom Landry Day," which included a parade that drew more than 100,000 people. After that, he mostly stayed out of the spotlight, except for his work with Christian organizations. Landry died of leukemia in February 2000 at the age of seventy-five. "I was fortunate enough to play 11 years for an incredible football coach and even more amazing man," said Roger Staubach. "Coach Landry was the kind of man we'd all like to be."[34]

MacArthur Lane led the NFL in rushing touchdowns with eleven in 1970, but soon fell out of favor with new coach Bob Hollway. The Cardinals suspended him for the 1971 regular-season finale after he criticized team ownership as part of a salary dispute, and then traded him to Green Bay the following season. Lane enjoyed a productive eleven-year career, finishing with Kansas City where he led the league in receptions with sixty-six in 1976. Lane played and coached in Canada and was also an assistant for the Chiefs. He has returned to his native Oakland where he works in the real estate business.

Bob Lilly retired after the 1974 season and was elected to the Hall of Fame in 1980. He was also named as one of the defensive tackles on the NFL's seventy-fifth anniversary team in 1994. Lilly dabbled in photography during his playing days and became an avid wildlife and outdoors photographer after his retirement, publishing books on photography and at one point opening a studio in New Mexico. He continues to live in his native Texas, less than fifty miles from his childhood home of Throckmorton. "I've seen a lot of good players," said his former teammate Lee Roy Jordan "and I'm not sure that Bob Lilly still isn't the best I've ever seen. If he had a mean streak, you would have [had] to outlaw him."[35]

John Mackey commented during the players' strike of 1970, "I've got broad shoulders and I can take a lot more abuse than I've already had."[36] Those broad shoulders were severely tested when repeated football concussions eventually led to dementia requiring full-time care. "You can't cry over spilled milk," said Mackey's wife Sylvia in 2007. "You have to look at how to make the best of the future."[37] The NFL and its Players Association responded by creating "The 88 Plan" (named after Mackey's old number) to help former players battling dementia. Mackey was elected to the Hall of Fame in 1992, and in 2001 an award was created in his name to honor the outstanding tight end in college football each season. He died in 2011 at the age of 69.

Jim Marshall played in four Super Bowls with the Vikings, but never won the big game. "I've never gotten over it," he said. "None of them. You never get over things like that. It still haunts me every day."[38] Marshall had a variety of jobs after leaving the NFL following the 1979 season, including stock broker and insurance salesman, but football injuries have greatly slowed him down in recent years. He still lives in the Twin Cities area, and often speaks to school-aged children. "I talk to them about choices," he says. "Working hard, concentrating on being the best they can be. Taking responsibility for one's life path."[39]

Don Meredith never played a single down in 1970, but he was one of the most important figures of that NFL season. It was Meredith who teamed with Howard Cosell to help turn *Monday Night Football* into a sporting and cultural institution in its inaugural season. Meredith worked two different stints at *MNF*, also teamed with Curt Gowdy at NBC, and acted in a variety of movies and television shows, but the fun-loving persona masked insecurities that troubled him almost his whole life. "Meredith has plenty of self-doubts," Tex Schramm said in 1968. "That facade is not his real nature. He's his own worst enemy, but he knows that."[40] After his retirement from broadcasting in 1985, Meredith dropped out of public view and preferred to spend his time secluded at his New Mexico home. He died of a brain hemorrhage in 2010 at the age of seventy-two.

Art Modell achieved his long-time dream of winning a Super Bowl championship when the Baltimore Ravens won Super Bowl XXXV following the 2000 season. After owning the franchise for forty-four years, Modell sold controlling interest of the Ravens to Maryland businessman Steve Bisciotti in 2003, although he retained a 1 percent share in the team. While Modell remained one of the most divisive figures in Cleveland sports history, he insisted that he had nothing but strong feelings for the city he left in 1995. "I left a good part of my soul [in Ohio]," he acknowledged. "I can never forget the kindness of the people of Cleveland."[41] Modell died in 2012 at the age of eighty-seven.

Earl Morrall played for six teams in a twenty-one-year career, leading Don Shula to say, "The good thing is that we always have a homecoming for him. He gets himself up for his old teams."[42] Morrall won three Super Bowl rings, but it's the one that got away that still haunts him. "Yeah, it's difficult," he said, referring to the Colts' loss to the Jets in Super Bowl III. "But it's there and it's not going to change."[43] In 2012 Morrall was living in south Florida, and described himself as semi-retired from his commercial leasing business.

Craig Morton played eighteen years in the NFL and shares with Kurt Warner the distinction of being the only quarterback to start a Super Bowl game for two different teams. Even though he lost both games, he said, "Playing in those two Super Bowls was a special honor. I had a long, fulfilling career in the NFL, but those Super Bowl experiences really made it extra rewarding."[44] Morton returned to his alma mater, the University of California, and worked as a fundraiser for the school's athletic department. He still remembers the nervousness he felt squaring off against Johnny Unitas in Super Bowl V. "I'm looking out at the field, and I see this gigantic, inflatable Johnny Unitas," Morton recalled. "I say to myself, 'What the heck am I doing playing against this guy?'"[45]

Joe Namath never got the Jets back in the Super Bowl, and spent the rest of his thirteen-year career battling injuries that eventually forced him to retire after the 1977 season. His persona was so large, and his success in Super Bowl III so indelible, that he was inducted into the Hall of Fame rather easily in 1985, despite ending his career with more interceptions than touchdown passes. It was natural that Namath would gravitate toward TV, and he has appeared in several television shows and movies. He has also made a comfortable living as a celebrity endorser. One television moment he undoubtedly would like to forget took place in December 2003, when an apparently inebriated Namath made advances toward reporter Suzy Kolber during a live sideline interview. It was the low point of Namath's long battle with alcohol, but his reputation survived, mainly because he continues to define an entire generation for football fans. "Broadway Joe was the coolest kid in America," Mark Kriegel wrote in his biography of Namath. "An object of affection for girls and gangsters, a source of bafflement for bookmakers everywhere. He walked off with Jagger's girls. He spilled drinks on Sinatra. He grinned his way through it all."[46]

Tom Nowatzke has the distinction of scoring the last Super Bowl touchdown in Baltimore Colts history. His 2-yard score in the fourth quarter of Super Bowl V tied the game and set the stage for Jim O'Brien's winning kick. "If you look back at the game, we should have won it going away," Nowatzke later said. But Super Bowl V was still "the roughest football game I've ever been in for two quarters, meaning the second half."[47] A former first-round pick of the Lions, Nowatzke ended his NFL career after the 1972 season and has become a successful businessman in the Detroit area. Tom Nowatzke Transport Equipment is one of the leaders in truck trailer sales and leasing in the country.

Jim O'Brien continues his work in the Los Angeles area as a project manager for a real estate company. There have been more famous—and more recent—game-winning Super Bowl kicks, including a couple by Adam Vinatieri of the Patriots. But Jim O'Brien was still the first. "All I remember is seeing the ball," he said in 2007. "I didn't see the holder [Earl Morrall] put it down and I didn't hear anything. Everything was just silent. There was no noise or anything. I kicked it and that was it."[48]

Mel Renfro helped the Cowboys to two Super Bowl championships, and his fifty-two career interceptions earned him a spot in the Hall of Fame in 1996. He still lives in the Dallas area, working for a mortgage company and making personal appearances, but fourteen years in the NFL apparently took a physical toll. Renfro says the nine concussions he suffered ultimately led to clinical depression. "Even in the happiest of times, I'll wake up in the morning with a heavy head and with the depression," said Renfro in 2007. "It's to the point where I don't want to . . . face people. That's not the way I used to be."[49]

Lou Saban never could find a place to settle down and ended up holding twenty-seven different coaching jobs in a restless fifty-two-year career. "I made some quick moves in a lot of places, but I just figured if it's not a good fit and it's not going to work, why hang around?,"[50] he said. His greatest success came in Buffalo, where in addition to the two AFL titles, he coached O. J. Simpson to the first 2,000-yard rushing season in NFL history in 1973. Saban also served as president of the New York Yankees in 1981–1982 at the request of his friend George Steinbrenner. "He's going to coach as long as he can breathe," said Steinbrenner in 2001, when Saban took his last coaching position at tiny Chowan University in Murfreesboro, North Carolina, at the age of eighty.[51] After two seasons, Saban finally retired for good. He passed away in 2009 at the age of eighty-seven.

Gale Sayers played only two games in 1971 before knee injuries forced his retirement at the age of twenty-eight. Even though he played in the NFL for parts of only seven seasons, he still holds records for touchdowns in a game and career kickoff return average. In 1977 he became the youngest inductee into the Hall of Fame. "It was a gift," Sayers says of his running style. "And trust me, it was easy. It was so easy, I can't even explain it."[52] He built a solid business career after leaving the NFL and today runs Sayers, a $100 million information technology company in Chicago. He has also been heavily involved with charity work, and The Gale Sayers Center focuses on after, school programs for disadvantaged adolescents.

Don Shula coached his first game for the Miami Dolphins in 1970. He didn't coach his last game for the team until 1995, at which point he held the NFL record for most coaching victories with 347 and games coached with 526 (including playoffs). Shula coached thirty-three years, won two Super Bowls, and had only two losing seasons. In retirement, he has created a line of steak houses, done some television endorsements, and occasionally offers commentary on the NFL. "What Babe [Ruth] was to baseball, Shula is to football coaching," said former NFL coach Marv Levy. "There are certain figures in sports who are larger than the games they play or coach, and Don Shula is one of those."[53]

Charles "Bubba" Smith played nine years in the NFL, his career cut short by a devastating knee injury that saw him play out the string with Oakland and Houston. Smith was never one to take such things too seriously. "Bubba didn't have an attitude about anything," said Mike Celizic. "He took life as it came and enjoyed new experiences. He wasn't out to please anyone but himself."[54] After retiring in 1976, Smith turned to acting and appeared in variety of television shows, commercials, and movies, including the popular *Police Academy* series. Smith died suddenly in August 2011 at the age of sixty-six.

Jackie Smith retired as the all-time receiver among tight ends with 480 receptions for 7,918 yards and forty touchdowns, and those numbers won him election to the Hall of Fame in 1994.[55] But it's the catch he didn't make that defines his career. Smith played his last season in Dallas and helped the Cowboys reach Super Bowl XIII; unfortunately his drop of a Roger Staubach pass in the end zone was a key play in the Cowboys' 35–31 loss to Pittsburgh. "I just missed it," he said later. "I slipped a little but still should have had it. I've dropped passes before, but never any that were so important."[56] Today, Smith is an avid fisherman and kayaker who also enjoys singing; he has sung the National Anthem and various venues and political rallies.

Roger Staubach seriously thought about leaving the Cowboys after the loss in Super Bowl V and gave an ultimatum to Tom Landry, asking for a trade if he did not get a chance to start in 1971. It took until midseason of that year before Staubach became the full-time starter, and then he led Dallas to ten straight wins, including a Super Bowl victory. Staubach won two Super Bowls for the Cowboys in his Hall of Fame career, which ended in 1979, and earned the nickname "Captain Comeback" for his frequent late-game heroics. He also built a reputation of moral integrity, prompting *Sports Illustrated* to call him "the Galahad of the Gridiron, the NFL's own personal St. Francis of Assisi, the straightest arrow in the quiver."[57] His former teammate Drew Pearson said, "There is nothing I would or could ever say bad about Roger. He's the only player I've played with who everything they say about him is true."[58] Staubach created a hugely successful real estate business in Dallas and also chaired the effort to bring Super Bowl XLV to north Texas.

Fran Tarkenton never thought of himself as a scrambler. "These wild sideline-to-sideline scrambles have become my trademark," he said in 1967, "and people have forgotten the simple truth of the matter, which is that I'm basically a pocket passer."[59] Tarkenton played eighteen years in the NFL but never won a championship, losing three Super Bowls after his return to Minnesota in 1972. Although his records have since been broken, Tarkenton retired as the NFL's all-time leader in touchdown passes and was elected to the Hall of Fame in 1986. He became a TV host and football analyst in retirement, but in 1994 created his own company and has branched out in insurance, financial planning, and computer technology. In 1999 Tarkenton had to pay more than $150,000 in restitution to the Securities and Exchange Commission, which accused him of fraudulently inflating the value of his company.

Duane Thomas never played a game for the San Diego Chargers after being traded to the team in 1972. A year later, he was traded to the Washington Redskins, but personal problems ended his NFL career at the age of twenty-seven in 1974. In 1989 he wrote a book about his Dallas experiences called *Duane Thomas and the Fall of America's Team*, but he seems to have made peace with his troubled past. He now lives in Arizona and enjoys writing and painting. Asked if he had any regrets about his NFL career, Thomas replied, "No, I really don't. You can't have regrets on that. That's where I was in my life. You can't really look back and I don't."[60]

Johnny Unitas was almost universally acknowledged as the best quarterback in NFL history when he retired after the 1973 season. Other quarterbacks—including Joe Montana, Dan Marino, and John Elway—have since laid claim to that title, but there still remains a mystique about Unitas. "Johnny U was an American original, a piece of work like none other, excepting maybe Paul Bunyan and Horatio Alger," wrote Frank Deford, when Unitas passed away in 2002.[61] Unitas had a difficult post-football career, as bad investments cost him $4 million and forced him to declare bankruptcy. He also suffered from crippling injuries caused by his eighteen-year NFL career. He was voted into the Hall of Fame in 1979, and the award for the best college quarterback each season is named the "Johnny Unitas Golden Arm Award."

Gene Washington, the 49ers receiver, finished his playing career after the 1979 season but returned to the NFL in 1994 as Director of Operations, where he was in charge of enforcing league playing rules. He retired from that position in 2009 and currently serves as a director for several companies listed on the New York Stock Exchange. In the 1980s Washington worked in the athletic department at his alma mater, Stanford University, where he met faculty member Condoleezza Rice, who went on to become U.S. secretary of state. Washington escorted Rice to several state dinners, but denied any romantic involvement, "We're great friends, we're comfortable with each other and we enjoy each other's company," he said in 2003. "She can relax with me. We've known each other for so long she doesn't have to break me in."[62]

NOTES

Chapter 1. The War

1 Peter Golenbock, *Cowboys Have Always Been My Heroes: The Definitive Oral History of America's Team* (New York: Warner Books, 1997), 762.

2 Tim Cowlishaw, "How 'Bout Them Cowboys?," *Dallas Morning News*, January 18, 1993, http://www.dallasnews.com/sharedcontent/dws/spt/football/cowboys/classic/recordbook/yearbyyear/1992/01189349ers.html (accessed July 22, 2010).

3 Randy Galloway, "'Niners Choke on Jimmy's Words," *Dallas Morning News*, January 24, 1994, http://www.dallasnews.com/sharedcontent/dws/spt/football/cowboys/classic/recordbook/yearbyyear/1993/012494galloway.html (accessed July 25, 2010).

4 Golenbock, *Cowboys Have Always Been My Heroes*, 762.

5 Mike Ozanian, "Dallas Cowboys Lead NFL with $2.1 Billion Valuation," *Forbes*, September 5, 2012, http://www.forbes.com/sites/mikeozanian/2012/09/05/dallas-cowboys-lead-nfl-with-2-1-billion-valuation/ (accessed September 27, 2012).

6 Will McDonough, *75 Seasons: The Complete Story of the National Football League, 1920–1995* (Atlanta: Turner Publishing, 1994), 25.

7 David Bauder, "Super Bowl Ratings Record: Giants-Patriots Game is Highest-Rated TV Show in US History," *huffingtonpost.com*, February 6, 2012, http://www.huffingtonpost.com/2012/02/06/super-bowl-ratings-record-tv-giants-patriots_n_1258107.html (accessed September 28, 2012).

8 The WFL went so far as to offer injured Jets quarterback Joe Namath a $4 million contract to play for its Chicago franchise, an offer he eventually turned down. Today, that offer would be worth more than $16 million. Jerry Kirshenbaum, "Scorecard," *Sports Illustrated*, April 28, 1975, http://sportsillustrated.cnn.com/vault/article/magazine/MAG1089767/index.htm (accessed June 12, 2011).

9 "The World Football League," *NFL Lost Treasures*, NFL Films, November 25, 2003.

10 Tommy Reamon, interview by Richie Franklin and Jim Cusano, "WFL Interviews," *worldfootballleague.org*, July 10, 1999, http://www.worldfootballleague.org (accessed June 14, 2010).

11 Gordon Forbes, "Ex-Maulers to Honor Their USFL Year in Pittsburgh," *USA Today*, June 8, 1994, C3; and Gordon Forbes, "Memories Linger in Liberty City; Philadelphia's USFL Reunion Unites 150 Stars," *USA Today*, June 12, 1989, C6.

12 Gordon Forbes, "Check Left Mark on USFL; Ex-Executive Holds Memory," *USA Today*, March 16, 2000, C18.

13 Ibid.

14 Larry Weisman, "USFL Lives on in Memories," *USA Today*, July 8, 1993, C2.

15 "The World Football League." Gary Davidson was also behind the creation of the World Hockey Association and the American Basketball Association. Both organizations strongly challenged the established NBA and NHL, and forced those leagues to expand and absorb individual teams. By contrast, the WFL and its teams vanished almost without a trace.

16 Stan Grosshandler, "All America Football Conference," *The Coffin Corner* 2, no. 7 (February 7, 1980) http://www.profootballresearchers.org/Coffin_Corner/02-07-035.pdf (accessed June 1, 2010).

17 It should be noted that the APFA had black players as early as the inaugural season of 1920. In 1946 both Woody Strode and Kenny Washington played for the Los Angeles Rams.

18 The original Baltimore Colts lasted only one season in the NFL before folding in 1951.

19 Dick Heller, "Browns NFL Debut in '50 Left Eagles Flying Low," *Washington Times*, January 19, 2004, C3.

20 Ibid.

21 McDonough, *75 Seasons*, 118.

22 Jim Morrison, "The American Football League's Foolish Club," *The Smithsonian*, January 14, 2010, http://www.smithsonianmag.com/history-archaeology/The-American-Football -Leagues-Foolish-Club.html (accessed June 4, 2010).

23 Lee Lowenfish, *Branch Rickey: Baseball's Ferocious Gentleman* (Lincoln: University of Nebraska Press, 2007), 564.

24 Tex Maule, "On With the Golden Game," *Sports Illustrated*, September 12, 1966, 54.

25 "Replay! The History of the NFL on Television," NFL Films, 1998.

26 Much like the USFL tried 20 years later, the AFL also sued the NFL on anti-trust grounds. In 1962 a federal judge ruled in the NFL's favor.

27 Furman Bisher, "Linked on Draft Day, Falcons' First Picks Took Different Paths," *Atlanta Journal-Constitution*, April 23, 2009, http://blogs.ajc.com/furman-bisher-blog/2009/04/23 /linked-on-draft-day-falcons-first-picks-took-different-paths/ (accessed August 1, 2010).

28 "Times They Are a Changin'," *Full Color Football: The History of the American Football League*, NFL Films, September 23, 2009.

29 Jarrett Ball, "From Upstart to Big Time, How the AFL Changed the NFL," *USA Today*, June 14, 2009, http://www.usatoday.com/sports/football/nfl/2009-06-14-sw-afl-cover_N.htm (accessed June 30, 2010).

30 George Blanda and Jack Olsen, "A Decade of Revenge," *Sports Illustrated*, July 26, 1971, 36.

31 Larry Felser, *The Birth of the New NFL: How the 1966 NFL/AFL Merger Transformed Pro Football* (Guilford, CT: Lyons Press, 2008), 167.

32 Ibid.

33 "Times They Are a Changin'."

34 "Pro Football: That Kansas City Beef," *Time*, December 9, 1966, http://www.time.com/time /magazine/article/0,9171,898482,00.html (accessed May 5, 2011).

35 Nate Davis, "Chiefs Were the Toast of the AFL ... After They Left Dallas," *USA Today*, June 28, 2009, http://usatoday30.usatoday.com/sports/football/nfl/chiefs/2009-07-27-sw-afl-chiefs _N.htm (accessed June 22, 2010).

36 Ed Gruver, "The AFL's First Super Team," Professional Football Researchers Association, 2007, http://www.mmbolding.com/Unplayed/Unplayed_Gruver.htm (accessed June 1, 2010).

37 John Jeansonne, "Chargers vs. Bears: A Makeup Game," *Newsday*, 1980, http://www.mmbolding .com/Unplayed/Unplayed.htm (accessed May 30, 2010).

38 "The Two Pro Football Leagues Must Meet," *Sports Illustrated*, December 16, 1963, 27. The use of the phrase "World Series" of football shows how dominant baseball was in the public conscious-ness. Today, mega-events of any type are commonly referred to as the "Super Bowl" of that event.

39 Tex Maule, "Ridiculous! The NFL by 50 points," *Sports Illustrated*, December 16, 1963, 32.

40 "Times They Are a Changin'."

41 Ken Rappoport, "The AFL-NFL Merger was Almost Booted ... By a Kicker." *nfl.com*, August 2009, http://www.nfl.com/news/story?id=09000d5d81206b90 &template=without-video -with-comments&confirm=true (accessed July 11, 2010).

42 "Times They Are a Changin'."

43 Tex Maule, "Here's How it Happened," *Sports Illustrated*, June 20, 1966, 15.

44 Rappoport, "The AFL-NFL Merger was Almost Booted."

45 Maule, "Here's How it Happened," 19.

Chapter 2. The Peace

1 Davis's bitterness and resentment against the NFL would fester for decades and would lead him to file a lawsuit against his fellow owners when they forbid him to move his Raiders franchise to Los Angeles. In 1982 a federal district court ruled for Davis, and the Raiders played in L.A. for thirteen seasons before returning to Oakland.

2 Felser, *The Birth of the New NFL*, 167.

3 Ibid., 99.

4 Ibid., 168.

5 Unlike sportswriters, the NFL didn't officially use the term until Super Bowl IV. "We didn't particularly like the term Super Bowl," said Jim Kensil, assistant to Pete Rozelle. "We felt it was a little too presumptuous." Associated Press, "Vikings Don't Escape Cold," January 7, 1970.

6 Marty Ralbovsky, *The Super Bowl: Of Men, Myths and Moments* (New York: Hawthorne Books, 1971), xv.

7 Mark Gaughan, "Could '64 Bills Have Won 'Super Bowl' Against Browns?" *Buffalo News*, May 29, 2005, http://www.mmbolding.com/Unplayed/ Unplayed_Gaughan.htm (accessed July 12, 2011).

8 The outspoken Gilchrist often complained about his role in Buffalo, resulting in his trade to the Denver Broncos in 1965. He later played for the Miami Dolphins.

9 Bill Toland, "Obituary: Carlton Chester 'Cookie' Gilchrist; Outspoken, Brackenridge-born star running back," *Pittsburgh Post-Gazette*, January 11, 2011, http://www.post-gazette.com/pg /11011/1117039-122.stm (accessed February 20, 2011).

10 Ralbovsky, *Super Bowl*, 6.

11 Jon Kendle, "Players Boycott AFL All-Star game," *Pro Football Hall of Fame*, February 18, 2010, http://www.profootballhof.com/history/2010/2/18/players-boycott-afl-all-star-game / (accessed February 19, 2011).

12 Peter King, "The Afl," *Sports Illustrated*, July 13, 2009, http://sportsillustrated.cnn.com/vault/article/magazine/MAG1157664/3/index.htm (accessed February 20, 2010).

13 Ibid.

14 Ibid.

15 Edwin Shrake, "Firewater for some Fired-Up Chiefs," *Sports Illustrated*, January 9, 1967, 14–15.

16 Ed Bagley, "Famous Quotes by Vince Lombardi," 2007, http://ezinearticles.com/?Famous -Quotes-by-Vince-Lombardi-During-Footballs-Annual-Bowl-Season&id=901905 (accessed July 22, 2010).

17 Jerry Kramer, *Instant Replay: The Green Bay Diary of Jerry Kramer*, ed. Dick Schaap (New York: World Pub. Co. 1968), xvii.

18 Ibid.

19 San Diego's LaDainian Tomlinson broke Hornung's record in 2006 by scoring thirty-one touchdowns, good for 186 points.

20 As rookies in 1966, Anderson and Grabowski were among the last of the college "bonus babies"; players who received enormous salaries because of the bidding war between the NFL and AFL. Anderson signed a $600,000 contract, while Grabowski signed for $400,000, figures that caused some hard feelings among Packer veterans who made far less money. Taylor was especially critical, noting the rookies "didn't come to play football; they came to count their money." With the merger and a common draft, the rookies of 1967 would make much less money. "Last Year for the Big Bonus Babies," *Ebony*, November 1966, 121.

21 Golenbock, *Cowboys Have Always Been My Heroes*, 262.

22 Robert Thomas, "Jim Lee Howell, Ex-Giants Coach, Dies at 80," *New York Times*, January 6, 1995, http://www.nytimes.com/1995/01/06/obituaries/jim-lee-howell-ex-giants-coach-dies-at -80.html (accessed June 21, 2010).

23 From 1960 through 1969, the Playoff Bowl in Miami matched up the teams that finished in second place in the two NFL conferences. It was officially named the Bert Bell Benefit Bowl, in honor of the former NFL commissioner, and proceeds went to the players' pension fund. The

game had no real meaning in terms of the standings or statistics, and partially for that reason, Lombardi called it a "hinky-dink football game, held in a hinky-dink town, played by hinky-dink players." The Playoff Bowl formally came to an end when the NFL and AFL began playing a common schedule in 1970. Richard Sandomir, "Little Consolation in Third-Place Game," *New York Times*, February 5, 2011, http://www.nytimes.com/2011/02/06/sports /football/06sandomir.html?_r=1&ref=sports (accessed June 13, 2011).

24 Golenbock, *Cowboys Have Always Been My Heroes*, 276.

25 Murray Olderman, "The Winningest Ones," *Newspaper Enterprise Association*, August 1970.

26 Edwin Shrake, "Texas Gentleman," *Sports Illustrated*, August 5, 2008, http://sportsillustrated .cnn.com/vault/article/magazine/MAG1152197/2/index.htm (accessed May 5, 2011).

27 Gary Cartwright, "Cowboys Blunder, Browns Win, 24-17," *Dallas Morning News*, November 22, 1965, http://www.dallasnews.com/sharedcontent/dws/spt/football/cowboys/classic /recordbook/yearbyyear/1965/112265browns.html (accessed August 11, 2010).

28 Edwin Shrake, "A Cowboy Named Dandy Don," *Sports Illustrated*, September 16, 1968, 117.

29 Gary Cartwright, "Tom Landry: Melting the Plastic Man," *Texas Monthly*, November 1973, 68–69.

30 "Dallas Effort Real Great," *Milwaukee Sentinel*, January 2, 1967.

31 Ralbovsky, *Super Bowl*, 2.

32 Ibid., 3.

33 "Green Bay Packers," *America's Game: The Super Bowl Champions*, NFL Films, December 22, 2006.

34 Ralbovsky, *Super Bowl*, 7.

35 "Replay!"

36 Ibid.

37 Cleon Walfoort, "Super Battle of Vowels Winds Up in Draw," *Milwaukee Journal*, January 16, 1967, 16.

38 Dusty Saunders, "Broken Record: NFL Ratings on Endless Rise," *Denver Post*, February 6, 2011, http://www.denverpost.com/sports/ci_17306686 (accessed June 13, 2011).

39 Oliver Kuechle, "Lombardi Gets Game Ball, a Tribute From His Team," *Milwaukee Journal*, January 16, 1967.

40 Ralbovsky, *Super Bowl*, 31.

41 Ibid.

42 "Green Bay Packers," *America's Game*.

43 On August 8, 1961, the young AFL had sought to establish some credibility by playing an exhibition game against a Canadian Football League team. Using a mixture of AFL and CFL rules, the Hamilton Tiger-Cats embarrassed the Buffalo Bills, 38–21 in Hamilton. In the 1950s and early 1960s, NFL teams went 6-0 against the CFL in a series of pre-season games, but no NFL/AFL team has played a CFL team since 1961.

44 "The Summer of the Little Super Bowls," August 5, 1967, http://www.mmbolding.com/BSR /Detroit_Lions_vs_Denver_Broncos_August_5,_1967.htm (accessed August 5, 2011).

45 Ibid.

46 Ibid.

47 Ibid. Despite its pre-season success, Denver went only 3-11 in the regular season.

48 Mark Mulvoy, "The AFL Has a Taste of Glory," *Sports Illustrated*, September 4, 1967, 14.

49 Ibid., 12.

50 Edwin Shrake, "Now the AFL Owns the Football," *Sports Illustrated*, January 27, 1969, 31.

51 Edwin Shrake, "Another Old Pro Kicks for Sixteen," *Sports Illustrated*, January 8, 1968, 17.

52 Although it should be noted that the AFC Championship game between the Chargers and Bengals on January 10, 1982, in Cincinnati had wind chill temperatures estimated between thirty and fifty degrees below zero. The game, won by the Bengals, 27–7, became known as the "Freezer Bowl."

53 Chuck Johnson, "Packers Move 1 Foot to Miami," *Milwaukee Journal*, January 2, 1968, 20.

54 Tex Maule, "The Old Pro Goes In For Six," *Sports Illustrated*, January 8, 1968, 15.

55 Lombardi took over as Packers general manager in 1968, but the lure of coaching was too great, and in 1969 he resigned and became head coach in Washington. The Redskins, who had a losing record in 1968, went 7-5-2 in Lombardi's only season. He never had a losing record in ten years as an NFL coach.

56 Ralbovsky, *Super Bowl*, 63.

57 Tex Maule, "Say It's So, Joe," *Sports Illustrated*, January 20, 1969, 10.

58 Robert Boyle, "Show-Biz Sonny and His Quest for Stars," *Sports Illustrated*, July 19, 1965, 66.

59 Ralbovsky, *Super Bowl*, 74.

60 It was the second dramatic meeting between the Jets and Raiders during the 1968 season. Their first meeting was on November 17 in Oakland. With just a minute to play, the Jets kicked a field goal to take the lead, 32–29. Right after the kick, at exactly 7 p.m. eastern time, NBC switched from the game to its regularly scheduled program, a movie called *Heidi*. Frustrated fans could not see the last minute of the game, in which the Raiders scored two touchdowns to win, 43–32. The game became known as "The Heidi Bowl."

61 Ralbovsky, *Super Bowl*, 74.

62 "New York Jets," *America's Game*, NFL Films, April 2, 2007.

63 Associated Press, "Bubba Admits Pique at Jibes by Namath," January 9, 1969.

64 Chuck Johnson, "Welcome to the AFL, Says Turner," *Milwaukee Journal*, January 13, 1969, 13.

65 Maule, "Say It's So, Joe," 12.

66 New England holds the current record with 16 straight regular season wins in 2007. The Patriots won two playoff games but lost the Super Bowl to the Giants to finish at 18-1.

67 Ralbovsky, *Super Bowl*, 125.

68 "Tarkenton Convinced by Chiefs," *Milwaukee Journal*, January 12, 1970, 13.

69 Ralbovsky, *Super Bowl*, 137. Coming off his first season coaching the Redskins, Lombardi would be diagnosed that summer with colon cancer and die on September 3, 1970. The trophy that goes to the winning Super Bowl team was named the Vince Lombardi Trophy in his honor.

70 Ralbovsky, *Super Bowl*, 130.

71 Ibid., 143.

72 AFL Films was created, in part, so as not to offend sensitive AFL owners who did not want their games shot by NFL Films people. The name was misleading because NFL Films continued to shoot both NFL and AFL games.

73 In 1970 former NFL player James "Yazoo" Smith sued the NFL, claiming that the draft violated the Sherman Anti-Trust Act. He won his case, and then the appeal, but the decision became moot when the NFL Players Association signed a new collective bargaining agreement that explicitly approved a draft of college players.

74 The Chicago Bears also went 1-13 in 1969, but the Steelers won a coin flip for the rights to the top pick.

75 Notable draftees that went on to fame in other sports included hurdler Willie Davenport, taken in the twelfth round by the Saints. Davenport bypassed the NFL for track and won two Olympic medals, including gold in 1968. That same Olympics, sprinter John Carlos was suspended from the games for his black power salute after a bronze medal effort in the 200 meters. Carlos was drafted in the fifteenth round by the Eagles and played one season in Philadelphia and two in Canada before knee injuries ended his career. In the eighth round, the Cardinals drafted quarterback Mike Holmgren, and while he never played in the league, Holmgren won a Super Bowl title in 1997 as head coach of the Packers.

76 Bill Plaschke, "Realignment Sparks Owner Unrest," *Los Angeles Times*, March 21, 1994, http://articles.latimes.com/1994-03-21/sports/sp-36767_1_nfl-meetings (accessed June 1, 2010).

77 "Packers in Same Division," *Milwaukee Journal*, January 16, 1970, 15.

78 The Hall of Fame game began in 1962 and until 2009 had traditionally been the opening game of the NFL preseason. In 1971 the Rams beat the Oilers, 17–6 in the first of thirty-eight straight years in which an AFC team played an NFC team. New Orleans won the 1970 Hall of Fame game, beating Minnesota, 14–13.

79 Tom Flores started the 1969 season in Buffalo, but joined the Chiefs after injuries to Dawson and backup Jacky Lee. Flores threw exactly one pass in the Chiefs' Super Bowl season—a 33-yard touchdown to Robert Holmes in a regular season game against Houston. It was the last pass of his pro career.

80 William Nack, "A Name on the Wall," *Sports Illustrated*, July 23, 2001, http://sportsillustrated .cnn.com/vault/article/magazine/MAG1023026/1/index.htm (accessed July 17, 2010).

81 Ibid.

Chapter 3. Week One: Kansas City Chiefs at Minnesota Vikings

1 Associated Press, "A Texas Stunner: Win Over Cowboys," September 9, 2002, http://www .sptimes.com/2002/09/09/Sports/A_Texan_stunner__win_.shtml (accessed September 1, 2010). The Texans became only the second expansion team in NFL history to win their first game. In 1961 the Minnesota Vikings beat the Chicago Bears, 37–13.

2 Heller, "Browns NFL Debut in '50 Left Eagles Flying Low."

3 Ibid. Eagles coach Greasy Neale complained that the Browns won simply because they threw the ball so much. When the teams met for rematch later that season in Cleveland, the Browns won 13–7 without throwing a single pass.

4 Tex Maule, "The Future Moves Into the Past," *Sports Illustrated*, September 28, 1970, 28.

5 Ibid.

6 Joe Kapp and Jack Olsen, "A Man of Machismo," *Sports Illustrated*, July 20, 1970, 27–28.

7 Ralbovsky, *Super Bowl*, 117. Kapp looked like anything but a plumber when he threw seven touchdown passes in a 52–14 win over Baltimore on September 28, 1969. The seven touchdown passes tied an NFL record that still stands today.

8 Tex Maule, "The Purple Gang Rubs Out L.A.," *Sports Illustrated*, January 5, 1970, 14.

9 Tex Maule, "Kapping the Browns," *Sports Illustrated*, January 12, 1970, 12.

10 Fran Tarkenton and Jack Olsen, "Dear Norm: I Cannot Return," *Sports Illustrated*, July 31, 1967, 40.

11 Marshall Smith, "A Green Rookie Learns to Live Dangerously," *Life*, November 17, 1961, 154.

12 The Grey Cup was the CFL version of the Super Bowl, but much older. The first Grey Cup was played in 1909.

13 Maule, "The Future Moves Into the Past," 28. Cuozzo was intelligent enough to play football and go through dental school at the same time.

14 Dick Gordon, "Cuozzo is Second to None, the Vikings Crow," *The Sporting News*, December 5, 1970, 3.

15 Incredibly, the Vikings did not run a single offensive play in Super Bowl IV that utilized a man in motion.

16 Tex Maule, "Wham, Bam, Stram!" *Sports Illustrated*, January 19, 1970, 10.

17 Both records have since been broken—by punter Jeff Feagles (most consecutive games, 352) and quarterback Brett Favre (most starts, 297, which ended in 2010).

18 Sid Hartman, "Marshall Burned Money on Keep Alive on Trek," *Minneapolis Star-Tribune*, February 1, 1971, http://blogs2.startribune.com/blogs/oldnews/archives/145 (accessed August 10, 2010).

19 "History: Wrong Way Run," *Sportz Ink*, 1999, http://min.scout.com/ 2/11652.html (accessed July 28, 2010).

20 "Bill Brown of the Minnesota Vikings: A Man of Old Leather," *Sports Chat Place*, 2010, http://archive.sportschatplace.com/sports-history/244-sports-history-articles/40506-bill -brown-of-the-minnesota-vikings-a-man-of-old-leather.html (accessed August 3, 2010).

21 Ibid.

22 Giants' linebacker Lawrence Taylor won the league MVP in 1986. No other defensive players have been so honored since the NFL began awarding a Most Valuable Player in 1957.

23 Maule, "The Future Moves Into the Past," 28.

24 Ibid.

25 Metropolitan Stadium had an odd configuration in that both teams' benches were on the same sideline. Marshall later admitted that during extremely cold games Minnesota players would run by the sideline heaters of the other team, hoping to warm up briefly before heading to their own bench.

26 It marked the twentieth straight game in which Cox had kicked a field goal, an NFL record, and he would eventually run the streak to thirty-one games. The current record holder is Matt Stover, who kicked a field goal in thirty-eight straight games for the Baltimore Ravens from 1999 to 2001.

27 Mark Starr, "Fumbling Away the Game," *Newsweek*, December 12, 1993, http://www.thedailybeast .com/newsweek/1993/12/12/fumbling-away-the-game.html (accessed August 12, 2010). Yepremian would do nothing to help his reputation in Super Bowl VII against Washington. After the Redskins blocked a field goal attempt, Yepremian picked up the ball and attempted a pass, but he managed only to bat the ball into the air. The Redskins' Mike Bass picked off the bobble and ran for a touchdown. Thankfully for Yepremian, the Dolphins held on to win, 14–7, and completed their perfect 1972 season.

28 Steve Christie is the current Super Bowl record holder, with a 54-yard field goal in Super Bowl XVIII. The kick was made indoors at Atlanta's Georgia Dome, where Christie's Bills lost to Dallas, 30–13.

29 For example, Ken Vinyard of the Falcons hit only nine of twenty-five field goal attempts in 1970 for a success rate of 36 percent.

30 Maule, "The Future Moves Into the Past," 31.

31 United Press International, "Revenge Sweet as Vikings Defeat Kansas City, 27-10," September 21, 1970.

32 Jack Olsen, "He Goes Where the Trouble Is," *Sports Illustrated*, October 19, 1970, 22.

33 Maule, "The Future Moves Into the Past," 31.

34 Ibid.

35 Ibid.

36 So desperate, in fact, that the Patriots would select Heisman Trophy winning quarterback Jim Plunkett of Stanford with the number one overall pick in the 1971 draft.

Chapter 4. Week One: New York Jets at Cleveland Browns

1 Chuck Johnson, "Starr Builds Lead, Pack Holds It, 14-10," *Milwaukee Journal*, September 29, 1964, Part 2, Page 10.

2 William Johnson, "After TV Accepted the Call, Sunday Was Never the Same," *Sports Illustrated*, January 5, 1970, 23. CBS won the bid with an offer of $28.2 million, which amounted to $14.1 million per year, compared to $4.65 million per year under the old CBS contract. In 2011 the NFL signed a new contract worth $28 billion over nine years.

3 Ibid., 29.

4 When Howard Hughes failed to gain control of ABC in 1968, he then worked to create a competing fourth network, but such plans never materialized and the Hughes Sports Network instead focused on producing and distributing selected sports programming, such as Big 10 basketball games and occasional pro golf events.

5 Ibid.

6 Michael MacCambridge, *America's Game*, 2004.

7 Bill Carter, "Roone Arledge, 71, a Force in TV Sports and News, Dies," *New York Times*, December 6, 2002, http://www.nytimes.com/2002/12/06/business/roone-arledge-71-a-force -in-tv-sports-and-news-dies.html?pagewanted=all&src=pm (accessed July 31, 2010).

8 Edwin Shrake, "What Are They Doing With The Sacred Game of Pro Football?" *Sports Illustrated*, October 15, 1971, 96.

9 Frank Deford, "TV Talk," *Sports Illustrated*, February 8, 1971, 12. Martha Mitchell was the wife of John Mitchell, who served as U.S. Attorney General under President Richard Nixon. She loved to talk, and her gossiping with Washington's power elite may have played a role in divulging some Watergate secrets.

10 Norman Chad, "Howard Cosell, Signing Off," *Sports Illustrated*, February 3, 1992, http://sportsillustrated.cnn.com/vault/article/magazine/MAG1141596/2/index.htm (accessed September 1, 2010).

11 Shrake, "Sacred Game of Pro Football?," 98.

12 Golenbock, *Cowboys Have Always Been My Heroes*, 375.

13 Roone Arledge, *Roone: Memoir* (New York: HarperCollins, 2003), 111.

14 Jeffrey Denberg, "Dandy Don Meredith Can Do It All, Fans," *Miami News*, November 14, 1970, B1.

15 Arledge, *Roone: Memoir*, 113.

16 Ibid.

17 Ibid.

18 Wells Twombly, "Cosell Will Never Disappoint You," *The Sporting News*, November 7, 1970, 14.

19 Cosell even starred in his own ABC variety show, *Saturday Night Live with Howard Cosell*, which ran from September 1975 to January 1976. *TV Guide* called the show "dead on arrival, with a cringingly awkward host." "Saturday Night Live with Howard Cosell." *TV Guide*, September 20, 1975, http://www.tvguide.com/tvshows/saturday-night-live-howard-cosell /204224 (accessed July 28, 2010).

20 "Replay!"

21 Ibid.

22 Robert Boyle, "TV Wins On Points," *Sports Illustrated*, November 2, 1970, 14–15.

23 Ibid.

24 "Replay!"

25 Robert Edelstein, "Monday Night Football," *Broadcasting & Cable*, October 19, 2009, http://www.broadcastingcable.com/article/365645-Monday_Night_Football.php (accessed October 15, 2010). Ebersol played a key role in helping Arledge and ABC create the *Monday Night Football* package.

26 In 1935 nearly 125,000 people shoehorned into Cleveland Municipal Stadium for the midnight mass of the Roman Catholic Church's Seventh Eucharistic Congress hosted by the Diocese of Cleveland. Many of the attendees sat on temporary seats on the field.

27 "Cleveland Indians Attendance Data," *Baseball Almanac*, 2011, http://www.baseball-almanac .com/teams/cleiatte.shtml (accessed June 14, 2011).

28 Getting the three million dollar bonus from the league was one of the main reasons Modell decided to move the Browns from the NFL to the AFC in 1970.

29 "Replay!"

30 Charles Babington and Ken Denlinger, "Modell Announces Browns' Move to Baltimore," *Washington Post*, November 7, 1995, http://www.washingtonpost.com/wp-srv/sports /longterm/memories/1995/95nfl4.htm (accessed August 22, 2010).

31 Peter Schmuck, "Art Modell on LeBron James' Fallen Status in Ohio," *Baltimore Sun*, July 12, 2010, http://www.cleveland.com/cavs/index.ssf/2010/07/art_modell_on_lebron_james _fal.html (accessed July 7, 2010).

32 Ibid.

33 In 1946 Frank Filchock and Merle Hapes were suspended by the NFL for being approached by gamblers prior to the championship game. In 1963 Rozelle suspended both Alex Karras and Paul Hornung for the entire season after they admitted to betting on NFL games.

34 William Johnson, "Mod Man Out," *Sports Illustrated*, June 16, 1969, 23.

35 It would not be the last time Namath threatened to quit prematurely. New York sportswriter Pete Axthelm called the threats "an annual preseason performance . . . kind of jockstrap Shakespeare-in-the-park." Pete Axthelm, "The Third Annual Permanent Retirement of Joe Namath," *New York Magazine*, July 19, 1971, 47.

36 Dave Anderson, "I Don't Want to Play—Namath," *Miami News*, August 7, 1970, 2D.

37 The only other significant offensive change in 1970 was that Al Woodall became the primary backup to Namath, replacing Vito "Babe" Parilli, who retired after fifteen pro seasons.

38 Don Smith, "Leroy Kelly," *The Coffin Corner* 16, no. 5 (1994) http://www.profootballresearchers .org/Coffin_Corner/16-05-579.pdf (accessed October 1, 2010).

39 Bob Oates, "National Conference," *The Sporting News*, March 7, 1970, 45.

40 "American Central," *Sports Illustrated,* September 21, 1970, 40.

41 Richard Sandomir, "One Night in 1970, the Revolution was Televised," *New York Times*, November 23, 2005, http://www.nytimes.com/2005/11/23/sports/football/23monday.html ?pagewanted=all&_r= (accessed September 5, 2010).

42 Larry Felser, "AFC Eastern," *The Sporting News*, October 10, 1970, 41.

43 Associated Press, "Officials, Not Stars, Move Ball in Professional Game," September 21, 1970.

44 Chuck Heaton, "85,703 See Browns Win, 31-21," *Cleveland Plain-Dealer*, September 21, 1970, http://www.cleveland.com/brownshistory/plaindealer/index.ssf?/browns/more/history /19700921BROWNS.html (accessed August 30, 2010).

Chapter 5. Week Two: Pittsburgh Steelers at Denver Broncos

1 McDonough, *75 Seasons*, 194.

2 Mike Klis, "Former Broncos Boss Saban Dies at 87," *Denver Post*, March 3, 2009, http://www.denverpost.com/broncos/ci_12026331 (accessed February 11, 2011).

3 Wayne Coffey, "One For the Aged," *New York Daily News,* November 11, 2001, http://www.nydailynews.com/archives/sports/2001/11/11/2001-11-11_one_for_the_aged___lou_saban.html (accessed February 12, 2011).

4 In 1968 Denver made Marlin Briscoe the first starting black quarterback in pro football history. Briscoe threw fourteen touchdown passes in eleven games, but switched to wide receiver the following season. Briscoe still holds the Broncos' team record for touchdown passes by a rookie quarterback (fourteen), eclipsing even John Elway (seven).

5 Edwin Shrake, "A Love Affair With a Loser," *Sports Illustrated*, March 29, 1965, 27.

6 Al Abrams, "Sidelights on Sports," *Pittsburgh Post-Gazette*, March 1943. Rooney's windfall would be worth more than $3 million today.

7 That did include one post-season game in 1947 when the Steelers and Eagles tied for the NFL East title with 8-4 records. The Eagles beat Pittsburgh in a divisional playoff, 21–0, but then lost the NFL Championship game to the Chicago Cardinals.

8 Rob Ruck, Maggie J. Patterson, and Michael P. Weber, *Rooney: A Sporting Life* (Lincoln: University of Nebraska Press, 2010), 113.

9 Gary Ronberg, "I Wanted To Go With a Loser," *Sports Illustrated*, February 9, 1970, 25.

10 Ruck, Patterson, and Weber, *Rooney: A Sporting Life*, 378.

11 Associated Press, "Broncos Use Rally to Defeat Steelers," September 28, 1970.

12 Al Levine, "Terry Bradshaw was so Excited..." *Miami News*, August 10, 1970.

13 Tex Maule, "Tomorrow's Generals," *Sports Illustrated*, February 15, 1971, 24.

14 Ruck, Patterson, and Weber, *Rooney: A Sporting Life*, 447.

15 Klis, "Former Broncos Boss Saban Dies at 87."

16 Christopher Smith, "Where Are They Now? Billy Van Heusen," *Broncos Magazine*, March 14, 2008, http://forums.denverbroncos.com/showthread.php?t=113126 (accessed May 6, 2011).

Chapter 6. Week Three: San Diego Chargers at Los Angeles Rams

1 William Wallace, "Sid Gillman, 91, Innovator of Passing Strategy in Football," *New York Times*, January 4, 2003, http://www.nytimes.com/2003/01/04/sports/sid-gillman-91-innovator-of -passing-strategy-in-football.html (accessed May 30, 2010).

2 "War and Peace," *Full Color Football*, NFL Films, September 30, 2009.

3 Jerry Magee, "Chargers' Alworth Ran Like a Deer, Played Like a Legend," *San Diego Union-Tribune*, December 26, 1999, http://www.signonsandiego.com/sports/sdbest/19991226-0010 _1s26bambi.html (accessed June 1, 2010).

4 Ibid.

5 Gruver, "The AFL's First Super Team."

6   The stadium opened in 1967 as San Diego Stadium but was renamed Jack Murphy Stadium upon Murphy's death in 1980. Qualcomm purchased naming rights in 1997, and the stadium, still in use by the Chargers today, is known as Qualcomm Stadium. For a ten-day period in 2011, it was called Snapdragon Stadium as part of a Qualcomm advertising promotion.

7   George Allen and Joe Marshall, "A Hundred Percent is Not Enough," *Sports Illustrated*, July 9, 1973, 74–75.

8   Alfred Wright, "You Win! You're Fired!" *Sports Illustrated*, September 7, 1970, 34.

9   Edwin Shrake, "A Private Eye on the New Rams," *Sports Illustrated*, October 3, 1966, 36.

10 Allen and Marshall, "A Hundred Percent is Not Enough," 79.

11 As a solo act, Jones sang on *The Hollywood Palace* in 1967 and 1968, and on the *Merv Griffin Show* in 1970.

12 Jerry Crowe, "Deacon Jones: 'Secretary of Defense' was King of the Sack," *Los Angeles Times*, April 21, 2009, http://articles.latimes.com/2009/apr/21/sports/sp-crowe21 (accessed June 2, 2010).

13 Ibid.

14 Ibid.

15 Tex Maule, "The Young Generals," *Sports Illustrated*, September 30, 1968, 20.

16 The previous week 45,988 came to the dedication of the stadium. In San Diego's first meeting with an NFL team, the Lions beat the Chargers, 38–17.

17 Al Larson, "Rams Frolic 50-7; Chiefs Next Victim?" *Long Beach Press-Telegram*, August 27, 1967, http://www.mmbolding.com/BSR/Interleague_San%20Diego%20Chargers_Los _Angeles_Rams_1967.htm (accessed June 5, 2011).

18 Snow's son J. T. would go on to have a fourteen-year career in major league baseball.

19 Mal Florence, "Chargers Just Another Team to Rams," *Los Angeles Times*, October 5, 1970, F7. When he retired after the 1974 season, Josephson started an acting career. His roles included the popular movie *Heaven Can Wait*, and the television show *The Six Million Dollar Man*.

20 Bob Oates, "Chargers Still Not in Rams' League, Lose, 37-10," *Los Angeles Times*, October 5, 1970, F1.

21 Florence, "Chargers Just Another Team to Rams," F7.

22 Magee, "Chargers' Alworth Ran Like a Deer, Played Like a Legend."

23 Florence, "Chargers Just Another Team to Rams," F7.

24 Tex Maule, "How the West was, Uh, Tied," *Sports Illustrated*, December 7, 1970, 24.

25 Jack Tobin and Gilbert Rogin, "A Marriage that was Doomed," *Sports Illustrated*, January 6, 1969, 22.

26 Jackson, "Roman Gabriel."

27 Tobin and Rogin, "A Marriage that was Doomed," 23.

28 Ibid.

29 Allen returned to the Rams as head coach in February 1978, but it was a short and bizarre homecoming. Carroll Rosenbloom, who owned the Rams at the time, was just as quick-tempered as Reeves. He fired Allen on August 13, just two games into the preseason schedule.

30 Jeff Meyers, "Allen Created a Mess: Traded Draft Choices," *The Sporting News*, January 16, 1971, 12.

31 The Rams' only Super Bowl appearance in Los Angeles came under coach Ray Malavasi, who had taken over for George Allen before the 1978 season. Malavasi and the Rams lost to the Steelers in Super Bowl XIV, 31–19.

Chapter 7. Week Four: Cincinnati Bengals at Cleveland Browns

1   "They Said It," *Sports Illustrated*, October 18, 1970, 12.

2   "Paul E. Brown Museum Kicks Off Fundraising Campaign," *Paul E. Brown Museum*, 2007, http://www.paulbrownmuseum.com/ (accessed October 3, 2010).

3 Phil Berger, "Paul Brown, One of Pro Football's Primary Architects, Dead at 82," *New York Times*, August 6, 1991, http://www.nytimes.com/1991/08/06/sports/paul-brown-one-of-pro -football-s-primary-architects-dead-at-82.html (accessed October 6, 2010).

4 Michael Freeman, *Jim Brown: The Fierce Life of an American Hero* (New York: William Morrow, 2006), 30.

5 "Revenge Games," *NFL Top 10*, NFL Films, November 20, 2010.

6 George Cantor, *Paul Brown: The Man Who Invented Modern Football* (Chicago: Triumph Books, 2008), 175.

7 Ibid., 181.

8 Maule, "Rude Welcome Back for Paul," 27.

9 As an indication of the rift between Modell and Brown, Modell claimed credit for getting approval of the Cincinnati franchise. "I was the key to Paul Brown returning to football," Modell said years later. "Jim Rhodes came to me and said he would like to get an NFL franchise for Cincinnati." Morris Eckhouse, "The Rivalry," *The Coffin Corner* 9 no. 9, (1987), http://www.profootballresearchers.org/Coffin_Corner/09-09-316.pdf (accessed September 28, 2010).

10 Before Riverfront Stadium opened, the Bengals played two seasons at Nippert Stadium on the University of Cincinnati campus.

11 By contrast, the Cowboys had paid $1 million when they joined the NFL in 1960. By 2002, the fee had gone up to $700 million for the Houston Texans.

12 Tex Maule, "Rude Welcome Back for Paul," *Sports Illustrated*, August 12, 1968, 29.

13 "Revenge Games."

14 Ibid.

15 Robinson won All-Pro honors in 1968 and 1969, and remains the only rookie player to rush for more than a thousand yards with an expansion team.

16 Maule, "Rude Welcome Back for Paul," 24.

17 Andrew O'Toole, *Paul Brown: The Rise and Fall and Rise Again of Football's Most Innovative Coach* (Cincinnati: Clerisy Press, 2008), 299.

18 Robert Boyle, "The Year of the Rookies—Bigger, Faster, Smarter," *Sports Illustrated*, October 20, 1969, 32.

19 "One Shot Wonders," *NFL Top 10*, NFL Films, May 30, 2007.

20 Ibid.

21 Ibid.

22 Tex Maule, "No One's Holding These Tigers," *Sports Illustrated*, September 27, 1971, 30.

23 Sam Wyche was often described as a coach on the field and he went into coaching full-time in 1979. In 1984 Paul Brown personally introduced him as the Bengals' new head coach, and he coached the team for eight seasons. He led the Bengals to Super Bowl XXIII, which the 49ers won 20–16 on a touchdown pass from Joe Montana to John Taylor with just thirty-five seconds to play.

24 Like Cook, Reid was destined to have a short Bengals career. An avid musician, he abruptly retired after the 1974 season to focus on songwriting and performing. He wrote or recorded several popular country music songs, including a Grammy Award winner in 1984.

25 Charles Heaton, "Browns Capture Crown, 27-0," *Cleveland Plain-Dealer*, December 27, 1964, http://www.cleveland.com/brownshistory/plaindealer/index.ssf?/browns/more/history /19641227BROWNS.html (accessed October 1, 2010).

26 Eckhouse, "The Rivalry."

27 Ibid.

28 Ibid.

29 Ibid.

30 O'Toole, *Paul Brown: The Rise and Fall and Rise Again*, 316.

31 Cantor, *Paul Brown: The Man Who Invented Modern Football*, 187.

32 O'Toole, *Paul Brown: The Rise and Fall and Rise Again*, 317.

33 Chuck Heaton, "Browns Nip Cincy, So do Birds," *Cleveland Plain-Dealer*, October 11, 1970, http://www.cleveland.com/brownshistory/plaindealer/index.ssf?/browns/more/history /19701011BROWNS.html (accessed October 3, 2010).

34 Associated Press, "Paul Brown Returns and Loses to Browns," October 12, 1970.

35 Heaton, "Browns Nip Cincy, So do Birds."

36 O'Toole, *Paul Brown: The Rise and Fall and Rise Again*, 318.

37 Ibid.

38 Ibid.

39 Patrick F. Putnam, "No Clink and No Clank in Cincinnati," *Sports Illustrated*, September 15, 1969, 26.

Chapter 8. Week Five: Baltimore Colts at New York Jets

1 Ralbovsky, *Super Bowl*, 149.

2 Jack Olsen, "The Rosenbloom-Robbie Bowl," *Sports Illustrated*, November 9, 1970, 27.

3 Ralbovsky, *Super Bowl*, 162.

4 Ibid., 167.

5 Larry Felser, "AFC Eastern," *The Sporting News*, January 30, 1971, 9.

6 When the Colts did win the Super Bowl thanks to a last-second O'Brien kick, the team changed its mind about cutting the rookie's hair. "We just couldn't do it to the kid," said center Bill Curry. "1970 Baltimore Colts," *America's Game*, NFL Films, February 9, 2007.

7 In 1970 four NFL teams employed place kickers who also played non-kicking positions. Besides O'Brien, there were Gene Mingo (running back, Steelers), Gino Cappelletti (receiver, Patriots), and George Blanda (quarterback, Raiders). Several teams also had punters play other positions, such as receiver Billy Van Heusen with Denver. Former Heisman Trophy winner Steve Spurrier punted for San Francisco but also backed up John Brodie at quarterback. Steelers' quarterback and top draft pick Terry Bradshaw punted three times during the year, all in the season finale against the Eagles. One punt was blocked and recovered for a touchdown.

8 Felser, "AFC Eastern," January 30, 1971, 9.

9 In 1966 the Major League Baseball Players Association hired Marvin Miller, who was instrumental in helping the union negotiate a minimum salary and collective bargaining agreement in 1968. That same year, the NFLPA was officially recognized by league owners.

10 The Chicago College All-Star Game began in 1934 matching a team of college all-stars against the defending NFL champions in Chicago. It started as a fundraiser for various charities in Chicago and was initially popular. But interest waned as the NFL dominated the series, winning thirty-one games against only nine losses and two ties. The last game in the series was played in 1976 and it stopped in the third quarter because of a downpour.

11 Joe Jares, "The One Night Season," *Sports Illustrated*, August 10, 1970, 12.

12 Ibid., 9.

13 Skip Myslenski, "I'm a Football Player, Not a Worker," *Sports Illustrated*, August 10, 1970, 10.

14 Morton Sharnik, "For an Opening, He Might Come Out and Growl," *Sports Illustrated*, January 18, 1971, 19, 23.

15 The $13,000 would be worth approximately $75,000 in 2012 dollars.

16 Jares, "The One Night Season," 11.

17 Labor issues cut short NFL seasons in 1982 and 1987 and threatened the entire 2011 season.

18 Olsen, "The Rosenbloom-Robbie Bowl," 27.

19 Sam Lacy, "Are the Colts that Bad?" *Baltimore Afro-American*, September 29, 1970, 18.

20 "1970 Baltimore Colts," *America's Game*, NFL Films, 2006.

21 Ibid.

22 Ibid.

23 "Namath Loses But Wins Colt Praise," *Baltimore Afro-American*, October 20, 1970, 12.

24 Namath's six interceptions were not the NFL record, which was set by Chicago Cardinals quarterback Jim Hardy in 1950 when he threw eight interceptions in a game against the Eagles.

25 "Joe Namath's Broken Wrist to be in Cast Six Weeks," *Meriden (CT) Morning Record*, October 21, 1970, 10.
26 Ralbovsky, *Super Bowl*, 162.
27 "Namath Loses," 12.
28 Ibid.
29 Associated Press, "Logan Sparks Colts," October 19, 1970.
30 Al Levine, "Morrall's Flashbacks Now Unitas' Show," *Miami News*, January 12, 1971.
31 Olsen, The Rosenbloom-Robbie Bowl," 23.
32 Ibid.
33 Larry Felser, "AFC Eastern," *The Sporting News*, December 12, 1970, 28.
34 Ralbovsky, *Super Bowl*, 147.
35 Felser, "AFC Eastern," December 12, 1970, 28.

Chapter 9. Week Six: Dallas Cowboys at Kansas City Chiefs

1 Golenbock, *Cowboys Have Always Been My Heroes*, 339.
2 Ibid.
3 Maule, "The Purple Gang," 17.
4 Golenbock, *Cowboys Have Always Been My Heroes*, 412–13.
5 Tex Maule, "Big Ifs in Big D," August 31, 1970, 13.
6 Golenbock, *Cowboys Have Always Been My Heroes*, 425.
7 Ralbovsky, *Super Bowl*, 153.
8 Golenbock, *Cowboys Have Always Been My Heroes*, 428.
9 Although usually overshadowed by fellow defensive tackle Bob Lilly, Pugh enjoyed a solid fourteen-year career. He played more seasons for the Cowboys than any other players except for Ed Jones, Bill Bates, and Mark Tuinei.
10 Cliff Harris ended up playing in eleven games and returned in time for the playoffs. He intercepted two passes on the season and in the Super Bowl recovered a fumble. Harris was a six-time Pro Bowler and three-time All-Pro in his ten-year career.
11 John Eisenberg, *Cotton Bowl Days: Growing Up with Dallas and the Cowboys in the 1960s* (New York: Simon & Schuster, 1997), 31.
12 Arthur Donovan and Bob Drury, *Fatso: Football when Men Were Really Men* (New York: Avon Books, 1987), 130.
13 Eisenberg, *Cotton Bowl Days*, 34.
14 Ibid., 38.
15 Golenbock, *Cowboys Have Always Been My Heroes*, 400.
16 Eisenberg, *Cotton Bowl Days*, 40.
17 Ibid., 51.
18 Ibid., 51–52.
19 Tex Maule, "Almost Too Good to Play," *Sports Illustrated*, November 6, 1967, 29.
20 It was part of a thirty-nine year NFL career for Dan Reeves, who in 1981 took over as head coach of the Denver Broncos. Reeves would take the Broncos to the Super Bowl three times, but his teams lost the game each time. He coached the Atlanta Falcons to their only Super Bowl appearance but also lost that game.
21 Maule, "Almost Too Good to Play," 30.
22 Tex Maule, "Dallas Cowboys," *Sports Illustrated*, September 12, 1966, 74.
23 Ralbovsky, *Super Bowl*, 161.
24 Rich Koster, "NFC Eastern," *The Sporting News*, October 10, 1970, 43.
25 The Chiefs-Dolphins game also set another record: longest game in NFL history. Miami won with 7:20 left in the second overtime, 27–24 on a field goal by Garo Yepremian. The game eclipsed the 1962 AFL Championship game in terms of length, which means the Chiefs/Texans franchise has played in the two longest games in pro football history.
26 Eisenberg, *Cotton Bowl Days*, 229.
27 "1971 Dallas Cowboys," *America's Game*, NFL Films, 2006.

28 Bob St. John, "Cowboys Leave Tepee Ablaze, 27-16," *Dallas Morning News*, October 26, 1970, http://www.dallasnews.com/sharedcontent/dws/spt/football/cowboys/classic/recordbook/yearbyyear/1970/102670chiefs.html (accessed July 22, 2010).

29 Ibid.

30 Rich Koster, "NFC Eastern," *The Sporting News*, October 17, 1970, 59.

31 Associated Press, "Raiders Gain Tie on Penalty Ruling," November 2, 1970.

Chapter 10. Week Seven: New York Giants at New York Jets

1 The Montreal Canadiens of the NHL won twenty-one Stanley Cup titles between 1923 and 1979. The Canadiens have twenty-four total Stanley Cups, while the Yankees have won twenty-seven World Series championships. The Boston Celtics have seventeen NBA titles, including eight in a row between 1959 and 1966.

2 Peter Golenbock, *Bums—An Oral History of the Brooklyn Dodgers* (New York: Pocket Books, 1984), 464.

3 "Team Turnarounds," *NFL Top 10*, NFL Films, April 29, 2008.

4 Frank Gifford and Peter Richmond, *The Glory Game: How the 1958 NFL Championship Changed Football Forever* (New York: Harper Books, 2008), 6.

5 Jimmy Breslin, "It's Metsomania," *Saturday Evening Post*, June 13, 1964, 22.

6 "I'll never make the mistake of being 70 again," Casey said after his firing. Jack Kenney, "'Major' Ralph Houk was Smart when it Counted," *New American*, July 22, 2010, http://www.thenewamerican.com/index.php/culture/biography/4108-major-ralph-houk-was-smart-when-it-counted (accessed August 31, 2010). It was one his many endearing comments that became part of his unique way of talking with the media. Sportswriters called his rambling monologues "Stengelse." "My God," said a reporter hearing him for the first time, "he talks the way James Joyce writes." Robert Creamer, "The Man Who Always Made Sense," *Sports Illustrated*, October 13, 1975, 41.

7 Coincidence or not, the Yankees' slide started at the same time they were purchased by CBS. The television conglomerate bought the team in 1964 for $11 million, and took a loss when it sold the Yankees to George Steinbrenner in 1973. A group of investors headed by Steinbrenner bought the Yankees for $8.6 million. When Steinbrenner died in 2010, the club and its holdings were valued at $1.6 billion.

8 Joe King, "The Quarterback," *The Sporting News*, March 25, 1967, 43.

9 Ibid.

10 Ralbovsky, *Super Bowl*, 91.

11 Alex Kroll, "The Last of the Titans," *Sports Illustrated*, September 22, 1969, 112.

12 Ralbovsky, *Super Bowl*, 91.

13 Boyle, "Show-Biz Sonny," 71.

14 Ralbovsky, *Super Bowl*, 92.

15 And don't forget that the New York Knicks, who won their first NBA championship in 1970, beat the Baltimore Bullets that season in the first round of the playoffs.

16 "1969 World Series," *Baseball Almanac*, http://www.baseball-almanac.com/ws/yr1969ws.shtml (accessed May 3, 2010).

17 Ralbovsky, *Super Bowl*, 72.

18 John Branch, "A Rivalry That Everyone Has Forgotten to Remember," *New York Times*, September 7, 2007, http://www.nytimes.com/2007/10/07/ sports/football/07giants.html?_r=3&adxnnl=1&ref=joe_namath&adxnnlx=1277641284-J7O48ORInSoo9xxoAw62Uw (accessed July 15, 2010).

19 Associated Press, "New York Jets vs. New York Giants," August 17, 1969, http://www.mmbolding.com/BSR/Interleague_New_York_Giants_ New_York_Jets_1969.htm (accessed July 29, 2010).

20 Ibid.

21 "Revolution," *Full Color Football*, NFL Films, October 7, 2009.

22 Associated Press, "New York Jets vs. New York Giants."

23 Branch, "A Rivalry."

24 "National Eastern," *Sports Illustrated*, September 21, 1970, 51.

25 Rich Koster, "NFC Eastern," *The Sporting News*, October 24, 1970, 31.

26 Michael Eisen, "Comeback over Eagles Reminiscent of Another Giants Rally in '70," Giants.com, September 20, 2006, http://www.giants.com/news/headlines/story.asp?story _id=18935 (accessed September 4, 2010).

27 Ibid.

28 The NFL's blackout policy had become very controversial, in part because it made it impossible for thousands of fans to watch the Super Bowl. For example, Super Bowl I in Los Angeles was blacked out in the large L.A. market. Congress passed a law in 1973 amending the policy to allow blackouts only if the team had not sold out its home game seventy-two hours in advance of kickoff. In 2012 the league amended the policy to lift blackouts for teams that had sold 85 percent of their tickets.

29 Associated Press, "Fight Arouses Giants for Victory Over Jets," November 2, 1970.

30 Dave Anderson, "Tarkenton Rallies Giants for 22-10 Victory Over Jets Before 63, 903 Fans," *New York Times*, November 2, 1970.

31 Rich Koster, "NFC Eastern," *The Sporting News*, November 21, 1970, 13.

32 Anderson, "Tarkenton Rallies."

33 The dramatic November 10, 1974, meeting would end with a 26–20 Jets' victory in overtime. A gimpy Namath hobbled across the goal line on a quarterback bootleg to tie the score late in the game, and then in overtime threw a 5-yard touchdown pass to Emerson Boozer.

34 Eisen, "Comeback over Eagles."

35 Ibid.

Chapter 11. Week Eight: Detroit Lions at New Orleans Saints

1 To indicate how ground-oriented offenses were in 1970, the current NFL record for passing yards in a season is 5,476 set by the Saints' Drew Brees in 2011. The record for most touchdown passes in a season is held by Tom Brady of New England, who threw fifty in 2007. See Appendix II for more information.

2 Tex Maule, "There's Gold In Them Thar Spills," *Sports Illustrated*, October 26, 1970, 20.

3 Bob Oates, "NFC Western," *The Sporting News*, October 10, 1970, 39.

4 Peter Finney, "What Can Saints New Boss Do for an Encore?," *The Sporting News*, November 21, 1970, 5.

5 Morton Sharnik, "This Saint Has Been Called a Sinner," *Sports Illustrated*, June 1, 1970, 18.

6 Toland, "Obituary: Carlton Chester 'Cookie' Gilchrist."

7 Michael MacCambridge, *America's Game: The Epic Story of How Pro Football Captured a Nation* (New York: Random House, 2004), 229.

8 Tex Maule, "Some New Saints in the NFL Temple," *Sports Illustrated*, August 14, 1967, 32.

9 Ibid., 31.

10 Ibid., 30.

11 Joe Marshall, "Look Who's Marching In," *Sports Illustrated*, November 12, 1979, 86.

12 "They Said It," *Sports Illustrated*, April 13, 1970, 19.

13 The same George Wilson who coached the expansion Dolphins for four seasons before giving way to Don Shula.

14 Tex Maule, "All Hail the Lusty Lions," *Sports Illustrated*, January 6, 1958, 11.

15 According to legend, when the Lions traded quarterback Bobby Layne to the Steelers in 1958, Layne put a curse on the team, saying Detroit "would not win [a championship] for 50 years." Through 2012, Layne's curse held true as the Lions won no championships and exactly one playoff game in fifty-four years. Tom Kowalski, "Lions to Superbowl? Layne Curse is Finally Over," *mlive.com*, February 16, 2008, http://www.mlive.com/lions/indes/ssf/2008/02/did _former_qb_curse_lions.html (accessed June 5, 2011).

16 Maule, "All Hail the Lusty Lions," 10.

17 Jerry Green, "Kappless Vikings? Then Hungry Lions Might Win," *The Sporting News*, September 19, 1970, 57.

18 Ibid., 56.

19 Jerry Green, "Munson Trapping Victims for Hungry Lions," *The Sporting News*, November 14, 1970, 3.

20 Ibid.

21 Associated Press, "Lions Rally in 2nd Half to Beat the Bears, 28-14," October 5, 1970.

22 George Plimpton, "Meet Mr. Twinkletoes and His Friends," *Sports Illustrated*, October 12, 1970, 29.

23 Bob Oates, "NFC Western," *The Sporting News*, November 21, 1970," 7.

24 Ibid.

25 Associated Press, "Saints Kicker Seeks Perfection," November 10, 1970.

26 Associated Press, "Dempsey's 63 Yard Kick Breaks Record and Lions," November 9, 1970.

27 Joe Scarpati, "A Moment in Time," *ESPN*, 2011, http://espn.go.com/nfl/feature/flash/_/id/5753078/tom-dempsey-moment-time. Scarpati said he put the ball back eight yards instead of the customary seven because he knew Tom Dempsey needed the extra distance to drive it harder.

28 Tom Dempsey broke the record of 56 yards set by Bert Rechichar in 1953. The record of 63 yards has since been tied three times: by Jason Elam of the Broncos in 1998, Sebastian Janikowski of the Raiders in 2011, and David Akers of the 49ers in 2012.

29 "They Said It," *Sports Illustrated*, November 23, 1970, 18.

30 Jerry Crowe, "Tom Dempsey's Kick was Beyond Belief, But Not His Range," *Los Angeles Times*, October 31, 2010, http://articles.latimes. com/2010/oct/31/sports/la-sp-crowe-20101101-11 (accessed May 7, 2011).

31 Peter Finney, "What Can Saints New Boss Do for an Encore?" *The Sporting News*, November 21, 1970, 5.

32 Associated Press, "Dempsey's 63 Yard Kick."

33 Peter Finney, "What Can Saints New Boss Do for an Encore?" *The Sporting News*, November 21, 1970, 5.

34 Alan Donnes, *Patron Saints: How the Saints Gave New Orleans a Reason to Believe* (New York: Hachette Books, 2007), x.

Chapter 12. Week Eight: Cleveland Browns at Oakland Raiders

1 George Blanda and Jack Olsen, "That Impossible Season," *Sports Illustrated*, August 2, 1971, 31.

2 Patrick Patterson, "Oakland Raiders: What's After Al Davis?" *San Francisco Examiner*, January 20, 2009, http://www.examiner.com/x-514-Oakland-Raiders-Examiner~y2009m1d20-Oakland-Raiders-Whats-after-Al-Davis (accessed September 22, 2010).

3 "Raider Quotes," *Raiderkids.net*, 2009, http://www.raiderkids.net/joomlatrial/index.php?option=com_content&view=article&id=82&Itemid=76 (accessed July 28, 2010).

4 Ralbovsky, *Super Bowl*, 43.

5 Edwin Shrake, "Thunder Out of Oakland," *Sports Illustrated*, November 15, 1965, 91.

6 "Al Davis Leads His Raiders into Super Bowl XV, but Not for the Love of Pete," *People*, January 26, 1981, http://www.people.com/people/archive/article/0,.20078465,00.html (accessed July 22, 2010).

7 Ibid.

8 Tex Maule, "Let George Do It and He Does," *Sports Illustrated*, November 23, 1970, 30.

9 Blanda and Olsen, "That Impossible Season," 32.

10 Associated Press, "Raiders Gain Tie."

11 "Sport: George Blanda is Alive and Kicking," *Time*, November 23, 1970, http://www.time.com/time/magazine/article/0,9171,943328-1,00.html (accessed October 2, 2010).

12 Associated Press, "Blanda, Like Fine Wine, Getting Better With Age," November 9, 1970.

13 Blanda and Olsen, "That Impossible Season," 33–34.

14 Jim Scott, "Over 40 Crowd Applauds Blanda, Mr. Big of the AFC," *The Sporting News*, January 16, 1971, 9.

15   Blanda and Olsen, "That Impossible Season," 34.

16   Dave Eisenberg, "Football is Blanda's Life," *The Sporting News*, November 14, 1970, 46.

17   Ibid.

18   The Dallas Texans beat Blanda and the Oilers, 20–17 in two overtimes to win the 1962 AFL Championship.

19   The modern player who probably got closest to Blanda's longevity is punter Jeff Feagles, who played twenty-two seasons in the NFL and retired in 2009 at the age of forty-three. Feagles set an NFL record by playing in all 352 regular season games in his NFL career.

20   Eisenberg, "Football is Blanda's Life," 46.

21   "Blanda Studies Foe While on Sidelines," *The Sporting News*, January 16, 1970, 10.

22   "Sport: George Blanda." Jim Otto and George Blanda were two of eight Raider players, coaches, and team executives on the 1970 Oakland team that eventually made the Hall of Fame. Another Raider on the roster, rookie linebacker Carl Weathers, played only two seasons in the NFL, but went on to an acting career of some note. Weathers played Apollo Creed in the series of *Rocky* movies.

23   Blanda and Olsen, "That Impossible Season," 35.

24   Blanda and Olsen, "Decade of Revenge," 45.

25   Associated Press, "Collier of Browns Says He'll Retire," December 2, 1970.

26   Ibid.

Chapter 13. Week Thirteen: Green Bay Packers at Chicago Bears

1   Jerry Kramer, "Death by Inches," *Sports Illustrated*, August 4, 1969, 52.

2   Tex Maule, "Never Rule Out an Old Champ," *Sports Illustrated*, October 1968, 30.

3   Kramer, "Death by Inches," 53.

4   Terry Bledsoe, "Crowd Boos as Lions Run Wild in Opener," *Milwaukee Journal*, September 21, 1970, 13.

5   The 16–3 loss in Dallas was symptomatic of the Packers' recent luck. Backup quarterback Don Horn didn't play in the game, but blew out a knee warming up on the sidelines.

6   Terry Bledsoe, "It's No Secret: Packers Itching to Scratch Bears," *Milwaukee Journal*, December 11, 1970, 24.

7   Tex Maule, "The Bears Upend the Giants," *Sports Illustrated*, January 6, 1964, 15. Under Halas, Chicago beat Washington, 73–0 to win the 1940 NFL championship in what remains as the most lopsided game in league history.

8   Gary D'Amato and Cliff Christl, *Mudbaths & Bloodbaths: The Inside Story of the Bears-Packers Rivalry* (Black Earth, WI: Prairie Oak Press, 1997), 4.

9   Dave George, "Halas and Lombardi Epitomized Bears-Packers Rivalry," *Palm Beach Post*, January 22, 2011, http://www.palmbeachpost.com/sports/dolphins/commentary-halas-and -lombardi-epitomized-bears-packers-rivalry-1202786.html?viewAsSinglePage=true (accessed October 30, 2010).

10   Ibid.

11   Bledsoe, "It's No Secret," 24.

12   "They Said It," *Sports Illustrated*, October 28, 1974, 22.

13   Sam Smith, "Bears Crush the 49ers, 61-20 at Muddy Wrigley Field," *Chicago Tribune*, November 1, 1987, http://articles.chicagotribune.com/1987-11-01/sports/8703230162_1 _charlie-krueger-bears-gale-sayers (accessed November 4, 2010).

14   "Tradition," 2010, http://www.chicagobears.com/tradition/hof-sayers.asp (accessed February 1, 2011).

15   "National Central," *Sports Illustrated*, September 21, 1970, 52.

16   Robert F. Jones, "The View From the Bottom," *Sports Illustrated*, October 27, 1969, 23.

17   Carter never played a down for the Bills, but was sent to Cincinnati where he became the Bengals' starter.

18 Bruce W. Thielemann, "Gale Sayers and Brian Piccolo," *Christianity Today*, May 16, 2000, http://www.christianitytoday.com/moi/2000/003/may/16.16.html (accessed November 5, 2010).

19 "National Conference," *Sport Illustrated*, September 21, 1970, 52.

20 Jim Slocum, "Starr Injury Foils Pack," *Milwaukee Sentinel*, December 14, 1970.

21 Ibid.

22 Ibid., 5. George Farmer caught 119 passes and scored ten touchdowns in a modest six-year NFL career.

23 Stuart Shea, *Wrigley Field: The Unauthorized Biography* (Washington, DC: Brassey's, 2004), 244.

24 Bud Lea, "Barney Burns Packers, 20-0," *Milwaukee Sentinel*, December 21, 1970.

25 Chuck Johnson, "Some Players Criticize Bengston, Others Defend Him," *Milwaukee Journal*, December 23, 1970, 16.

26 Arin Karimian, "Packers Celebrate Super Bowl With 56,000 at Lambeau Field," *USA Today*, February 8, 2011, http://www.usatoday.com/communities/thehuddle/post/2011/02/nfl -packers-super-bowl-xlv-celebration-parade/1 (accessed February 22, 2011).

Chapter 14. Week Fourteen: St. Louis Cardinals at Washington Redskins

1 Dave Fleming, "Pottsville Maroons Won't Give Up Fight," *Pottsville Republican-Herald*, October 25, 2009, http://republicanherald.com/ sports/pottsville-maroons-won-t-give-up -fight-1.352192 (accessed May 7, 2011).

2 To this day, people in Pottsville believe their Maroons were cheated out of a title, and several books and documentaries have been made about the "stolen championship" of 1925. Carr suspended the Pottsville franchise, only to reinstate it the next year, but the Maroons were out of the NFL for good by 1929.

3 Jack Olsen, "The Unhappiest Millionaire, *Sports Illustrated*, April 4, 1960, 36.

4 Warner Wolfner offered George Halas a million dollars on one occasion.

5 Olsen, "The Unhappiest Millionaire," 36.

6 "War and Peace." Namath eventually signed for a then-record $427,000.

7 "National Eastern," *Sports Illustrated*, September 21, 1970, 51.

8 Mark Mulvoy, "Peach Fuzz With a Difference," *Sports Illustrated*, November 27, 1967, 37–38.

9 Golenbock, *Cowboys Have Always Been My Heroes*, 436.

10 Rich Koster, "New Big Red Machine-The Tank," *The Sporting News*, October 31, 1970, 3.

11 Ibid.

12 In 1935 the New York Giants shut out three straight opponents, and four overall, on their way to the NFL championship. The Akron Pros shut out ten opponents in the 1920 season, including five in a row to open the season.

13 Bob St. John, "Redbirds Chirp, Bye, Bye Cowboys," *Dallas Morning News*, November 17, 1970, http://www.dallasnews.com/sharedcontent/dws/spt/football/cowboys/classic/recordbook /yearbyear/1970/111770cardinals.html (accessed May 31, 2010).

14 Rich Koster, "NFC Eastern," *The Sporting News*, October 24, 1970, 31.

15 "Larry Wilson," *St. Louis Sports Hall of Fame*, 2010, http://www.stlouissportshalloffame.com /index.php?option=com_content&view=article&id=22&Itemid=210 (accessed September 9, 2010).

16 Rich Koster, "NFC Eastern," October 24, 1970, 31.

17 Vic Gold, "Redskins' Revenge," *The Washingtonian*, August 1, 2002, http://www.washingtonian .com/articles/sports/6524.html (accessed September 11, 2010).

18 William Johnson, "Arararararargh!" *Sports Illustrated*, March 3, 1969, 33.

19 Ibid.

20 Robert Lipsyte, "Vince Lombardi Without Tears," *Miami News*, September 7, 1970.

21 "National Eastern," *Sports Illustrated*, September 21, 1970, 51.

22 Rich Koster, "NFC Eastern," *The Sporting News*, August 29, 1970, 48.

23 It's possible that Jerry Smith's alleged homosexuality has kept him out of the Hall. Although Smith never admitted his sexual preference, Dave Kopay, a former teammate of Smith and the

first NFL player to admit he was a homosexual, wrote in his autobiography that Smith was also a homosexual. Jerry Smith died of AIDS in 1986.

24 "National East," *Sports Illustrated*, September 20, 1971, 46.

25 Ibid., 49.

26 Rich Koster, "NFC Eastern," *The Sporting News*, January 2, 1971, 21.

27 Rich Koster, "NFC Eastern," *The Sporting News*, January 9, 1971, 12. Charley Winner coached five seasons in St. Louis and later coached two years with the Jets. His record as NFL head coach was 44-44-5.

28 John Gilliam went on to have an especially productive career after his trade to Minnesota, making the Pro Bowl four straight years and helping the Vikings to play in three Super Bowls.

29 Eisenberg, *Cotton Bowl Days*, 230.

30 Koster, "NFC Eastern," January 2, 1971, 21.

31 Gold, "Redskins' Revenge."

32 According to the Elias Sports Bureau, Allen is third in winning percentage at .712 behind John Madden (.759) and Vince Lombardi (.739). The list also includes other 1970 coaches, including Blanton Collier (.691, fourth), Don Shula (.677, sixth), Paul Brown (.624, thirteenth), and Bud Grant (.621, fifteenth).

33 Gold, "Redskins' Revenge."

Chapter 15. Week Fourteen: Houston Oilers at Dallas Cowboys

1 Bob St. John, "And the Cowboys Go Tumbling Down," *Dallas Morning News*, November 9, 1970, http://www.dallasnews.com/sharedcontent/dws/spt/football/cowboys/classic (accessed May 22, 2010).

2 Bob St. John, "Redbirds Chirp, Bye, Bye Cowboys," *Dallas Morning News*, November 17, 1970, http://www.dallasnews.com/sharedcontent/dws/spt/football/cowboys/classic/recordbook /yearbyyear/1970/111770cardinals.html (accessed May 31, 2010).

3 Ibid.

4 Edwin Shrake, "Why is this Man Laughing?" *Sports Illustrated*, September 18, 1972, 133.

5 Bob St. John, *Landry: the Legend and the Legacy* (Nashville: Word Pub, 2000), 281. Rentzel pleaded guilty to indecent exposure the following April and received five years probation. Released by Dallas, he went to the Rams, but in 1973 was busted for marijuana possession and subsequently suspended for the entire season by Commissioner Rozelle. Rentzel retired after the 1974 season.

6 Eisenberg, *Cotton Bowl Days*, 437.

7 Ibid.

8 Golenbock, *Cowboys Have Always Been My Heroes*, 437–38.

9 Eisenberg, *Cotton Bowl Days*, 452.

10 Ibid., 454.

11 Edwin Shrake, "Almost Alone at the Top," *Sports Illustrated*, December 25, 1967, 16–17.

12 Ed Fowler, *Loser Takes All: Bud Adams, Bad Football & Big Business* (Atlanta, GA: Longstreet Press, 1997), 5.

13 Stram coached the Texans/Chiefs for fifteen years, while Landry's mark of twenty-nine consecutive seasons coaching the Cowboys is an NFL record.

14 Edwin Shrake, "A Difference of Opinion in the Gentle State of Texas," *Sports Illustrated*, September 8, 1969, 20.

15 Sam Allis and Kurt Anderson, "The Best Little Rivalry in Texas," *Time*, November 20, 1981, http://www.time.com/time/magazine/ article/0,9171,925046,00.html (accessed June 30, 2010).

16 Because Neely signed with Houston before his college eligibility had expired, he was not allowed to play in the Sooners' bowl game that season. Neely's Oklahoma teammate and future Dallas teammate Lance Rentzel was also ruled ineligible because he too had prematurely signed a pro contract.

17 *Houston Oilers, Inc. v. Ralph Neely*, 361 F.2d 36 (10th Circuit, 1966).

18 Shrake, "Difference of Opinion," 18.

19 Ibid., 20.

20 Ibid., 21.

21 Ibid., 20.

22 "American Central," *Sports Illustrated*, September 21, 1970, 40.

23 Which is why Houston took Santa Clara quarterback Dan Pastorini with the third overall pick in the 1971 NFL draft.

24 Maule, "Big Ifs in Big D," 10.

25 Rich Koster, "NFC Eastern," *The Sporting News*, January 2, 1971, 21.

26 On October 9, 1966, at the Cotton Bowl, Meredith threw five touchdown passes in a 56–7 win over the Eagles. He finished the day twenty-five of thirty-eight for 447 yards and no interceptions.

27 Bob St. John, "Cowboys' Wildcatter Blows in Gusher," *Dallas Morning News*, December 21, 1970, http://www.dallasnews.com/sharedcontent/dws/spt/football/cowboys/classic/recordbook /yearbyyear/1970/122170oilers.html (accessed August 2, 2010).

28 "Worst Teams," *NFL Top 10*, NFL Films, September 29, 2007.

29 Ibid.

30 Carlton Stowers, "Dallas Number Up; Oilers Count 'Em Out in 30-24 Win," *Dallas Morning News*, November 23, 1979, http://www.dallasnews.com/sharedcontent/dws/spt/football /cowboys/classic/recordbook/yearbyyear/1979/ (accessed September 1, 2010).

31 Thomas George, "NFL Owners Approve Move to Nashville by the Oilers," *New York Times*, May 1, 1996, http://www.nytimes.com/1996/05/01/sports/ pro-football-nfl-owners-approve -move-to-nashville-by-the-oilers.html (accessed September 3, 2010).

32 Ibid.

33 Associated Press, "Triumphant Return for Titans, Adams," December 30, 2002, http://articles.latimes.com/2002/dec/30/sports/sp-titans30 (accessed September 14, 2010).

34 "Titans Owner Apologizes for Gesture to Former Houston Mayor," *CBC News*, November 10, 2000, http://www.cbc.ca/sports/story/2000/05/11/owner000511.html (accessed September 14, 2010).

Chapter 16. The Playoffs

1 "Top 40 Memorable Moments in Bengals History," Bengals.com, 2011, http://www.bengals .com/team/40-memorable-moments-6-10.html (accessed July 21, 2011).

2 That record would be more lopsided (40-18-1) if not for the old NFL teams that played in the AFC (Pittsburgh, Cleveland, and Baltimore). Seven NFL teams went undefeated against AFL rivals and no AFL team was better than even against NFL competition.

3 Roy Blount, "The Good Humor Men," *Sports Illustrated*, November 6, 1972, 21.

4 Larry Felser, "AFC Eastern," *The Sporting News*, October 3, 1970, 39.

5 Dave Eisenberg, "Fastest-Rising of Pro QBs? Watch the Dolphins' Griese," *The Sporting News*, October 31, 1970, 10.

6 Larry Felser, "Amazing Power," *The Sporting News*, November 7, 1970, 14.

7 John Crittenden, "Fast Dolphin Finish Erases 4 Losing Years," *The Sporting News*, January 2, 1971, 17.

8 Ibid.

9 "They Said It," *Sports Illustrated*, June 29, 1970, 13.

10 Lea, "Barney Burns Packers."

11 Ibid.

12 John Steadman, "Colts Stampede Behind Blue-Ribbon Bull," *The Sporting News*, January 9, 1971, 15.

13 Associated Press, "Bengal 4 Wants to Meet Unitas," December 24, 1970.

14 Steadman, "Colts Stampede," 15.

15 Ibid.

16 Bob St. John, "Close-Fisted Cowboys Tight-Rope Past Lions," *The Sporting News*, January 9, 1971, 13.

17   Ibid.

18   Ibid.

19   Ibid.

20   Ibid.

21   Dick Young, "Young Ideas," *The Sporting News*, January 16, 1971, 17.

22   Tex Maule, "Rushing to Stake a Claim," *Sports Illustrated*, January 4, 1971, 15.

23   Ibid.

24   Sandy Padwe, "When Trust is Betrayed," *Sports Illustrated*, June 27, 1988, 80.

25   Ibid.

26   Dick Gordon, "No Viking Alibis—49er Defense Just Too Tough," *The Sporting News*, January 9, 1971, 19.

27   Ibid.

28   Associated Press, "Victory Over Vikings Puts 49ers Closer to 1st Title," December 28, 1970.

29   Maule, "Rushing to Stake a Claim," 15.

30   Al Levine, "Garo's Just No Mudder," *Miami News*, December 28, 1970.

31   Jim Scott, "Field More Suited for Dolphins, but Raiders Made Big Splash," *The Sporting News*, January 9, 1971, 10.

32   Brown was in the middle of another Pro Bowl season, his ninth, and would eventually intercept fifty-four passes in a sixteen-year Hall of Fame career. Interestingly, during his career Brown would return only two interceptions for touchdowns in the regular season. But he had two touchdown returns in the playoffs, including a 75-yarder against Fran Tarkenton and the Vikings in Super Bowl XI, a game the Raiders won, 32–14.

33   Associated Press, "Brown Theft is Key Play," December 28, 1970.

34   Ibid.

35   Scott, "Field More Suited," 10.

36   Ibid.

37   Maule, "Rushing to Stake a Claim," 15.

38   Associated Press, "Snow 1st, Raiders 2nd for Colt Fans," January 2, 1971.

39   "Night Before Session Plots Woes for Colts," *Baltimore Afro-American*, January 2, 1971, 16.

40   "1970 Baltimore Colts," *America's Game*.

41   Robert Jones, "To Kill a Memory That Still Hurts," *Sports Illustrated*, January 11, 1971, 20.

42   Ibid., 18.

43   The Colts played at Memorial Stadium until moving to Indianapolis in 1984. The stadium hosted the Baltimore Ravens for one season in 1997, but it was demolished in 2001.

44   Jones, "To Kill a Memory," 21.

45   Ibid.

46   "Unitas, 37, Still the Master," *New York Times Service*, January 4, 1971.

47   Jones, "To Kill a Memory," 21.

48   Ibid., 20.

49   Larry Felser, "AFC Eastern," *The Sporting News*, January 16, 1971, 21.

50   Maule, "Big Ifs in Big D," 10.

51   Mark Mulvoy, "On Paper, Dallas is the Best," *Sports Illustrated*, December 6, 1971, 31.

52   United Press International, "Brodie's Passing Worries Landry," January 2, 1971.

53   Ibid.

54   Rich Koster, "NFC Eastern," *The Sporting News*, January 9, 1971, 12.

55   Donovan and Drury, *Fatso*, 22–23.

56   Ibid., 22.

57   Dwight Chapin, "Kezar Memories: Seagulls and Brawls," *San Francisco Chronicle*, January 3, 2001, http://football.ballparks.com/NFL/ SanFrancisco49ers/oldindex.htm (accessed October 3, 2010).

58   Wells Twombly, "Kezar: The Wonderful Dump," *The Sporting News*, January 9, 1971, 12.

59   Dick O'Connor, "Cowboys Make Their Critics Dine on Crow," *The Sporting News*, January 16, 1971, 3.

60 Tex Maule, "Witnesses for the Defense," *Sports Illustrated*, January 11, 1971, 16.

61 O'Connor, "Dine on Crow," 3.

62 Chapin, "Kezar Memories." Nolan was right—the 49ers reached the playoffs the following two seasons, only to lose again to Dallas both times. "Dick Nolan against Tom Landry was like Tom Landry against Vince Lombardi," Nolan said. "Landry couldn't get past Lombardi, and I didn't get past Landry" (ibid.).

63 O'Connor, "Dine on Crow," 3.

64 Terry Bledsoe, "Cowboys Win a Big One," *Milwaukee Journal*, January 4, 1971, 9.

65 Maule, "Witnesses for the Defense," 16.

Chapter 17. Super Bowl V

1 Eisenberg, *Cotton Bowl Days*, 239.

2 Ralbovsky, *Super Bowl*, xi.

3 Ibid., 165.

4 Dick Young, "Young Ideas," *The Sporting News*, January 16, 1971, 17.

5 "Colts Can Be Unwanted Champs," *Miami News*, January 2, 1971.

6 Al Levine, "Only Memories Remain of Old-Time Spirit," *Miami News*, January 16, 1971.

7 Leonard Koppett, "It's No Longer the Super Bowl," *The Sporting News*, January 30, 1971, 4.

8 "NFL Blackout Sticks," *New York Times Service*, January 14, 1971.

9 Sam Lacy, "Colts AFRO Pick in Super Bowl," *Baltimore Afro-American*, January 16, 1971, 13.

10 Ralbovsky, *Super Bowl*, 155.

11 Ibid., 169.

12 John Steadman, "Once and for All, Morrall Erases that Loser Image," *The Sporting News*, January 30, 1971, 6.

13 Dave Eisenberg, "Foot Back in Football," *The Sporting News*, January 14, 1971, 50.

14 Mark Mulvoy, "On Paper, Dallas is the Best," *Sports Illustrated*, December 6, 1971, 32.

15 Robert Jones, "An Act, Followed by an Act, Followed by an Act," *Sports Illustrated*, January 18, 1971, 20. Paul Brown began calling plays in the early 1950s by using "messenger guards"—linemen who would shuttle in and out of the game on each play carrying the signal to quarterback Otto Graham. The Browns also experimented with a radio helmet that allowed Brown to speak directly to the quarterback. The NFL outlawed its use in 1956, but the radio helmet returned in 1994 and is now used by all NFL teams.

16 Jamie Aron, *Dallas Cowboys: The Complete Illustrated History* (Minneapolis: MBI Publishing, 2010), 122.

17 Joe Falls, "Super Bowl Visitor's Diary," *The Sporting News*, January 30, 1971, 2.

18 "Sport: Into the Pride Bowl," *Time*, January 18, 1971, http://www. time.com/time/magazine /article/0,9171,942461-1,00.html (accessed September 30, 2010).

19 Ibid.

20 Falls, "Super Bowl Visitor's Diary," 2.

21 Lacy, "Colts AFRO Pick," 13.

22 Ralbovsky, *Super Bowl*, 171.

23 It was a policy the league started in Super Bowl I, but as the number of media outlets grew, the two weeks before the Super Bowl were often viewed as overkill. Thus, in some seasons, the NFL mandated only a week between the conference championships and the Super Bowl. In 2002, for example, Tampa Bay won Super Bowl XXXVII over the Raiders only a week after the NFC Championship game.

24 Falls, "Super Bowl Visitor's Diary," 2.

25 Lowell Reidenbaugh, "Super Bowl V-Great, if you Like Volleyball," *The Sporting News*, January 30, 1971, 3.

26 Rating is a measurement of how many homes are watching a particular show versus homes with television sets. Thus the game attracted almost 40 percent of viewers in homes with televisions.

27 "NFLs Sticky TV Problem," *The Sporting News*, January 16, 1971, 17.

28 John Crittenden, "Miami Mayor Blanked on Super Bowl Ducats," *The Sporting News*, January 30, 1971, 6.

29 Taking inflation into account, the $100 per day in 1970 would be $562 today; the $35 million would be around $200 million.

30 Tom Barrett, "A True Feast for Super Bowl Fans," *The Sporting News*, January 30, 1971, 8.

31 John Underwood, "New Slant on the Mod Squad," *Sports Illustrated*, November 15, 1971, 38.

32 Crittenden, "Miami Mayor Blanked on Super Bowl Ducats," 6.

33 William Johnson, "Goodbye to Three Yards and a Cloud of Dust," *Sports Illustrated,* January 27, 1969, 37.

34 Ibid., 33.

35 The debate over injuries and artificial surface continues today, and dozens of studies have been conducted with often conflicting results. Perhaps the most telling incident occurred on October 10, 1993, when receiver Wendell Davis of the Bears tore up both knees after going up for a pass and landing on the AstroTurf at Philadelphia's Veterans Stadium. "They found my kneecaps up in my thighs," said Davis. Peter King, "A Fight Over Turf," *Sports Illustrated*, November 1, 1993, 32.

36 Todd Neale, "AAOS: Artificial Turf Injuries Still More Likely in NFL," *MedPage Today*, March 15, 2010, http://www.medpagetoday.com/ MeetingCoverage/AAOS/19020 (accessed October 11, 2010).

37 Larry Felser, "Meddlers Eager to Undercut Patriots' G.M. Bell," *The Sporting News*, January 1, 1972, 21.

38 Wells Twombly, "A Jar of Silly Putty," *The Sporting News*, January 30, 1971, 11.

39 Penalties such as intentional grounding and holding were 15 yards in 1970. Such penalties were changed to 10 yards in 1974 in an effort to encourage offense and scoring.

40 Golenbock, *Cowboys Have Always Been My Heroes*, 460.

41 Reidenbaugh, "Super Bowl V," 6.

42 John Steadman, "Unitas Plagued by Headache for Weeks," *The Sporting News*, January 30, 1971, 3.

43 Bob Oates, "Not-So-Super Colts Still Get $15,000 Apiece," *The Sporting News*, January 30, 1971, 5.

44 Tex Maule, "Eleven Big Mistakes," *Sports Illustrated*, January 25, 1971, 17.

45 Golenbock, *Cowboys Have Always Been My Heroes*, 461.

46 St. John, *Landry*, 284.

47 Terry Bledsoe, "Colts Survive Stupor Bowl," *Milwaukee Journal,* January 18, 1971, 10.

48 Ralbovsky, *Super Bowl*, 180.

49 Jim Murray, "Best of Murray," *The Sporting News*, January 30, 1971, 22.

50 "1970 Baltimore Colts," *America's Game*.

51 Larry Felser, "American Football Conference," *The Sporting News*, January 30, 1971, 9.

52 Reidenbaugh, "Super Bowl V," 3.

53 Ibid.

54 Golenbock, *Cowboys Have Always Been My Heroes*, 463.

55 Felser, "AFC Eastern," January 30, 1971, 9.

56 Chuck Howley remains the only player from a losing team honored as the Super Bowl MVP.

57 Sportswriter Bob Oates called it "the best throw of the day." "I was totally embarrassed," said Lilly. To the Baltimore player who returned his helmet, Lilly said, "I'm so sorry. I hope it didn't hit you" (Eisenberg, *Cotton Bowl Days*, 253).

58 Ibid., 244.

59 Sam Blair, "Acme of Futility, Cowboys Blow it All in Blooper Bowl," *The Sporting News*, January 30, 1971, 10.

60 Bob Oates, "Not-So-Super Colts Still Get $15,000 Apiece," *The Sporting News*, January 30, 1971.

61 Murray, "Best of Murray," 22.

62 Bob St. John, "Super Day Dribbles Away, 16-13," *Dallas Morning News*, January 18, 1971, http://www.dallasnews.com/sharedcontent/dws/spt/football/nfl/superbowl/thegame/stories /073010dnspoclassicsuperbowl 1971.6a33261.html (accessed November 1, 2010).

63 Melvin Durslag, "What a Bargain!," *The Sporting News*, January 30, 1971, 8.

64 "Morrall the Hero This Time," *Milwaukee Journal*, January 18, 1971, 10.

65 Twombly, "Jar of Silly Putty," 11.

66 Maule, "Eleven Big Mistakes," 12.

67 Ralbovsky, *Super Bowl*, 186.

68 Bob Oates, "Not-So-Super Colts Still Get $15,000 Apiece," *The Sporting News,* January 30, 1971.

69 Twombly, "Jar of Silly Putty," 11.

70 "1970 Baltimore Colts," *America's Game.*

71 Ibid.

72 Ibid.

73 Ibid.

Chapter 18. The Aftermath

1 McCafferty took over the Lions in 1973 and went 6-7-1 in his only season in Detroit. He died of a heart attack in the summer of 1974 at the age of fifty-three.

2 Hank Gola, "Former Baltimore Colts Kicker Jim O'Brien Boots Himself Into History," *New York Daily News*, February 6, 2010, http://www.nydailynews.com/sports/football/2010/02/06/201006_former_baltimore_colts _kicker_jim_obrien_boots_himself_into_history_.html (accessed November 11, 2010).

3 E. M. Swift, "Now You See Him, Now You Don't," *Sports Illustrated*, December 15, 1986, 87.

4 John R. O'Neill, "Robert Irsay's Legacy: Era of Change," *Indianapolis Star*, January 15, 1997, http:// www2.indystar.com/library/factfiles/people/i/irsay_jim/stories/1997_0115.html (accessed November 12, 2010).

5 The elder Irsay died in January 1997.

6 Ann Hornaday, "Colts Left Town, But Film Salutes the Band That Played On," *Washington Post*, October 8, 2009, http://www.washingtonpost.com/ wp-dyn/content/article/2009/10 /07/AR2009100704004.html (accessed November 12, 2010).

7 Golenbock, *Cowboys Have Always Been My Heroes*, 464.

8 The Cowboys traded Morton to the New York Giants following the 1974 season for a number one draft pick that turned into Hall of Fame defensive tackle Randy White. Morton went to Denver in 1977 where he led the Broncos to the Super Bowl against Dallas. Facing his old team, Morton had a miserable day, completing just four of fifteen passes with four interceptions, as the Cowboys easily won Super Bowl XII, 27–10. "It took Craig Morton 12 years," sportswriter David Israel wrote after the game, "but he finally won a Super Bowl for Dallas." Kevin Gleason, "Day V: Q&A With Super Bowl Marathon Man," Hudsonvalley.com, February 2, 2008, http://blogs.hudsonvalley .com/hudson-valley-sports-kevin-hudson/page/5/ (accessed December 4, 2010).

9 Golenbock, *Cowboys Have Always Been My Heroes*, 404–5.

10 Bob St. John, "Super Cowboys Bowl 'em Over," *Dallas Morning News*, January 17, 1972, http://www. dallasnews.com/sharedcontent/dws/spt/football/cowboys/classic/recordbook /yearbyyear/1971/011772 dolphins.html (accessed November 13, 2010).

11 Golenbock, *Cowboys Have Always Been My Heroes*, 464.

12 NFL Films gave Dallas the name "America's Team" in the Cowboys' 1978 highlight film.

13 The Cowboys' rushing record was broken when the Redskins ran for 280 yards in Super Bowl XXII.

14 The highest-scoring year in NFL history came in 1948, when teams averaged 23.2 points per game.

15 "Things That Changed the Game," *NFL Top 10*, NFL Films, May 13, 2008.

16 Ibid.

17 Frank Henderson and Mel Olson, *Football's West Coast Offense* (Champaign, IL: Human Kinetics, 1997), vii.

18 Paul Zimmerman, "Did He Pass? Did He Ever. Give Him an 'A.'" *Sports Illustrated*, September 10, 1984, 15–16.

19 Paul Zimmerman, "Out of the Running," *Sports Illustrated*, October 8, 1990, 57. In the same 1984 season that saw Marino smash several NFL passing records, the Rams' Eric Dickerson broke O. J. Simpson's single-season rushing record, running 379 times for 2,105 yards. In 2012 the Vikings' Adrian Peterson came within just 9 yards of breaking Dickerson's record, rushing for 2,097 yards on 348 carries. Thus the running game is alive and well in the NFL.

20 David Maraniss, *When Pride Still Mattered: A Life of Vince Lombardi* (New York: Simon & Schuster, 1999), 387.

21 Donovan and Drury, *Fatso*, 120–21.

22 Golenbock, *Cowboys Have Always Been My Heroes*, 242.

23 Peter Gent chronicled many of these darker issues in his novel *North Dallas Forty*, published in 1973. Although the book was fictional, it was based on Gent's experiences with the Cowboys, which he characterized as a team divided by drug use and racial issues. *North Dallas Forty* refers to the fact that most of the Cowboys' white players lived in north Dallas, while the black players were segregated in south Dallas. The book has been called one of the greatest sports novels ever written, and it was turned into a popular movie in 1979.

24 "National East," *Sports Illustrated*, September 21, 1970, 51.

25 "Lost Treasures of the NFL, Volume 5," NFL Films, 1999.

26 John Underwood, "He's Burning to be a Success," *Sports Illustrated*, September 20, 1971, 92.

27 Ibid., 100.

28 John Underwood, "The Desperate Coach," *Sports Illustrated*, August 25, 1969, 66.

29 Mark Mulvoy, "On Paper, Dallas is the Best," *Sports Illustrated*, December 6, 1971, 31. When Thomas also called general manager Tex Schramm "sick, demented and completely dishonest," Schramm wryly replied, "That's not bad—he got two out of three" (ibid.).

30 A vow he pretty much kept until Super Bowl VI. In the victorious Dallas locker room after the game, Tom Brookshier of CBS asked, "Are you as fast as you seem to be?" Thomas simply replied, "Evidently."

31 Golenbock, *Cowboys Have Always Been My Heroes*, 483.

32 "They Said It," *Sports Illustrated*, July 16, 1973, 12.

33 Don Banks, "The Top Five: Move over, Moss and T.O. — These are the Real Bad Boys of NFL Lore," *Sports Illustrated*, January 14, 2005, http://sportsillustrated.cnn.com/2005/writers/don_banks/01/14/top.five/ (accessed May 9, 2011).

34 Among the many players the Raiders rescued from the scrapheap of the NFL were Hall of Famers Ted Hendricks and Bob Brown, and Super Bowl MVP Jim Plunkett.

35 Curry Kirkpatrick, "They Don't Pay Nobody to be Humble," *Sports Illustrated*, November 13, 1989, 56.

36 Robert Boyle, "And then the Clock Showed 0:00," *Sports Illustrated*, September 27, 1982, 14.

37 The season was reduced from sixteen games to nine, and a special round-robin playoff format was used involving sixteen teams instead of the usual ten.

38 Paul Zimmerman, "When Push Came to Shove," *Sports Illustrated*, October 5, 1987, 39. This time, the strike lasted only twenty-four days, forced the cancellation of only one game, and aside from the novelty of playing games with "scab" players, the season continued with minimal disruption.

39 The $23,000 in 1970 is comparable to around $127,000 in 2011.

40 Jack Olsen, "He Goes Where the Trouble Is," *Sports Illustrated*, October 19, 1970, 22.

41 Kapp eventually signed with the Boston Patriots for a contract that was estimated at $100,000 a year for five years, but 1970 was his last season in the NFL. He finished the year throwing only three touchdown passes compared to seventeen interceptions.

42 Judd Zulgad, "Favre in Line for Big Pay Bump," *Minneapolis Star-Tribune*, August 18, 2010, http://www.startribune.com/sports/vikings/100951754.html?elr=KArksUUUU (accessed November 1, 2010).

43 Ibid.

44 Bill Lubinger, "Remember When … Off-Season was Work Time for the Cleveland Browns?" *Cleveland Plain-Dealer*, May 26, 2010, http://www.cleveland.com/browns/index.ssf /2010/05/remember_when_ offseason_was_wo.html (accessed November 2, 2010).

45 Ibid.

46 Ibid.

47 "Professionals," *Best Ever*, NFL Films, 1981.

48 Roger Mills, "The First 100 Days," *St. Petersburg Times*, May 29, 2002, http://www.sptimes.com /2002/05/29/Bucs/The_first_100_days.shtml (accessed November 4, 2010).

49 Bigger, faster athletes also means a greater risk for serious injury, particularly related to concussions. As of 2013, more than four thousand former players had sued the NFL seeking damages for their concussive injuries. "There needs to be changes," said Chris Nowinski of the Sports Legacy Institute, which studies brain injuries in sports. "People just aren't going to do well with those types of injuries. You're not going to keep your best players on the field." Hal Habib, "Miami Dolphins' Channing Crowder: NFL Campaign Against Helmet-to-Helmet Hits Makes the Game Less Manly," *Palm Beach Post*, October 19, 2010, http://www.palmbeachpost.com/sports/dolphins/miami-dolphins-channing-crowder-nfl -campaign-against-helmet-981382.html (accessed January 13, 2011).

50 Michael Rosenberg, "The 2011 NFL Hateability Index," cnnsi.com, September 9, 2011, http://sportsillustrated.cnn.com/2011/writers/michael_rosenberg/09/07/hateability.index /index.html (accessed September 9, 2011).

51 "They Said It," *Sports Illustrated*, October 12, 1970, 12.

52 Bil Gilbert, "Problems in a Turned-On World," *Sports Illustrated*, June 23, 1969, 66.

53 Lyle Alzado, "I'm Sick and I'm Scared," *Sports Illustrated*, July 8, 1991, 22.

54 Shrake, "Sacred Game of Pro Football," 99.

55 Germany's Bundesliga soccer league ranks second with an average attendance of 41,904.

56 Sean Leahy, "HDTV and Technology Pit NFL Stadiums vs. Fans Living Rooms," *USA Today*, September 1, 2010, http://www.usatoday.com/sports/football/nfl/2010-08-31-nfl-hd-tv -stadium-or-living-room_N.htm (accessed November 4, 2010).

57 The NFL had experimented with occasional Thursday night games, but did not make it a permanent feature until 2006.

58 Joe Saumarez-Smith, "NFL Should Change its Opposition to Betting," *Bloomberg*, February 6, 2009, http://www.bloomberg.com/apps/news?pid=newsarchive&sid=aRi2yDLKXa.o (accessed November 10, 2010).

59 Ibid.

60 Anthony Bruscas, "Going Blog Wild: Anyone With a Computer and an Opinion Can Launch a Media Startup," *Seattle Post-Intelligencer*, February 24, 2004, http://seattlepi.nwsource.com /othersports/161835_blog24.htm (accessed January 13, 2007).

61 "Replay!"

62 Mark Maske and Thomas Heath, "NFL's Economic Model Shows Signs of Strain," *Washington Post*, January 8, 2005, http://www.washingtonpost.com/ac2/wp-dyn/A57668-2005Jan7 ?language=printer (accessed October 19, 2010).

63 Jerry Green, "NFC Central," *The Sporting News*, October 24, 1970, 36.

64 Bob Oates, "National Football Conference," *The Sporting News*, January 30, 1971, 10.

65 Bill Richardson, "AFC Western," *The Sporting News*, October 24, 1970, 30.

66 Ibid. An analysis that was still technically correct even after the Dolphins went 14-0 in 1972.

67 Frank Deford, "Parity or Mediocrity?," *cnnsi.com*, September 8, 1999, http://sportsillustrated .cnn.com/inside_game/deford/news/1999/09/08/deford/ (accessed November 9, 2010).

68 Ted Lewis, "NFL Achieves Parity; Tricky Part is Maintaining Long-Term Success," *New Orleans Times-Picayune*, February 6, 2010, http://www.nola.com/saints/index.ssf /2010/02/nfl_has_parity_trick_is_mainta.html (accessed November 11, 2010).

69 Ibid.

70   Martin Gough, "NFL Takes UK Seriously," *BBC Sport*, October 26, 2007, http://news.bbc
     .co.uk/sport2/hi/other_sports/american_football/7062729.stm (accessed November 8, 2010).

71   Ibid. In 2012 the NFL played regular season games in London and Toronto. The Jacksonville
     Jaguars committed to play one home game in London from 2013 to 2016, and the league said
     it was working to add a second game there each season.

72   "NFL Europa Closes," *NFL.com*, http://www.nfl.comnews/story?id=09000d5d801308ec
     &template=without-video&confirm=true (accessed November 15, 2010).

73   Kevin Baxter, "NFL's Popularity in Mexico Continues to Grow," *Los Angeles Times*, January 29,
     2010, http://articles.latimes.com/2010/jan/29/sports/la-sp-nfl-mexico29-2010jan29 (accessed
     August 5, 2010). In the fall of 2010, NFL Commissioner Roger Goodell indicated the league is
     planning a permanent presence in Europe. "I think the next step will be multiple games [in
     Europe]. And if that's successful then I think the idea of a franchise here is realistic" (Gough,
     "NFL Takes UK Seriously").

74   Mark Mulvoy, "On Paper, Dallas is the Best," *Sports Illustrated*, December 6, 1971, 37.

75   George Vecsey, "The Most Crucial Battles Will Be Off the Field," *New York Times*, September
     4, 2010, http://www.nytimes.com/2010/09/05/sports/football/05vecsey.html?_r=1 (accessed
     November 15, 2010).

76   Adjusted for inflation, a $5 ticket in 1970 would cost $28.13 in 2012. The New York Jets lead
     the NFL in ticket prices, with an average ticket in 2012 costing fans more than $117.

77   Michael McCarthy, "NFL: Attendance Likely to Fall for Third Straight Season in 2010, to
     Lowest Level Since 1998," *USA Today*, September 1, 2010,
     http://:content.usatoday.com/communities/thehuddle/post/2010/ 09/nfl-attendance-likely-to-
     fall-for-third-straight-season-in-2010-to-lowest-level-since-1998/1 (accessed November 17,
     2010).

78   Aaron Kuriloff and Curtis Eichelberger, "NFL 2009 Season Signals End of Parity That Helped
     Build League," *Bloomberg*, September 10, 2009, http://www.bloomberg.com/apps/news
     ?pid=newsarchive&sid=a17GOPMiGywY (accessed November 17, 2010).

Appendix III. 1970 Pro Bowl

1   Tex Maule, "Goodbye to the Alka-Seltzer and Aspirin Bowl," *Sports Illustrated*, February 1,
     1971, 50.

2   Ibid.

Appendix V. The Men of 1970: Where Are They Now?

1   Brent Foster, "NFLPA Chief: Settlement with Retired Players a First Step at Unification," *USA
     Today*, June 6, 2009, http://www.usatoday.com/sports/football/nfl/2009-06-05-nflpa-press
     -conference_N.htm (accessed November 29, 2010).

2   Associated Press, "George Allen, Coach, Dead at 72; Led Redskins to Super Bowl," January 1, 1991,
     http://query.nytimes.com/gst/fullpage.html?res=9D0CE2DA1330F932A35752C0A967958260
     (accessed November 30, 2010).

3   Neil White, ed., *Mississippians* (Taylor, MS: Nautilus Publishing, 2010), 64.

4   George Blanda and Jack Olsen, "I Keep Getting My Kicks," *Sports Illustrated*, July 19, 1971, 26.

5   Maule, "Tomorrow's Generals."

6   Bob Sansavere, "Gracious to the End, Bill Brown Gets His Due," *St. Paul Pioneer-Press*,
     September 24, 2004.

7   "Bill Brown," *Sports Chat Place*.

8   Sam Farmer, "Living Legend," *Los Angeles Times*, December 22, 2006.

9   Jim Gehman, "Where Are They Now: FB Norm Bulaich," *philadelphiaeagles.com*, May 17,
     2008, http://www.philadelphiaeagles.com/news/Story-WhereAreTheyNow.asp?story_id
     =15476 (accessed December 2, 2010).

10   McDonough, *75 Seasons*, 16.

11   "The Sportscasters: Behind the Mike," *The History Channel*, February 7, 2000.

12 Richard Deitsch, "Q & A Larry Csonka," *Sports Illustrated*, November 28, 2005, http://sportsillustrated.cnn.com/vault/article/magazine/MAG1114139/index.htm (accessed December 5, 2010).

13 Jeff Schultz, "Bill Curry Goes Back to Tuscaloosa a Changed Man," *Atlanta Journal-Constitution*, November 16, 2010, http://blogs.ajc.com/jeff-schultz-blog/2010/11/16/bill-curry-goes-back-to-tuscaloosa-as-a-changed-man/ (accessed December 5, 2010).

14 Tom E. Curran, "Curtis Still Stewing Over Super Bowl III Loss," *nbcsports.com*, January 26, 2009, http://nbcsports.msnbc.com/id/28861055/ns/sports-super_bowl_xliii/ (accessed December 10, 2010).

15 "Al Davis Voted As Most Disliked Sports Figure in America," *Kansas City Star*, February 6, 2011, http://www.kansascity.com/2011/02/06/2637001/al-davis-voted-as-most-disliked.html (accessed December 10, 2010).

16 Rick Reilly, "Commitment to Honesty," *espn.com*, October 14, 2011, http://espn.go.com/espn/story/_/id/7098616/rick-reilly-reflects-al-davis-commitment-honesty (accessed October 19, 2011).

17 Hank Gola, "From Record-Setting Boot to Katrina, Former Saint Tom Dempsey Still Gets a Kick Out of Life," *New York Daily News*, January 30, 2010, http://www.nydailynews.com/sports/football/2010/01/30/2010-01-30_tom_dempsey_saints_kicker.html (accessed December 11, 2010).

18 Jackson, "Roman Gabriel."

19 Bill Dwyre, "Pat Haden is USC's New Athletic Director," *Los Angeles Times*, July 21, 2010, http://articles.latimes.com/2010/jul/21/sports/la-sp-usc-garrett-haden-20100721 (December 11, 2010).

20 John Taylor, "Bob Griese Hangs Up Telestrator After Nearly Three Decades," *College Football Talk*, February 3, 2011, http://collegefootballtalk.nbcsports.com/2011/02/03/bob-griese-hangs-up-the-telestrator-after-nearly-three-decades/ (accessed December 11, 2010).

21 Ibid.

22 Robert Janis, "Whatever Happened To … Jim Hart," *Washington Times*, July 11, 2008, http://www.washingtontimes.com/weblogs/redskins-fan-forum/2008/jul/11/whatever-happened-to-jim-hart/ (accessed August 7, 2011).

23 Golenbock, *Cowboys Have Always Been My Heroes*, 574.

24 Bob Barnett and Bob Carroll, "Chuck Howley," *The Coffin Corner* 6, nos. 9 and 10 (1984), http://www.profootballresearchers.org/Coffin_Corner/06-09-196.pdf (accessed December 3, 2010).

25 "Message from Deacon," *Deacon Jones Foundation*, http://www.deaconjones.com/ssp/message (accessed May 30, 2010).

26 St. John, *Landry*, 349.

27 Ibid.

28 "CFL Greats Fight 'Most Bizarre Thing,'" *Canadian Broadcasting Corporation*, November 27, 2011, http://www.cbc.ca/sports/football/cfl/story/2011/11/27/sp-cfl-mosca-kapp-fight.html.

29 Associated Press, "'Webster' Star and Detroit Lions Legend Alex Karras near Death," October 9, 2012, http://www.foxnews.com/entertainment/2012/10/09/webster-star-and-detroit-lions-legend-alex-karras-near-death/ (accessed October 11, 2012).

30 Judd Zulgad and Patrick Reusse, "Vikings Great Karl Kassulke Succumbs to Heart Attack," *Minneapolis Star-Tribune*, October 29, 2008, http://www.startribune.com/?id=33455019&path=%2Fsports (accessed September 22, 2010).

31 Smith, "Leroy Kelly."

32 Kevin Sherrington, "The Curious Case of Former Cowboy Steve Kiner and his Missing Cotton Bowl Watch," *Dallas Morning News*, June 1, 2010, http://www.dallasnews.com/sports/headlines/20100518-Sherrington-The-curious-case-of-9746.ece (accessed January 6, 2013).

33 Glenn Dickey, "Where Are They Now? Daryle Lamonica—'The Mad Bomber'—Quarterback Guided Raiders' Long-Ball Attack," *San Francisco Chronicle*, December 19, 2004,

http://www.sfgate.com/sports/article/WHERE-ARE-THEY-NOW-Daryle-Lamonica-The
-Mad-2628069.php (accessed November 29, 2010).

34 Denne Freeman and Jamie Aron, *I Remember Tom Landry* (Dallas: Sports Publishing, 2001), vii.

35 Golenbock, *Cowboys Have Always Been My Heroes*, 236.

36 Alfred Wright, "The Owners and Players Fumble On in Philly," *Sports Illustrated*, August 3, 1970, 47.

37 James Kiatell, "John Mackey: From the NFL to Dementia," *CBS Evening News*, April 28, 2007, http://www.cbsnews.com/stories stories/2007/04/28/eveningnews/main2738666.shtml (accessed November 22, 2010).

38 "The Story of the 1998 Minnesota Vikings," *America's Game: Missing Rings*, NFL Films, 2008.

39 Matt McCabe, "Interview: Jim Marshall on the NFL, the Vikings, and the Purple People Eaters," *St. James (MN) Plaindealer*, October 20, 2010, http://www.stjamesnews.com/features/x1665089473/Interview-Jim-Marshall-on-the-NFL -the-Vikings-and-the-Purple-People-Eaters (accessed December 1, 2010).

40 Shrake, "A Cowboy Named Dandy Don," 120.

41 Timothy Heider, Tom Diemer, and Evelyn Theiss, "Browns Bolt; Modell Warned Mayor, Governor a Month Ago," *Cleveland Plain-Dealer*, November 7, 1995, http://www.cleveland .com/ohio-sportsblog/index.ssf/2010/11/art_modell_owner_who_moved_the.html (accessed July 7, 2010).

42 Tex Maule, "Many Substitutes for Victory," *Sports Illustrated*, November 25, 1968, 29.

43 Ralph Vacchiano, "Super Bowl III Still Lingers for Former Baltimore Colts QB Earl Morrall," *New York Daily News*, January 23, 2010, http://www.nydailynews.com/sports/football /jets/2010/01/23/2010-01-23_earl_morrall_colts_super_bowl_iii.html (accessed July 30, 2010).

44 Rudy Klancnik, "Two Starts, No Wins, Lots of Super Memories for Morton," *espn.com*, January 23, 2008, http://sports.espn.go.com/nfl/playoffs07/news/story?id=3207012 (accessed August 20, 2010).

45 Ibid.

46 Mark Kreigel, "Where Have You Gone, Joe Namath?" *Sports Illustrated*, August 9, 2004, 101.

47 Jim Sargent, "Tom Nowatzke, All-American," *The Coffin Corner* 25, no. 5 (June 16, 2003) http://www.profootballresearchers.org/Coffin_Corner/25-05-998.pdf (accessed December 5, 2010).

48 Gola, "Former Baltimore Colts Kicker."

49 Alan Schwarz, "An Answer to Help Clear His Fog," *New York Times*, May 31, 2007, http://www.nytimes.com/2007/05/31/sports/football/31renfro.html?_r=1 (accessed July 11, 2010).

50 Coffey, "One For the Aged."

51 Ibid.

52 Tim Layden, "Part III: The Icon," *Sports Illustrated*, August 23, 2010, http://sportsillustrated.cnn .com/vault/article/magazine/MAG1173398/3/index.htm (accessed October 24, 2010).

53 Marv Levy, "The Last of the Legends." *Sports Illustrated*, January 15, 1996, http://sportsillustrated .cnn.com/vault/article/magazine/MAG1007653/index.htm (accessed December 2, 2010).

54 Mike Celizic, *The Biggest Game of them All: Notre Dame, Michigan, and the Fall of '66* (New York: Simon & Schuster, 1992), 89, 219.

55 Tony Gonzalez now has all three records, with 1,242 catches, 14,268 yards, and 103 touchdowns after the 2012 season.

56 Joe Capozzi, "Super Bowl XIII Slipped Away From Dallas Cowboys and Jackie Smith," *Palm Beach Post*, February 2, 2010, http://www.palmbeachpost.com/ sports/super-bowl-xiii -slipped-away-from-dallas-cowboys-208508.html (accessed August 7, 2011).

57 Robert Jones, "A Do-Gooder Who's Doing Good," *Sports Illustrated*, September 4, 1978, 87.

58 Golenbock, *Cowboys Have Always Been My Heroes*, 552.

59 Fran Tarkenton and Jack Olsen, "Better to Scramble Than Lose," *Sports Illustrated*, July 17, 1967, 76.

60 Nick Eatman, "Former RB Duane Thomas Makes Surprising Visit," *dallascowboys.com*, July 26, 2008, http://www.dallascowboys.com/news/ news.cfm?id=62343770-B8AD-DCB4 -4CECE6E34DFF4C98 (accessed July 20, 2010).

61 Frank Deford, "The Best There Ever Was," *Sports Illustrated*, September 23, 2002, 97.

62 "Football-playing Beau for Condoleezza?," *Times of India*, June 6, 2003, http://www.freerepublic .com/focus/news/924379/posts (accessed August 22, 2010).

INDEX

278 *Index*

ABOUT THE AUTHOR

Dr. Brad Schultz has written four other books on sports media and broadcast journalism. He is currently an associate professor in the Meek School of Journalism and New Media at the University of Mississippi.

In 2011 Schultz produced *The Season: Oxford Chargers*, detailing the 2010 Oxford Chargers football team, which won a national Aurora award as best sports documentary. He has two children and resides in Oxford, Mississippi, with his wife, Darlene.